MODERN TECHNOLOGY OF EXTRUSION & EXTRUDED PRODUCTS

MODERN TECHNOLOGY OF EXTRUSION & EXTRUDED PRODUCTS

Written By :

EIRI Consultants and Engineers

ENGINEERS INDIA RESEARCH INSTITUTE

4449, Nai Sarak, Main Road, Delhi-110 006 (India)
Ph. : 91-11-23918117, 23916431, 45120361, 23947058
Fax : 91-11-23916431, 23918117
★ **E-Mail :** eiribooks@yahoo.com eiriprojects@gmail.com
★ **Website :** www.eiriindia.org www.eiri.in
eiribooksandprojectreports.com

Sole Distributor :
EIRI PROJECT CONSULTANTS & PUBLISHERS
4/54, Roop Nagar, Delhi-110007

Printed and Published by :

ENGINEERS INDIA RESEARCH INSTITUTE

4449, Nai Sarak, Main Road, Delhi-110 006 (India)

Ph. : 91-11-23918117, 23916431, 45120361, 23947058

Fax : 91-11-23916431, 23918117

✶ **E-Mail :** eiribooks@yahoo.com eiriprojects@gmail.com

✶ **Website :** www.eiriindia.org www.eiri.in

eiribooksandprojectreports.com

Distributed by :

EIRI PROJECT CONSULTANTS & PUBLISHERS

4/54, Roop Nagar, Delhi-110007

ISBN : 978-93-80772-04-2

Printed in New Delhi (India)

₹800

Printed and Published by Sudhir Gupta for "Engineers India Research Institute", 4449, Nai Sarak, Main Road, New Delhi-110 006 and Printed at Swastik Offset, Delhi

Preface

The book **'MODERN TECHNOLOGY OF EXTRUSION & EXTRUDED PRODUCTS'** covers various methods including Introduction of Extrusion Processes, Extrusion, Type of Dies for Film Extrusion, Extrusion of Plastic Films, Blown Film Extrusion :, Extrusion instabilities of variabilities, Blown Film Extrusion, Plants for Multilayer Films, Lamination, High Speed Production of Thin CPP Film, Linear Low Density Polyethylene Mulch Film, Extruder Operation, Details of Processing Equipements, Post Extrusion Process, Vacuum Metallizing, Co-extruded Film Manufacturing, Production of Breathable Films and Laminates, Manufacture of Extruded Thermoplsatic Foam, Plastic Pipe for Water Supply, New Opportunities with PP for Window Profiles, Corrugator Multilayer Pipe Technology, Option for Cable Conduit Systems.

The book has been written for the benefit and to prove an asset and a handy reference guide in the hands of new entrepreneurs and well established industrialists.

Director

ENGINEERS INDIA RESEARCH INSTITUTE

Nai Sarak, Main Road,
Delhi-110 006 (India)
E-mail : eirisidi@bol.net.in

LIST OF PUBLICATIONS/BOOKS PUBLISHED BY

ENGINEERS INDIA RESEARCH INSTITUTE 4449, NAI SARAK, MAIN ROAD, DELHI - 6 (INDIA)

DAIRY FARMING & MILK PROCESSING & ICE CREAM

Name of Books	₹	US$
* Dairy Formulations Processes & Milk Processing Industries	750/-	75
* Milk Processing and Dairy Products Industries	750/-	75
* Hand Book of Dairy Farming	375/-	50
* Hand Book of Ice Cream Technology and Formulae	525/-	75
* H.B.Milk Processing, Dairy Products and Packaging Technology	975/-	100

HERBS CULTIVATION/MEDICINES

Name of Books	₹	US$
* Herbs, Medicinal & Aromatic Plants Cultivation	650/-	65
* औषधीयए वंस ुगन्धितप ैधोंक ा व्यवसायिकक ृषिकरण(हिन्दी)	800/-	80
* Hand Book of Medicinal & Aromatic Plants	875/-	90
* Hand Book of Aromatic & Plants and Biodiesel (Jatropha)	1100/-	110

FOOD PROCESSING, PRESERVATION, FOOD DEHYDRATION, SNACK FOOD, MEAT PROCESSING

Name of Books	₹	US$
* Fruits & Vegetables Processing Hand Book	750/-	75
* Food Processing & Agro Based Industries	975/-	100
* Manufacture of Snacks Food, Namkeen,Pappad & Potato Products	750/-	75
* Agro Based and Food Processing with E.O.U	1300/-	130
* Preservation & Canning of Fruits and Vegetables	900/-	90
* Hand Book of Food Dehydration and Drying	650/-	65
* Meat Processing & Meat Products Hand Book	900/-	90
* Technology of Food Preservation and Processing	950/-	100
* Agro Based & Processed Food Products	1100/-	110
* Hand Book of Mushroom Cultivation, Processing & Packaging	550/-	60
* Potato & Potato Processing Technology	750/-	75
* Technology of Maize & Allied & Allied Corn Products	650/-	65
* Fruit Beverage & Processing with Mango Products	750/-	75
* Technology of Food Processing Indu.	975/-	100
* Technology of Sweets (Mithai) with Formulae	1050/-	105
* Citrus Fruits Cultivation and Processing Technology	1000/-	100

HOSIERY/TEXTILES/GARMENTS

Name of Books	₹	US$
* Hosiery, Ready-Made Garments & Textile Projects	1300/-	130
* Technology of Textiles (Spinning & Weaving, Dyeing, Scouring, Drying, Printing and Bleaching)	900/-	90
* Hand Book of Garments Manufacturing Technology	900/-	90

PRODUCT FROM WASTE

Name of Books	₹	US$
* Technology of Products From Waste	900/-	90

SOAP & DETERGENTS ACID SLURRY

Name of Books	₹	US$
* Household Soaps, Toilet Soaps & Other Soaps	750/-	75
* Profitable Small Scale Manufacture of Soaps & Detergents	375/-	40
* Hand Book of Synthetic Detergents with Formulations	900/-	90
* Modern Technology of Acid Slurry, Surfactants, Soap and Detergents with Formulae	900/-	90

COSMETIC (SYNTHETIC & HERBAL)

Name of Books	₹	US$
* Cosmetics Processes & Formulations Hand Book	900/-	90
* Herbal Cosmetics & Beauty Products with Formulations	750/-	75
* Profitable Small Scale Manufacture of Cosmetics (Synthetic & Herbal)	950/-	95
* Hand Book of Synthetic and Herbal Cosmetics	575/-	60
* Technology of Herbals Cosmetics & Toiletries Products with Formulae	1100/-	110

ESSENTIAL OILS & AROMATIC PLANTS

Name of Books	₹	US$
* Hand Book of Essential Oils Mfg. & Aromatic Plants	650/-	65
* Essential Oils Processes and Formulations Hand Book	650/-	65
* Modern Technology of Essential Oils	850/-	85
* Technology of Perfumes, Flavours & Essentials Oil	1175/-	120

PERFUMES AND FLAVOURS

Name of Books	₹	US$
* Hand Book of Perfumes & Flavours	600/-	60
* Technology of Perfumes & Flavours and Essential Oils	1175/-	120
* Hand Book of Perfumes with Formulations	750/-	75
* Hand Book of Flavour Technology	750/-	75
* Hand Book of Flavour & Food Colourants Technology	1400/-	140

OIL AND FATS

Name of Books	₹	US$
* Oils, Fats and Derivatives with Refining & Packaging Technology	950/-	95

BUILDING MATERIALS & CHEMICALS

Name of Books	₹	US$
* Technology of Building Materials & Chemicals with Processes	950/-	95

AGRO CULTIVATION, ANIMAL FARMING, AGRO PLANTATION & AGRO CHEMICAL/PESTICIDES

Name of Books	₹	US$
* Hand Book of Tree Farming	800/-	80
* Hand Book of Poultry Farming and Feed Formulations	450/-	45
* Hand Book of Pig Farming	400/-	40
* Agro Based H.B. of Plantation, Cultivation & Farming	500/-	50
* Agro-Based Plantation Cultivation & Farming	475/-	50
* Agro Based Industries (Plantation & Farming)	1300/-	130
* Technology of Modern Rice Milling and Basmati Rice	600/-	60
* Floriculture Hand Book (Flowers Growing Technology)	1000/-	100
* Hand Book of Goat Farming	450/-	45
* Modern Bee Keeping & Honey Processing	375/-	45

CONTENTS AND SUBJECT INDEX

1

Introduction of Extrusion Processes

Extrusion is the forming method used to produce continuous lengths of sheet, pipes, rod, profiles and so on, although the method is also sufficiently versatile to be adapted for the production of single items, such as bottles. As a result of this versatility, extrusion accounts for a very large percentage of the tonnage of plastic processed in the world. The total product made by this process is about 66 per cent of the total plastic processed through different processes in India.

The principle of extrusion is simple. Plastic granules fall from a hopper through an aperture in the barrel on to a rotating screw. The screw is similar to that in injection moulding machine in that it is usually of a fixed pitch but has a series of zones of different root diameter. As the screw rotates, the granules are transported along the heated barrel so that they are melted and mixed to form a uniform melt. The melt is pressurised by decreasing the channel depth and at the end of the screw, the plastic passes through a filter and eventually through a changeable die to form the desired shape pipe, sheet, film, rod and so on. After emerging from the die the plastic may pass through a former to produce the exact shape and size required.

The extrudate must, of course be cooled and this is accomplished with air jets or a water bath. In order to pull the extrudate through the cooling medium there is usually a take-off mechanism at the end of the extruder line. The speed of the take-off may be varied to control the drawdown of the extrudate. The final stage of the process is the storage of the product in some convenient form.

The size of an extruder is normally quoted in terms of the barrel, but the L/D ratio may also be used. This is the ratio of the length of the flighted portion of the screw to the inside diameter of the barrel. Most extruders have a ratio in the range 15:1 to 25:1 but large machines may have an L/D ratio 30:1, 40:1 or more. Screw design can be crucial to provide efficient moulding of different plastics. In general an extruder screw has a feed zone, a compression zone, and a metering zone, although the relative length ofthese zones depends on the material being processed. Other factors which need to be considered are the compression ratio. For example, the recommended screw design for nylon is an L/D ratio of at least 16:1, a compression ratio of 4:1, and a short compression zone (one screw flight). PVC on the other hand requires a compression zone which extends over the full length of the screw and the recommended L/D ratio is at least 20:1 with a compression ratio of about 3:1.

Although the vast majority of extruders are of the single screw type, twin and or for screw extruders are also in current use mainly for processing unplasticised PVC. The intermeshing screws may rotate in the same direction or be contra-rotating. The main advantage of this system is that the twin screw configuration gives a positive displacement rather than relying on friction as in the single screw system. This means that there is less work done on the melt and, hence, less possibility of degradation particularly important with PVC. Another advantage is that powdered material can be processed without difficulty whereas, in single screw machines there can be feeding problems. This is again important for PVC which is usually formulated as powder.

One of the recent developments in extrusion in which different materials, or various combinations of the same material, are extruded simultaneously to produce & laminar composite. This may be used for structural reasons to strengthen an inexpensive, but weak plastic with a thin strip or coating of stiff but expensive plastic. Or it may be done for decorative effect by coextruding plastics of different colours.

It has been found that screw driven extruders are not suitable for processing thermosets, mainly because of the difficulties of building up the pressures necessary for good quality products. Another drawback is the downtime associated with dismantiling and cleaning the system if the material cures in the barrel.

Thermosets are usually extruded on machines which are essentially reciprocating hydraulic press. The principle of operation is similar to a lunger type injection moulding machine in that during the back-stroke of the plunger the thermoset powder falls from the hopper into the relatively cool barrel. During the forward stroke the material is pushed along the barrel and the majority of the flow occurs in the transition between the barrel and the die. The die is heated and is very long so that the material taken in during each cycle is pressurised against the material already in the die. The required pressure is generated by the frictional resistance between the die wall and the curing plastic hence the need for a long die.

The efficient operation of the system depends to a large extent on the design of the die. High quality tool steel are required and these must be chrome-plated and highly polished on the working surfaces. With correct design and sufficient rigidity to withstand the high pressures involved, it is possible to extrude most profiles (including pipes) using thermosetting resins.

The extruder, which offers the advantages of a completely versatile processing technique, is unsurpassed in economic importance by any other processes. This continuously operating process, with its relatively low cost of operation, is predominant in the manufacture of shapes such as films, sheets, tapes, filaments, pipes, rods, and others. The basic processing concept is similar to that of injection moulding (IM), in that material passes from a hopper into a cylinder in which it is melted and dragged forward by the movement of a screw. The screw compresses, melts, and homogenises. When the melt reaches the end of the cylinder, it usually is forced through a screen pack prior to entering a die that gives the desired shape with no break in continuity (8-9, 85, 90-96, 100-106, 115-143) (Fig. 1.1).

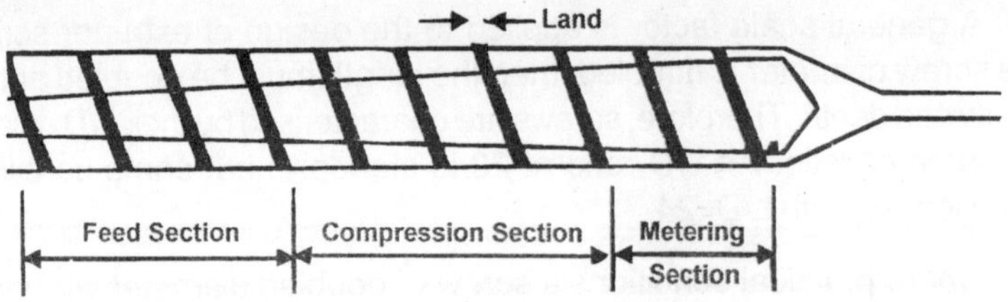

Fig.1.1: An extrusion screw for thermoplastics.

While general-purpose screws will extrude a wide range of thermoplastics, certain plastics impose special requirements on screw design. Crystalline polymers require a long feed zone, while plasticised vinyls, cellulosics, and some soft plastics require a very short feed zone since they can be compressed as soon as they enter the screw. Nylon melts quickly and requires only a short compression zone. Rigid vinyls are degraded by the heating effect of shear stresses in the metering zone, and no metering zone is provided for these plastics, or alternately, a deep channel is provided to reduce shearing effects. Shallower channels give more thorough mixing and generate more frictional heat in the polymer; therefore, the more viscous polymers can use deeper channels.

Most screws have a pitch equal to the diameter and a thread width equal to about one-tenth of the diameter. Clearance between screw and barrel is about 0.00 15 in./in. diameter. Since considerable torque is applied to the screw, its root diameter must be substantial to sustain torque loads.

A typical general-purpose screw in a 4½-in. diameter and pitch and 90 in. length would have the following design:

Feed zone	2 1/2 in.
Compression zone	45 in.
Metering zone	22 1/2 in.

The screw material is usually, a medium-carbon low alloy steel with hardened flights to resist wear. The screw is hollow so that if necessary it may be heated or cooled by circulating a fluid through it.

The screw is usually driven by an alternating-current motor. Continuous variation of screw speed is normally required. Production rate lies within the range of 5 to 15 pounds of product per hour per installed horsepower. A screw of smaller diameter must be operated at a faster speed than one of larger diameter. Speeds of operation range from well below 100 rpm to above 100 rpm.

Since the screw forces plastic through an exit die at high pressure, there is a considerable thrust to be absorbed by a thrust bearing. This thrust bearing requires roller bearings; ball bearings are not sufficiently rugged.

A major difference between extrusion and IM is that the extruder processes plastics at a lower pressure and operates continuously. Its pressure usually ranges from 200 to 1,500 psi (1.4 to 10.4 MPa) and could go to 5,000 or possibly 10,000 psi (34.5 or 69 MPa) (Table 1.1). In IM, pressures go from 2,000 to 30,000 psi (14 to 210 MPa). However, the most important difference is that the IM melt is not continuous; it experiences repeatable abrupt changes when the melt is forced into a mould cavity. With these significant differences, it is actually easier to theorise about extrusion and to process plastics through extruders, as many more controls are required in IM.

Table 1.1. Typical extruder die head pressures.

	Melt pressure at the die	
Extruded shape	*PSI*	*MPA*
Film-blown	1,000-5,000	6.9-34.5
Film-cast	200-1,500	1.4-10.4
Sheet	200-1,500	1.5-10.4
Pipe	400-1,500	2.8-10.4
Wire Coating	1,000-5,000	6.9-34.5
Filament	1,000-3,000	6.9-20.7

Good-quality plastic extrusions require homogeneity in terms of the melt heat profile and mix, accurate and sustained flow rates, a good die design, and accurately controlled downstream equipment for cooling and handling the product. Four principal factors determine a good die design: internal flow length, streamlining, the materials of construction, and uniformity of heat control. Heat profiles, such as those in Fig. 1.2, are preset via tight controls. To accomplish this control, cooling systems are incorporated in addition to heater bands. Barrels use forced air and/or water jackets. In some machines water bubbler channels are located within the screws.

On leaving the extruder, the product is drawn by a pulling device, and in this stage it is subject to cooling, usually by water or blown air. This is an important aspect of control if tight dimensional requirements exist and/or conservation of plastics is desired. Usually lines do not have adequate control of the pulling device. The processor's target is to determine the tolerance required for the pull rate and to see that the device meets the requirements. One should check with a supplier on the speed tolerances available. Even if tight dimensional requirements do not exist, the probability is that better control of the pull speed will permit tighter tolerances and reduce the material output. One should check the cost of replacing the puller.

As the molecules of the melt flow are aligned in the direction of the output from the die, the strength of the plastic is characteristically greater in than direction that at right angles. Depending on the product use, this may or may not be favourable. The degree of orientation can be controlled.

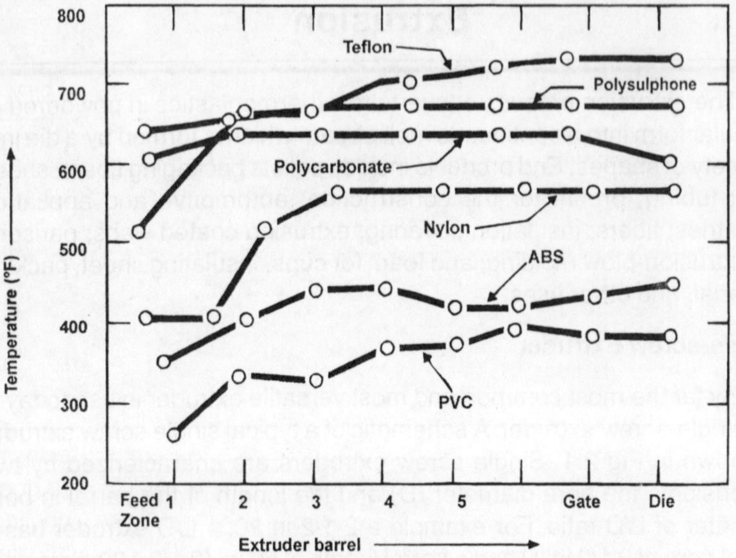

Fig. 1.2 : Temperature profiles of different plastics going through an extruder.

The success of any continuous extrusion process depends not only upon uniform quality and conditioning of the raw materials but also upon the speed and continuity of the feed of additives or regrind along with the virgin resin. Actually only thermoplastics go through extruders; markets have not developed to date for extruded thermosets. The variations in the bulk density of materials exist in the hopper, requiring controllers such as weight feeders and perhaps requiring some type of packing feed, such as rams, screw packers, and so on.

2

Extrusion

The extrusion process converts raw thermoplastics in powdered or granular form into a continuous melt stream which is formed by a die into a variety of shapes. End products include pellets packaging fibers; sheet; pipe; tubing; profile for the construction, automotive and appliance industries; fibers; insulation covering; extrusion coated webs; parisons for extrusion-blow molding; and foam for cups, insulating sheet, packing material, and other uses.

Single-screw Extruder

By far the most common and most versatile extruder in use today is the single-screw extruder. A schematic of a typical single screw extruder is shown in Fig 2.1. Single screw extruders are characterized by two dimensions; the bore diameter (D) and the length of the barrel in bore diameter of L/D ratio. For example a 2 1/2 in 20; 1 L/D extruder has a barrel bore of 2 1/2 in ID and a barrel length of 50 in. (2 1/2 x 20 diameters in length).

Common commercial sizes of extruders range from 2 to 8 in. Machines are available as small as 3/4 in for laboratory or specialized use and as large as 24 in or more on special order. common L/Ds range from about 5:1 minimum through 34: 1 and to 40 +.: 1 for some multiple venting application. Generally the shorter machines (through 20: 1) are applied to elastomer processing; the longer one (20: 1 L/D and above) are applied to thermoplastic processing.

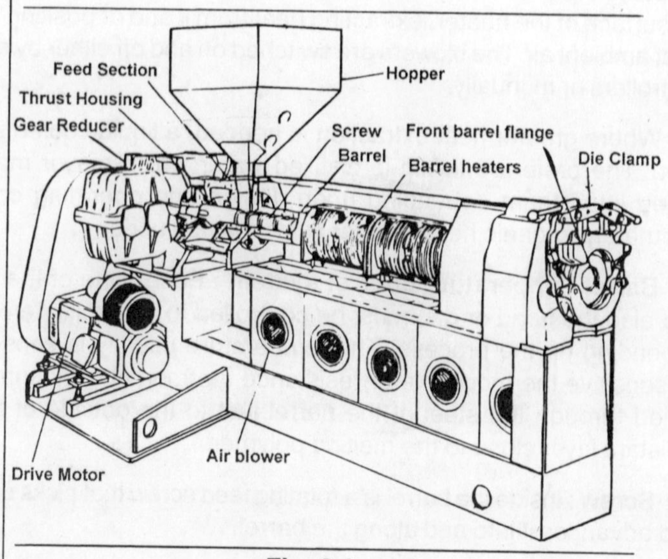

Fig. 2.1

Extruder barrel and feed section : The section barrel of single-screw extruder usually is a long thick-walled tube of alloy steel into which a hard, highly crystalline wear resistant alloy has been centrifugally cast After the casting the bimetallic tube is straightened and honed, usually to a tolerance of ± 0.001 in. on the ID The barrel must tolerate an internal pressure of 10,000 p.s.i. without elastic deformation above the 0.15% strain at which the internal alloy will cack in tension.

Attached to the feed end of the barrel (often as a separate casting) is an opening into the barrel bore for raw material feeding. It usually is jacketed for room temperature water cooling to prevent premature melting of polymer.

Barrel heat input and extraction mechanisms: The barrel must be provided with means to both add and extract heat. Though heaters vary in design, the most common ones are cast aluminum. The heater halves are clamped to the barrel to provide intimate contact between the steel of the barrel and the aluminum of the heater. The heat sink is either air of a liquid coolant.

The heaters are arranged in zones, often 4 to 5 on a 24: 1 L/D extruder. Auxiliary systems provide heat sinks for heat absorption. Probably the

Simplest is a blower mounted under each zone heater to blow air over the surface of the heater, extracting heat from it and depositing it into the plant ambient air. The blowers are switched on and off either by automatic controllers or manually.

Where greater heat extraction is needed, a liquid cooled system is used. The preferred liq'.lid is distilled water which mayor may not be boiled into steam depending upon design and operating conditions. Alternately, organic heat transfer fluids may be used.

Barrel temperature control system : Each zone of the extruder, and also the head or die, must be controlled to a specific temperature, depending on the process. The temperature usually is sensed with a tip-sensitive thermocouple or resistance thermometer mounted in hole drilled through the steel of the barrel just to the outside of the wear-resistant layer close to the melting polymer.

Screw : Inside the barrel is a rotating feed screw that picks up polymer and advances it into and along the barrel.

Gearbox and thrust bearing: Common operating speed of medium-size extruders range between 50 and 150 r.p.m. The speeds of medium-hp drive motors i.e. 40 to 200 hp., are usually 1750 r.p.m. Motor speed is reduced to the screw speed usually with a gear reducer which simultaneously increases the available torque as it reduces the speed.

The gearboxes supplied by extruder manufacturers may be horizontal or vertical, cast iron of welded. They may have helical, herringbone or worm gears, 2 1/2 in. and larger extruders use helical or herringbone gearboxes.

Drives : The most common extruder drives are statically rectified d.c. drives operating on 460v three-phase power. As the armature voltage is reduced from nameplate rating to zero, the speed reduces linearly to zero, while maintaining full load torque capability.

D.C. drives usually are equipped with tachometers and drive regulators which hold speed within 1% regulation and 2% long-term drift. The signals from these tachometers can be fed into coordinate modules and master references to drive the extruder speed up and down with process line speeds, tandem extruders, coextrusion extruders, etc.

Though the power factor drops off materially. d.c., drives tend to be relatively efficient in energy use. Other types of drives that are used include eddy current a.c. motors, and hydraulic drives.

Venting: Some polymers contain small amounts of volatile monomer moisture or entrapped gases which adversely affect the extruded product. These may be removed through vents in the barrel.

3

Type of Dies for Film Extrusion

1) **Side-fed Die for Blown Film :** In such die, polymer melt in fed to die from side and melt is divided in two streams. This has disadvantage of Joint/weld line, where film can be weak in strength.

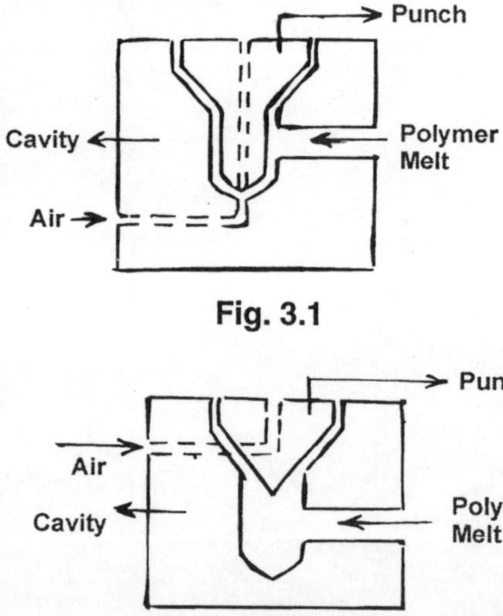

Fig. 3.1

2) **Bottom-fed Die for Blown Film :** In such die, polmer melt is fed to die from bottom of punch and hence does not involve any weld line problem. This is most common type of die.

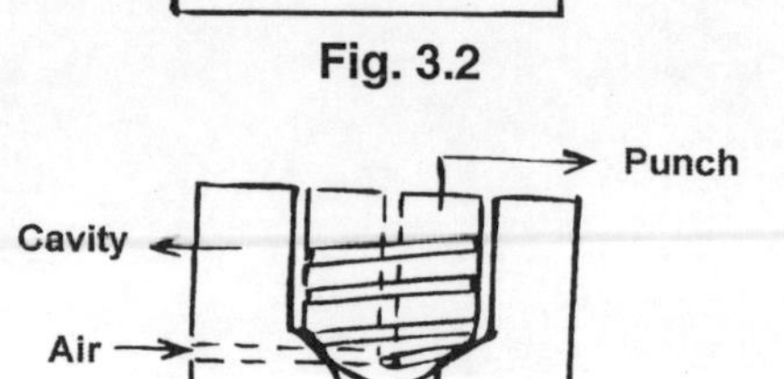

Fig. 3.2

3) **Spiral Flow Die :** There are different varieties such as 2 start, 4 start, 8 start, spiral flow dies. This spiral flow die gives distinct advantage of better homogenity of melt, even

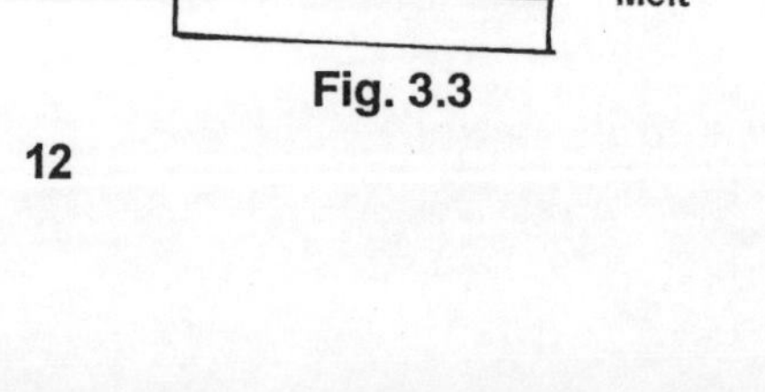

Fig. 3.3

distribution of melt pressure & better melt stability.

4. **T-Die (Coat Hanger Die) :** This type of die is generally used for :
   - Cast Film Extrusion
   - Slit tape extrusion for woven sacks.
   - Extrusion coating
   - BOPP film co-extrusion

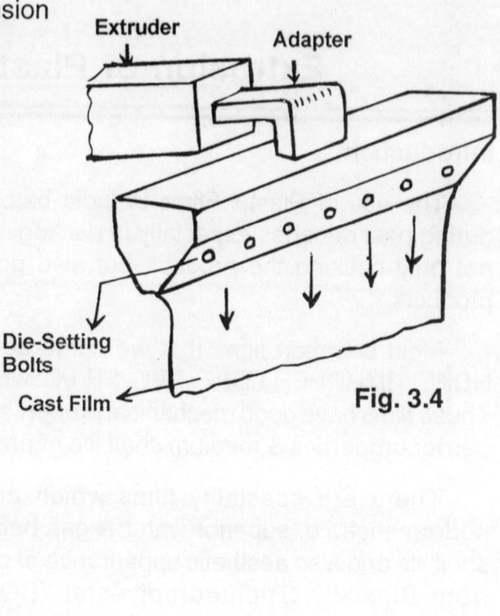

Fig. 3.4

4

Extrusion of Plastic Films

Introduction

The use of Plastic Films in India has shown phenomenal growth during past decades especially in packaging. Films play a major role in not only packing the product, but also protecting and displaying the products.

Most common films that we come across are made from LDPE, HDPE, HMHDPE, LLDPE, PVC, PP, etc. which form the commdity films. These films have good mechanical properties and reasonably good water barrier properties & medium shelf life of product packed.

There are speciality films which are higher priced and high performance i.e. superior water & gas barrier properties giving longer shelf life and also aesthetic appearance of printed films. These are made from Biaxially Oriented(polyester (BOPET), Bi-axially oriented polypropylene (BOPP), Mono-axially oriented Polypropylene, Cellophane, Oriented Nylon (OPA), Oriented Polystyrene (OPS).

There are high speciality plastics which impart excellent barrier properties to extend shlef life of production packed. They are very expensive and are normally used in combination with other commodity plastic films Such plastics, include polyvinylidene chloride (PVDC), Ethylene Vinyl Alcohol (EVOH) and Ionomers. These plastics are used with processing plastics by way of Blown film co-extrusion 3,5 and 7 layers.

Processing

Films are produced by a process called Extrusion, which comprises of converting plastic granules into a continuous uniform melt and forcing the melt through a die into various desired shapes such as film, sheet, tubing, pipes and rods. The process of extrusion is carried out in an extruder. Extruder consists of cylindrical barrel in which a screw rotates and help to convert solid plastic granules into homogenous molten plastic mass and to convey the same to the die continuously. The size of extruder is defined by diameter of its screw.

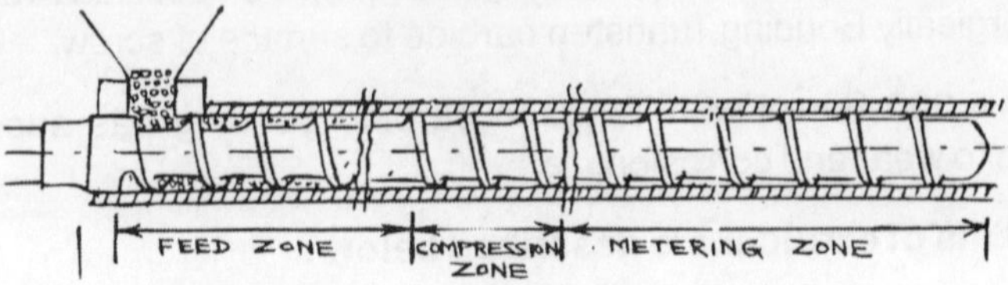

Fig. 4.1

Hopper Cooling Helps to avoid bridging.

<u>TEMPERATURE PROFILE :</u> (CAMEL BACK)

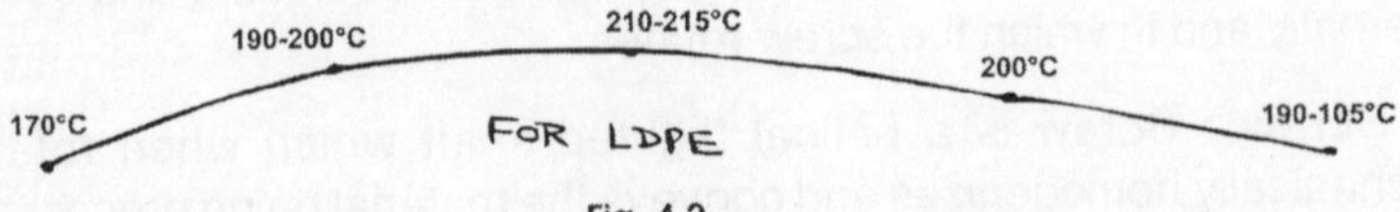

Fig. 4.2

For MDPE - 180°C to 220°C   For HDPE - 190°C to 230°C
For PP - 190°C to 240°C   For LLDPE - 190°C to 240°C

Table 4.1

Polymers	Screw Details		
	L/D Ratio	Compression Ratio	
LDPE	24:1 to 30:1	3.40: 1	
LLDPE	24:1 to 26 :1	2.5:1 to 3:1	PITCH =
MDPE	24:1 to 26:1	3.4 :1	DIAMETER
HDPE	24:1 to 26 :1	3 : 1 to 3.4 :1	HELIX ANGLE =
PP	24:1 to 26:1	3.5:1 to 3.8:1	16.5°TO 17°

Mixing Sections - Maddock Type
For Better Melt - Mixing Pins/Rings
Homogenisation - Grooved Barrels.

MATERIAL OF CONSTRUCTION:

Screw : Nitrided Steel or Carbide Metal

Barrel : Nitrided Steel

New Superior Materials: (A) Titanium Carbide Composites (FERROTIC) For Hard Facing (Trade Name "FERRO-TIC").

Cobalt - Nickel alloys are gaining accepRance for wear resistance.

No Abrasion Screw -Xaloy, Pulasky, USA, have Deposition Process for Metalurgically Bonding Tungsten carbide to surface of screw.

Xaloy - 800 Barrel with Tungsen carbide bonding has superior resistance to wear and corrosion.

Components of extruder are described below :

Hopper: It is mounted at the opening end of the barrel for the entry of raw material. The raw material passes through the vertical opening in the feed section into the extruder barrel.

Barrel: Barrel is a cylindrical housing, which is heated and cooled externally and in which the screw rotates.

Screw : Screw is a helical flighted shaft which when rotated mechanically homogenizes and conveys the material being processed.

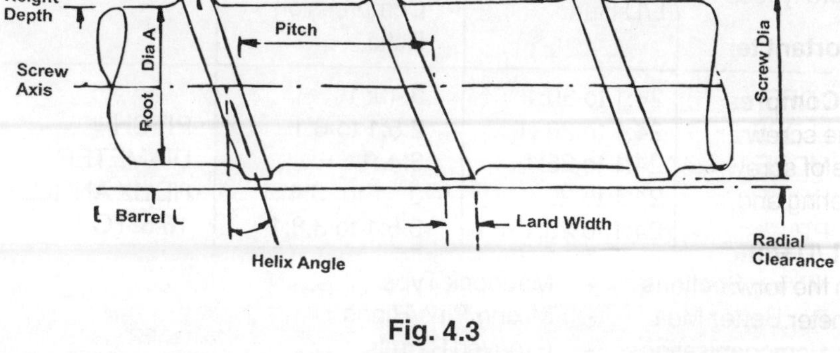

Fig. 4.3

Screw Flight : The helical melt thread of the screw.

Flight Land : The surface at the radial extremity of the flight constituting the periphery or outside diameter of the screw.

Screw Diameter: The diameter developed by rotation of flight land about the screw axis.

Helix Angle : The angle of the flight at the periphery relative to a plane perpendicular to the screw axis.

Ptich : Distance in axial direction between

Flight Depth : Distance in the radial direction from the periphery of the flight to the root.

Diameteral Screw Clearance : The difference in diameter between screw and barrel bore.

Screw Zones:

A typical screw is divided into three zones:

Feed Zone : The function of this zone is to receive material coming from hopper and feed it to compression zone. The root diameter in feed zone is minimum and is generally constant over the entire zone length.

Compression Zone : This zone has a gradual decreasing depth or decreasing pitch of screw, because of which material is gradually compressed and compacted. Transition of material from solid form to molten form takes place in this zone, because of heat and shearing action.

Metering Zone : This portion of screw acts as a pump and it delivers molten material to the die at a constant rate. Flight depth in this zone is generally less than that in feed zone and is constant throughout.

Important terms associated with the Screw Design

Compression Ratio (CR) : It can be expressed as a ratio of volume of the screw channel at feed opening to volume in the metering zone. In case of screws with constant pitch, CR is the ratio of depths at feed end metering end.

L/D Ratio: It is the ratio of length of the screw, which is the distance from the forward edge of feed opening to the screw tip, to the barrel bore diameter.

These two design parameters are specific to the type of polymer. The recommended values of L/D & CR for PE are 24 to 28 : 1 and 2.5 to 3.0 : 1 respectively. Many a times mixing sections in the screw are recommended for processing LLDPE.

Heating & Cooling Systems

Controlled heating is provided using external electrical resistance or induction heaters arranged in several groups or zones along the barrel. Thermocouples are fitted at regular intervals on barrel for temperature measurement and control. Cooling is done using blowers of cooling water jack-ets to remove excess heat from the polymer melt.

Breaker Plate & Screens

Breaker plate is to break spiral motion of melt and support screen pack. Screen pack, which is a combination of screens with different mesh sizes is used as a filter.

The screen pack combinations, which generally used are 40/60/40, 60/ 80/60 or 40/60/60/40 mesh.

Downstream Equipments :

Blowers, quench tank. guides. winders, cutter slitter etc. constitute the downstream equipments for an extruder, which change according to the type of extruder and also the product being processed.

Now film extruders with either oscillating platform, rotating die or oscillating haul-off (Take up) assembly are developed, which enable to obtain better quality hump free film Rolls.

Different types of Film processing techniques

Blown Film Process : It is a process in which a plastic tube after extruding through an annular die is inflated by air to desired diameter. cooled collapsed and wound in the form of rolls.

In India. Blown film extrusion process is found economical & is used by most of the processing units, In this process. there are two types :-

(1) Single layer blown film extrusion &

(2) Multi-layer (2 to 5 layers) blown film co-·extrusion.

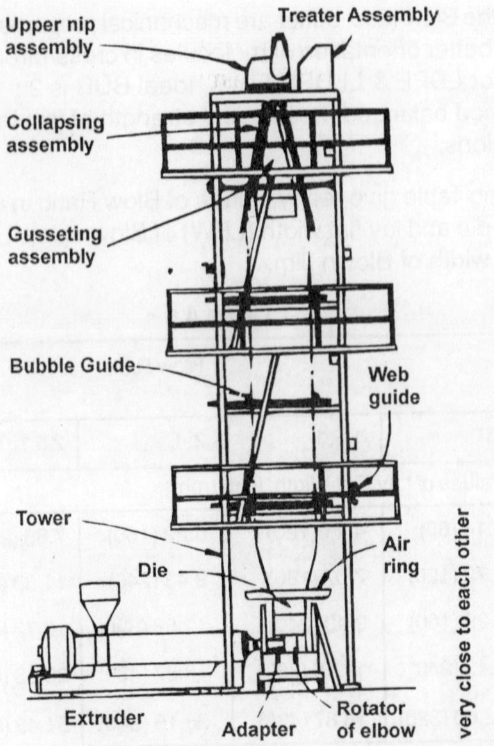

Fig. 4.4

The film properties achieved in this process are dependant on vari-ous processing conditions, such as Blow Ratio, Processing Temperature Profile, Draw Ratio, Relation of screw speed & haul-off speed, film thick-ness uniformity, Frost line height (FLH) and adjustment of cooling air through air ring. etc.

$$\text{BUR} = \frac{\text{Perimeter of bubble}}{\text{Perimeter of Die}} = \frac{\pi D}{\pi d}$$

where,

D = Diameter of Bubble

d = Diameter of Die

$$\pi = \frac{22}{7} = 3.14$$

Simplified approx formula is

$$d - \frac{\text{LFW}}{1.5 \times \text{BUR}}$$

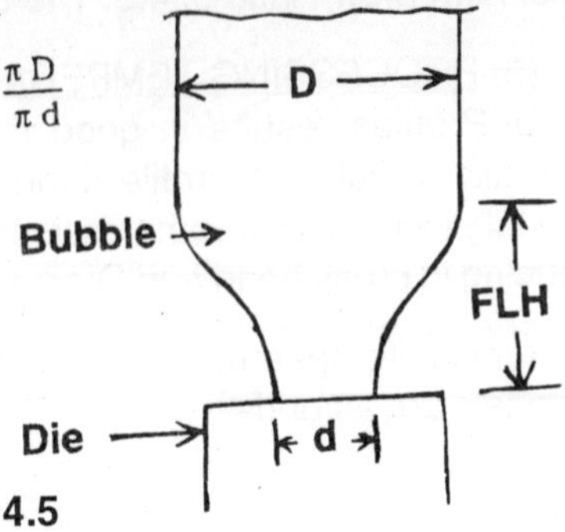

Fig. 4.5

Higher the Blow ratio, better are mechanical properties (Tensile. Impact etc.) due to better orientation of molecules in cross-direction (Transverse direction) For LDPE & LLDPE Films, Ideal BUR is 2 : 1 to 2.5 : 1 which results in good balanced mechanical strength of film in both machine & cross directions.

Following Table give ready values of Blow Ratio in relation to size of diameter of die and lay flat width (LFW) of Blown film . LFW of film is half of cut open width of Blown film.

Table 4.1

Die Diameter	Blow Ratio				
Inch (mm)	1:1	1.5: 1	2: 1	2.5:1	3: 1
	Values of Lay Flat Width, inch (mm)				
2 (50)	3.14 (80)	4.71 (120)	6.29 (160)	7.86 (200)	9.43 (240)
3 (75)	4.72 (120)	7.07 (180)	9.43 (240)	11.80 (300)	14.15 (360)
4 (100)	6.29 (160)	9.43 (240)	12.58 (320)	15.72 (400)	18.86 (480)
6 (150)	9.43 (240)	14.15 (360)	18.87 (480)	23.58 (600)	28.30 (720)
8 (200)	12.60 (320)	18.87 (480)	25.16 (640)	31.45 (800)	37.73 (960)

for LDPE, LLDPE and HDPE films, processing at Low Blow Ratio, (Some-times Less than 1:1) is not advisable, since orientation of molecules is insufficient & unbalanced, which results in inferior mechanical strength of the resultant films.

For TQPP film, normal blow ratio used is 1.2: 1 to 1.5: 1 For HMHDPE films, high Blow Ratio of 4.5: 1 to 5.5: 1 is used.

(2) PROCESSING TEMPERATURE PROFILES : Adequately high Temp. Profiles results in good mechanical properties of blow fIlms. Normally camel back profile is found useful. i.e. Lower in feed zone and gradually increasing in compression and metering zones and then gradually reducing in cross head and Die zones.

Typical Temperature Profiles for film extrusion for popular plastic materials are as under :-

Table 4.2

LDPE Film Grades	*Barrel Zones*	*Cross Head*	*Die Zones*
Heavy Duty (0.2MI)	170/195/205	200/190	185/180°C
Milk Pkg. (0.5MI)	160/185/195	190/85	180/170°C
General Purpose Pkg. (2MI)	160/180/185	185/180	170/160°C
(4MI)	150/170/170	160/155	150/145°C
Heavy Duty (1.OMI)	160/185/195	190/185	180/170°C
General Purpose (2MI)	160/180/185	180/175	175/170°C
HMHDPEFilm Grade,	170/220/230	210/220	200/190°C
TQPP Film Grade (1OMI)	170/195to 200/205	200/190	190/180°C

(3) FROST LINE HEIGHT (FLH) : This is the distance between the die and the zone where the bubble solidifies and assumes it's final diameter. This FLH is dependent on the rate of cooling by air from cooling ring. Higher the rate of cooling, Lower is FLH and Vice-Versa.

Normally recommended FLH for various plastic blown film materials are as under:-

(1) For LDPE and LLDPE blown film extrusion, one foot to two feet, de-pending on diameter of the bubble.

(2) For PP blown extrusion, 6 inches to 10 inches.

(3) For HDPE blown film extrusion, 6 inches to 15 inches.

(4) For_HMHDPE blown film extrusion, FLH is as high as two feet to four feet, depending on diameter of bubble.

(4) FILM THICHKNESS CONTROL: Film thickness is controlled by adjusting screw speed and Nip Roll speed.

(5) THICKNESS VARIATION CONTROL :-

It is very essential to control film thickness in narrow range, preferably within ± 5%. This variation is controlled by -

(a) Setting the die gap uniform all along the periphery, with help of the die setting bolts. It is ideal to have 8 to 10 Nos. die setting bolts.

(b) Adjusting air flow of air cooling ring.

The film with low variation in thickness has superior and reliable mechanical properties and is free from thick bands or humps on the roll, which enhances the printing quality of the film.

Cast Film Process: Polymer melt is extruded through a flat die either onto a rotating chilled roll or into a water quench tank, where the melt is rapidly cooled and frozen to form a film called the cast film.

Advantages of this process over blown film Extrusion are :

(1) Superior transparency & clarity of film

(2) 4 to 5 times higher output. since no limitations on cooling of film.

The only limitation of cast film process is relatively lower orientation and strength of film in transverse direction.

Coextrusion Film Process: It is a process in which two or more polymers processed on separate extruders are passed together through a common die to fonn a film. It can be either a blown or cast film process. This process is widely used for. producing barrier films, stretch films etc. Co-extrusion film process leads to a co-extruded film or multilayer film.

Such films offer specific advantages such as higher shelf-life superior mechanical properties of the film and pouches (Tensile strength. pucture resistance. Impact strength), better heat seal strength. better hot tack strength etc. due to the combination of dirrerent plastic materials used in the multilayer structures.

Some of the multilayer structures based on polyethylene and their applications :

MATERIAL COMBINATION	Important fields of Application
1. LDPE + LLDPE in 2 or 3 layers	Milk film, carrier bags, general packaging.
2. LDPE/EVA LLDPE/EVA	heavy duty bags, stretch, packaging, medical articles

	LLDPE/LEPE	
3.	HDPE/EVA	blood plasma, bakery goods, food stuffs.
4.	HDPE/LDPE or LLDPE LDPE/HDPE/LDPE LLDPE/HDPE/LLDPE	bakery goods, food-stuffs, tomato concentrate, pet food, cornflacks.
5.	LDPE/TL/Nylon-6/TL/LDPE or LLD PE /TL/Nylon -6 /TL/LDPE	Packing of meat, sausage, Cheese, ham, fish, ready-made meal.
6.	LDPE/HDPE	Vanaspati Ghee pouches.
7.	LLDPE/LDPE/HDPE	Edible oil pouches, short shelf-life
8.	LLDPE/TL/Nylon-6/TL/ IONOMER	Edible oil pouhces-longer shelf-life

STRETCH - EXTRUSION PROCESS

In this process, after primary extrusion. the product is again reheated & stretched/oriented in one or two directions (machine & transverse directions) in order to impart superior mechanical properties to final products :

1) Bi-axially oriented PP films and Polyester films, having superior mechanical properties and barrier properties.

2) Flat Tapes for HDPE & PP woven sacks also known as 'Raffia'.

3) PP & HDPE monofilaments, twines and sutli.

4) PP, Nylon-6 Box strappings.

In above process, the extruded product is reheated and then stretched in machine director and Transverse direction. The stretch ratio depends on type of Plastic, for example for PP it is 1:7 to 1:8 and for HDPE it is lower 1:5 to 1:6. After stretching the product is again heated (PP to about 130 to 135°C & HDPE to 100° to 120°C) for purpose of stress-Relaxation in the prodUct. After this, the product is ready for final winding.

In secondary operations, Flat tapes are taken on looms for weaving, monofilaments on Rope making machine, etc.

In the following schematic Diagram, Flat tape stretch extrusion line for PP Raffia is shown. This is versatile line, since with only the change of die other products monofilaments or Box strappings can also be produced.

Popular applications of BOPP Film are :

- Wrapping of cigarette cartons & tobacco packing.
- Packing of potato chips, noodles, sevia, etc.
- Packing of Bakery products.
- Paper print Laminations.
- Pressure sensitive adhesive tapes.
- Printed synthetic paper applications.
- Visiting cards, invitation cards, calenders, Technical Brochures etc.

Popular applications of HDPE woven Sacks & cloth are :

- Packing of fertilizers and chemical powders.
- Tarpaulin (Black or Blue) covers for protection on Trucks.

Polypropylene woven sacks are preferably used for packing of Cement, since same are more suitable to withstand hot-filling of cement powder. PP woven cloth is also preferred for Bulk Bags (250 kg., 500 kg. Bags) since the same is stronger than HDPE woven cloth.

The most important element of the extrusion machine is the extrusion screw. This delivers material through the die and also heats the thermoplastic by mechanically working it. The length of the screw may be divided into three zones (Fig. 1.1): feed, compression, and metering. The purpose of the feed zone is to pick up the pellets of thermoplastic from the feed hopper and to move them into the main length of the extruder. In this zone the cross-section of the screw channel is usually constant. In the compression zone the loosely packed pellets are compacted and softened to produce a continuous stream of molten plastic. In this section the depth of the screw or the pitch may be decreased. Finally the metering zone takes the molten plastic from the compression zone and feeds it at a controlled rate through the die. The metering zone has a smaller channel depth. It acts as a constant-volume metering pump, which explains the term metering zone.

At an open discharge, that is, without a die to create back pressure, the output of an extruder screw would be given by the formula :

$$Q = \frac{\pi^2 D^2 Nh}{2}$$

where Q = cubic inches per minute

D = diameter of screw in inches

N = rpm

h = depth of screw thread at metering zone.

It would seem that the extruder output should be directly proportional to the volume of the last flight of the screw and to the screw rotational speed. This is not quite the case, due to backpressure from the die and other factors.

A general scale factor is applied to the design of extruder screw: If the screw diameter is doubled, then the length must be doubled and also the thread depth. Therefore, screws are characterised by their L/D or length-to-diameter ratio. An L/D ratio of 20 is standard, but some screws are even longer, with L/D=24.

Under practical conditions a screw of doubled diameter will have an output increased by eight times. Output is also proportional to revolutions per minute.

5

Blown Film Extrusion : Trouble Shooter's Guide

Table 5.1

Faults	**Remedies**
Gels and fish eyes	-Increase the back pressure by using finer screen/adding another screen to improve homogeneity. - Prevent decomposition inside the system and burnt particles on die lips. clean die often. -Increase the Processing temperature.
Black/foreign particles	-Check for contamination in mateiral. -Keep hopper covered and full, to prevent dusty air entering the extruder. Carry out purging or cleaning of die set in case of suspected oxidation of polymer.
Die lines and scratches	-Check and remove nick and burnson die lips, if any. -Clean the die and also the head when necessary. - Purge sufficiently when changing

	to a material of different melt flow index. -Increase the head temperature -Avoid internal decomposition
Orange peel apperance	-Increae extrusion temperature. -Check the heaters which may be defective. -Increase the back pressure by adding screens.
Pot marks	-Usually due to high moisture content. Avoid stocking granules in open air, damp and cold buildings.
Ripples on film	-Check moisture in freshly opened bag and pre-dry granules in case of moisture content at 70-80°C. -Check land length of die and increase the same if necessary. -Inspect temperature profile. -Maintain proper freeze line height. - Control excessive output.
Uneven thickness around circumference	-Adjust die opening with the help of centring screws. -Check the uniformity of cooling air flow throughout the cirfumference of the bubble. -Check the defective heaters of other hot-cold spots on die. -Always maintain proper freeze line heights (FLH).
Variation in thickness of film im machine direction	-Check regularity of screw speed. -Check regularity of haul-off speed. -Maintain optimum processing temperatures.

Bubble instability (vibrating or shaky bubble)	-Check temperature and thickness uniformity of melt at the die. -Check constancy of air pressure inside the bubble. -Add additional bubble guide bars. - Decrease the air flow to the cooling ring. -Avoid outside drafts, shield the system from doors, windows and other air currents.
Wrinkles and creases (A) In blown film	-Check uneven thickness. -Check variation in width. -Reduce freeze line heights. -If film is too cold, reduce cooling or increae extrudate temperature or lower take off rolls. -Adjust & clean collapsing boards, check for smooth and drag free passage through flattener and nip rolls.
(B) On the reel of finished film	-Align the nip rolls correctly ensure that two nip rolls are parrallel and the pressure across the face of rolls is uniform. -Ensure that the winder shaft pulls the film at even and just adequate tension. -Use anti-crease or smoothing foils for remvoing creases. -In case of wrinkles due to static electricity on passage of film, use static eliminator.
Blocking	-Improve the cooling of bubble. -Reduce the temperatures at die and head.

(A) Internal surface	-Reduce pressure at nip rolls. -Supply cooling water to one of nip rolls.
(B) External surfaces	-Discharge the static electricity before wind up rolls. -Check for excessive intensity of corona treatment.
Poor strength	-Adjust relation of linear speed and blow ratio to correct balance. Extrude with tha blow ratio 2:1 to 2.5:1 -Lower the frost line. -Check for die lines which may weaken the film. -Use the polymer with lower melt flow index, if possible.
Poor optical properties	-Increase blow ratio between 2 to 2.5:1. -Raise frost line. -Raise melt temperature. -Reduce cooling rate by passing a lower volume of air.

Table 5.2 :

IMPORTED LDPE FILM GRADES

Grade	MFI	Density	Application
cdF Chinie, Qatar, Lotrene			
FB 3003	0.30	0.923	Heavy duty film, (HD).
FB 5026	0.50	0.922	Milk pouch film (MP).
FD 0374	3.50	0.922	General purpose film (GP).
TPC, Singapore, Cosmthene			
F 101	0.25	0.920	Heavy duty film (HD).
F 108-5	0.40	0.921	Milk pouch film (MP).
F 410-1	5.0	0.923	General purpose film (GP).

Interbras Brazil

NA 677	0.30	0.920	Heavy duty film.
NA 679/50	2.00	0.922	General purpose film.

Yuhwa, Korea

F 600	0.5	0.950	Milk pouch film (MP).

Hangyang, Koerea

3081	0.5	0.950	Milk pouch film (MP).

Dinalene

D 20	0.20		Heavy duty film.
D 65	3.50		General purpose film

Escorene, Exxon Chemicals

LD 150			Milk pouch Film.
LD 100			General purpose Film.

TABLE 5.3 : IMPORTED LDPE GRADES

	Heavy Duty Film Grades	**Milk Pouch Film Grades**	**General Purpose Film Grades**
(1) QUAPCO, QUATAR	FB 3003	FB 5026	FD 0374
(2) DINALENE IN A PETRO-CHEMICAL YUGOSLAVIA	D 20		D 65
(3) OKITEN CROATIA	R 2	R 5	R 3
(4) COSMOTHENE TPC SINGAPORE	F 101	F 108-5	F 410-1

(5) ESCORENE OF EXXON, CHEMICALS, SOUTHY ARABIA		LD 150	LD 100
(6) PETROTHENE POLIOFEFINAS BRÀZIL	NA 677		NA 679/50

TABLE 5.4 :
POPULAR FILM GRADES USED IN INDIA
LDPE GRADES.

Grade	MFI (g/10mm)	Density (g/cc)	Recommended Applications
IPCL, Indothene			
22 FA 002	0.2	0.920	Heavy duty packaging canal Lining Fil, Food Grain, Storage covers, Shrink Film, Detergent, & Salt Bags, Foam Films.
23 FY 005 1005 FY 20	0.5 0.5	0.923 0.920	Packing of Milk & Frozen Food Shrink films.
24 FS 040 1020 FS 20	4.0 2.0	0.923 0.920	Consumer Goods, Packing Grocery Bags, Snack Food Packing, Carrier Bags, Shopping Bags, etc.
FNS 2000	2.0	0.920	Lamination film.
Oswal, Othene			
OBFA-0790 OBFK-0114	0.30 2.0	0.920 0.918	Milk packaging. General purpose film.

Table 5.5 :
LLDPE (Butene) Grades

Grade		MFI (g/10 mm)	Density (g/cc)	Recommended Applications
RIL (Reclair)				
	Slip			
F 19010	Medium	0.9	0.918	Heavy duty, milk & other liquid packaging.
F 21010	No	0.9	0.918	Lamination film.
F 22020	High	1.7	0.918	General purpose films, blending.
IPCL (Indothene)				
	Slip			
LL 20 FS 010	High	1.0	0.920	Liners, drip laterals.
LL 20 FA 010	No	1.0	0.920	Stretch film, lamination film.
LL 20 FY 010	Medium	1.0	0.920	Milk Packaging
LL 20 FS 020	High	2.0	0.920	General purpose film.
Sabic, Ladene				
	Slip			
218 N	No	2.0	0.918	Lamination film
218 W	High	2.0	0.918	General purpose film
118 N	No	1.0	0.918	Lamination film
118 W	High	1.0	0.918	Heavy duty film
Exxon, Exocorene				
	Slip			
LL 1001XW	High	1.0	0.918	Heavy duty film

Table 5.6 :
LLDPE (Octene) Grades

Grade	MFI (g/10min)	Density (g/cc)	Recommended Applications
RIL Reclair			
0 19010	0.90	0.918	Speciality, Heavy Duty & Liquid Packaging Film.
0.21010	0.90	0.918	Speciality lamination Film.
Dow, Dowlex			
5056 01 E	1.00	0.920	Liquid Packaging Film.
5056 E	1.00	0.920	Speciality lamination Film.
2045 AC	1.00	0.920	Heavy Duty Applications.
NG 5056 E	1.10	0.920	Lamination Film, Bag-in Box, Linear, Liquid Food, Pkg.
Union Carbide Corp. "Tuflin" (Hexene) :			
HS-7028 NT 7	1.00	0.918	Liners, Trash Bags Stretch warp.
HS-7098 NT 7	1.00	0.918	High Impact Film, Ice Bags.
Mobil, Hexene Copolymer Gardes			
NTX 095	0.90	0.918	Industrial & Consumer Goods Packing
NTX 101	0.90	0.918	Blown stretch film super Impact & Tear Strength.

Table 5.7 :
HM HDPE Grades

Grade	MFI	Density	Applications
NOCIL, Pilene			
PM 4577 F	0.40 (5)	0.950	Paper like film, shopping bags, carrier bags, industrial liners etc.
Mobil			
HTA 001 HTA 002	0.5 (12) 16 (12)	0.948 0.952	Same as above
Sabic, Ladene			
F 00948	0.05 (12)	0.948	Same as above.
Mitsui, Hizex			
7000 F 8000 F	0.05 0.03	0.956 0.950	Same as above.
G-Lex Gail			
F 50 HM 0003	0.03	0.95	Same as above.

6

Extrusion Instabilities of Variabilities

In extrusion, as in all other processes, an extensive theoretical analysis has been applied to facilitate understanding and maximise the manufacturing operation. However, the "real world" must be understood and appreciated as well. The operator has to work within the many limitations of the materials and equipment (the basic extruder and all auxiliary upstream and downstream equipment). The interplay and interchange of process controls can help to eliminate problems and/or aid operation with the variables that exist. The greatest degree of instability is due to improper screw design (or using the wrong screw). Proper instrumentation, particularly barrel heat, is important to diagnosis of the problem(s). For uniform/stable extrusion, it is important to periodically check the drive system, the take-up device, and other equipment, and compare it to its original performance. If variations are excessive, all kinds of problems will develop. An elaborate process control system can help, but it is best to improve stability in all facets of the extrusion line. Examples of instabilities and problem areas include: (i) non-uniform plastics flow in the hopper; (ii) troublesome bridging, with excessive barrel heat that melts the solidified plastic in the hopper and feed section and stops plastic flow; (iii) variations in (a) barrel heat, (b) screw heat, (c) screw speed, (d) screw power drive, (e) die heat, (f) die head pressure, and the (g) take-up device; (iv) insufficient melting and/or mixing capacity; (v) insufficient pressure generating capacity; (vi) wear and/or damage of the screw and/or the barrel; (vii) melt fracture/sharkskin).

Finally one must check the proper alignment of the extruder and the downstream equipment. Proper alignment and isolation of the vibrators is a must for high-quality and high-speed output.

PLASTIC HANDLING

Care should be taken to prevent conditions that promote surface condensation of moisture on the plastic and moisture absorption by any existing pigments in colour concentrates. The surface condensation can be avoided by proper storage of the plastic and keeping it in an area at least as warm as the operating temperature for at least 24 h prior to its use. If moisture absorption by a colour concentrate is suspected, heating for 8 to 24 h in a 250 to 300°F (120 to 150°C) oven should permit sufficient drying. With hygroscopic resins, special precautions and drying are required. A hopper dryer's heat can be used to improve melt performance and extruder output capacity (Fig. 6.1). When the dryer preheat is insufficient, heat can be applied in the screw's solids conveying zone and/or the barrel feed throat (assuming the capability exists).

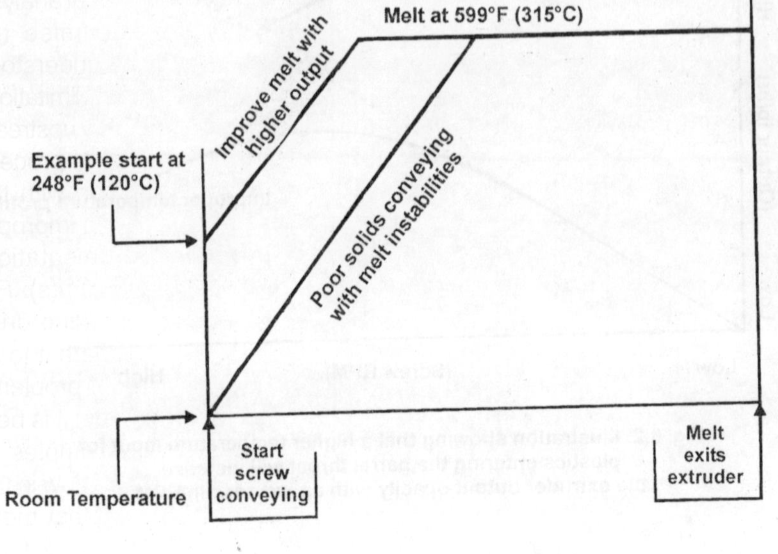

Fig. 6.1 : Technique for improving material and/or machine performance by preheating "solids" entering the extruder's feed throat.

A typical heat profile that is adequate at low screw speed may be inadequate when speeds are increased, because of the greater rate of material flow through the extruder. (In fact, the heat profile may even be inadequate at low speed.) The output may not increase at a linear rate with increasing speed unless the heat profile increases (Fig. 6.2). With a proper heat profile, a linear relationship between speed and output can be maintained through a wider operating range. However, too high a heat at low screw speed is likely to cause melting all the way back to the barrel throat, causing resin bridging and degradation.

Different techniques are used to improve feeding from the hopper-a ram stuffer, a tapered (larger) screw in the throat section, a grooved feed section, starved feeling, and so on. All have advantages and disadvantages, based on the capabilities of the machines and of the resin being processed. What may help with one machine in the plant may be useless in another machine using the same resin.

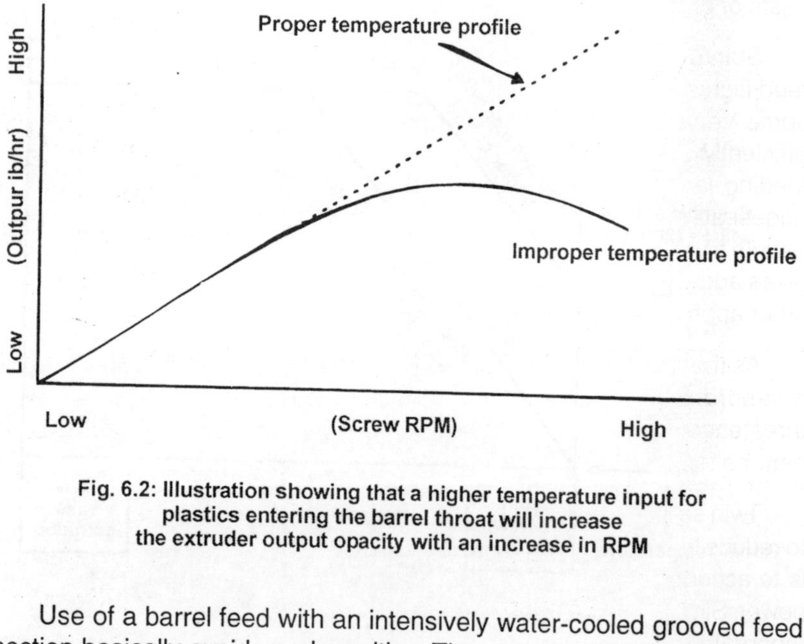

Fig. 6.2: Illustration showing that a higher temperature input for plastics entering the barrel throat will increase the extruder output opacity with an increase in RPM

Use of a barrel feed with an intensively water-cooled grooved feed section basically avoids early melting. The grooves impart better solids conveying for resins with a low coefficient off riction such as UHMWPE and other resins where additives make them extremely slippery. The grooves usually have right-angle profile and axial arrangements, although helical grooves are used for certain materials. Optimum sizing and dimensioning of the feed section and the correct control of cooling are necessary, as well as proper design of the feed screw, to achieve a high-output revolution with a low-friction load.

If a resin exhibit a feeding inefficiency (as the screw speed is increased, the output of the extruder does not measurably increase), grooved feed sections should be considered. Most materials feed well, as seen through moderate or high pressure levels early in the barrel, and the state of screw design has led to efficient "melting rate limited" extrusion. A grooved feed that is already limited by the melting rate will overdrive the screw and cause melt quality effects that must be corrected through the use of shallower screws. Should a material not be "melting rate limited" but feed reasonable well, a grooved feed will increase the output. Probably the next larger screw will accomplish the same result at a lower cost. One must consider economics, including the added maintenance and operational costs of grooves.

Starve or metered feeding devices do not allow equipment to run with feed flights completely filled; so this approach is best avoided, although some vented screws do use these devices. Machines will run most efficiently and with the best cleaning when feed flights are full. Starve feeding leads to flights that are partially empty for sole distance, an undesirable situation (wear problems, etc.). Some two-stage screws that handle a variety of resins may not be versatile enough, and then a feeder gives added control. When machines are having a feed problem, and no other approach is possible, starving can help.

As the feeder is adjusted, the screw's performance will at some point deteriorate so that the output consistency or the melt efficiency is threatened. Adjusting the screw design to preclude the need to starve is a better alternative, which usually is economically feasible.

Twin screw extruders producing profiles will often use starve feeders to reduce torque requirements. However, a better approach, when feasible, is to accomplish this via a screw design with adequate extruder torque power. Slight starving of twins may not seriously deteriorate the melt, but moderate to high levels of starving will reduce stability.

As already explained regrind can be a major problem. Many extruder lines, such as film trim and scrap, are reprocessed; the material is granulated and/or plasticised by a small extruder and fed back with virgin resin. The extrudability of the combination may be quite different from that of virgin resin. Problems also can develop in the blending of two or more different resins, such as LLDPE and LDPE, to improve specific performances. The LLDPE starts melting/breaking down at a lower heat than does LDPE, so their blend is more difficult to process than virgin/regrind blends. New screw designs overcome such problems.

MULTIPLE SCREW EXTRUDERS

Regardless of their particular designs, all extruders have the function of conveying plastic and converting it into a melt. For this purpose, both single and multiple screw extruders are suitable; but they all have individual characteristic features. Practical and theoretical data show that each type has its place. The single screw machine dominates and will be the focus of discussion in this chapter. However, other types are available, such as the twin screw extruders and they are often used to achieve improved dispersing and mixing, as in the compounding of additives.

Other claims for multi screws, most often twin screw designs, inslude a high conveying capacity at low screw speed, a positive and controlled pumping rate over a wide range of temperature and coefficients of friction, low frictional heat generation which permits low-heat operation, low contact time in the extruder, relatively low motor power requirements, and the ability to feed normally difficult feeding materials such as powders. Twin screw types, because of their low heat extrusion characteristics, have found increasingly wide usage in heat-sensitive PVC processing. The most popular and functional multiscrews are the twin screw designs.

Twin screw extruders with non-intermeshing counter-rotating screws are mostly used for compounding by resin manufacturers, including situations where volatiles must be removed during extrusion. Meshing twin screws have found a substantial market in difficult compounding and devolatilisation processes. To provide specialised compounding and mixing, particularly in the laboratory, different techniques are required, such as using interchangeable screw sections on a splined shaft.

Most of the commercial machines on the market and in the use today are intermeshing. One interesting feature of non-intermeshing twins is the possibility of running the two screws at different speeds, thus creating frictional relationships between them, which in some instances can be exploited for the rapid melting of powders. In some twins, one screw is significantly shorter than the other. This design is used for resins that may be adequately conveyed by a single screw once in the form of a melt, but which, because of low bulk density or very low coefficients of friction of the solid against the surrounding walls, are difficult to feed into screw flights. Thus, after melting by the twins, the resin moves through the single screw.

Constant screw diameters can be used, as in single designs. or the screws can be conical. A conical twin with a large-diameter rear feed zone has a volume capacity greater than the compression and metering zones capacity. This design allow a greater amount of powder to be moved to the feed zone per RPM while using the least possible clearance between flights, to provide a higher output rate with minimum shear and frictional heat accumulation. Different variables are involved in multi screw machines compared to singles, so multi screws generally are sized on the basis of lb/h rather than L/D and/or diameters.

With intermeshing screws, the relative motion of the flight of one screw inside the channel of the other acts as a wedge that pushes material from the back to the front of the channel and from screw to screw. This pattern keeps the screw moving forward, almost as if the machine were a positive displacement gear pump, which conveys material at rather low RPM with low compression and very little friction. The friction in a single screw that causes material to move forward also generates heat. Twin screws do not have the problem of frictional heat build-up because heat is not influenced by friction. Heat is controlled from an outside source (barrels)--an action that becomes very critical in the processing of heat-sensitive plastics, such as PVC. The multiple screws provide the advantages of higher output rates and very tight heat control, as required, for example, to produce large PVC pipes. However, single screws are also used to produce PVC pipe.

Although multiple screws are more expensive than single screws, there are some advantages to using multiscrews. Twins can be used effectively in handling PVC dry blends that are compounded in a plant, potentially offering a significant costs savings as compared to buying compounded PVC. With a multiple and its lower operating heat profile, lower levels of heat stabilisers can be used, with potential savings in material costs.

Other uses for twin screws include the processing of extruded Expandable polystyrene (EPS) sheet and high molecular weight polymers. For EPS, there might be cost advantages in using one machine rather than the usual tandem single screw setup. One machine mixes while the other extrudes, with the second machine providing the required cooling time period. Products such as high molecular weight polyolefins or some of the TFE-fluoroplastics can be gently melted in twin screws, and these high viscosity melts can be conveyed through a die without pulsations, a major advantage in processability.

In counter-rotating systems, the basic advantage is that the material that does pass through the nip of the two screws is subject to an extremely high degree of shear, just as if it were passing through the nip between two rolls of a two-roll mill. By varying the clearance (the free space that is left after the two screws have intermeshed), it is possible to vary the position of material that is carried through and just moves axially. The narrower the clearance between screws, the greater the shear force that will be exerted, and the larger the portion of material that remains in the "bank". With this action, it is easy to adjust the amount of shear to be applied.

In co-rotating twin screw extrusion, one screw transports the material around and up to the point where the screws intermesh. At that point two opposing and equal-velocity gradients exist, so nearly everything that one screw has carried is taken over by the other screw. In this system, plastics will follow an eight-shaped path along the entire barrel length. Advantages of co-rotating are: (i) chances are better statistically that all particles will be subjected to the same shear; (ii) with the relatively long eight-shaped path, the chances of influencing the plastic in terms of the melt heat are good; (iii) at the deflection point, the shear energy introduced can be regulated within very wide limits by adjusting the depths of the screw flights; and (iv) the system allows for a much greater degree of self-cleaning or self-wiping than in other designs, as one screw completely wipes the other screw. This latter performance is important, not so much in terms of keeping screws clean, but in permitting greater control over the residence time distribution, which is very important with heat-sensitive plastics.

To summarise the comparison of screw types, in a single extruder the screw rotating inside the barrel is not able by itself to push the material forward. If for some reason the material filling the channels adheres to the screw, it becomes a rotating cylinder and provides no forward motion. Material pushed forward should not rotate, or at least should rotate at a slower rate than the screw. The only force that can keep the material from turning with the screw and make it advance along the barrel is the friction between the material and inside surface of the barrel. The more friction, the less rotation of material with the screw; the less rotation, the more forward motion. To yield sufficient production with a low friction factor, the screw must have a large diameter and turn at high speed. However, a large¬diameter screw rotating at high speed develops very high shear. The heat produced may increase the melt temperature over its limit, so cooling is necessary during the process (water jacket and/or blown air over the barrel). A non-intermeshing twin screw functions like a single screw extruder, with friction as the prime mover. Twins with intermeshing screws operate on a completely different principle. The direction of rotation, whether co-rotating or counter-rotating, has a great influence on the way they operate.

Counter-rotating twins tend to accumulate and compress the material where the screws meet and remove material where they part, thereby creating zones of high and low pressure around the screws. Material that is forced by this pressure through small passages at high speeds is subjected to high localised shear. In co-rotating twins, material is transferred from one screw to the other without such high shear action.

In co-rotating twins, the screws act like a positive displacement gear pump and do not depend on friction against the barrel to move material forward. As there is no relationship between the screw speed and the output rate, they can work with starve feeding. The channel depth is three to four times greater than in a single screw, and, more important, the screw speed is much lower (use 15-20 rpm); so the total shear rate is much less (can be 80 per cent less in twin vs. single). The low screw speed accounts for the low shear rate, and this situation keeps material more viscous and the stock heat down. Consequently, any additional heat required has to be applied through the barrel heaters.

Unfortunately, there are losses as well as gains. The higher-cost multiple screw machines, with their more expensive and complicated drive systems, require constant preventive maintenance; otherwise, rather extensive down time (and repair costs) would occur. Regardless of the disadvantages, multi-screws have an important role in processing plastics. Their disadvantages should not influence their use if there are cost advantages.

SINGLE SCREW EXTRUDERS

The standard metering extrusion screw with its three zones (conveying, compression, and metering) basically operates like a conventional injection moulding (1M) screw. The nomenclature is the same for each, except that no valve is used at the end of the extrusion screw. As reviewed, extrusion screws operate at lower pressures and in a continuous mode (IM is repeatable with abrupt, completely on-off pressure changes and very fast cycles). Even though many variables must be considered, extrusion requires fewer controls and presents fewer problems than IM.

Single screw extruders have changed greatly over the years. Today's functional modular concept developed mainly for reasons of effectiveness and favourable cost comparisons. Their output rates have significantly surpassed those of older designs. The output rates can be used as a guide to predict the output rate of a process. The performance of all machines and production lines (film, profile, etc.) will depend on the many factors that have to be controlled and syncronised going from upstream through the extruder and the downstream equipment. The type of screw used has always been a major influence in the complete line.

The blown film extruder has typified the new generation of extruders. The most effective screw design, in most cases, has been an L/D of 25. Longer machines with a 30 to 33 L/D are chosen for venting or special requirements. High outputs are obtained with LDPE blown film or PP cast film extrusion. The 20 L/D machines now are almost always used only for heat-sensitive plastics. The 25 L/D version offers exactly the right compromise for obtaining a high output and preventing over heating and damage of thermally sensitive plastics.

Even in today's high technology world, the art of screw design is still dominated by trial-and-error approaches. However, computer models (based on proper input and experience) play an important role. When new materials are developed or improvements in old materials are required, one must go to the laboratory to obtain rheological and thermal properties before computer modeling can be performed effectively. New screws improve one or more of the basic screw functions of: melt quality, mixing efficiency, melting performance along the screw, melt heat level, output rate, output stability, and power usage or energy efficiency.

As previously reviewed, heating can be controlled by using different machine settings, which involve various trade offs. For example, in choosing the optimum rotation speed, a slow speed places the melt in contact with the barrel and screw for a longer time via heat conduction, and the slower speed produces less hear, so that dissipative heating is reduced, and properties of the plastic (particularly of a film) are enhanced. Sometimes an internal heat control is used with a screw (Fig. 6.3). This type of screw is characterised by deeper channels, steeper helical angles, and an internal heating element. Its internal heating lowers the amount of viscous heating needed to process the material. As a result, the melt heat can be reduced by 50°F.

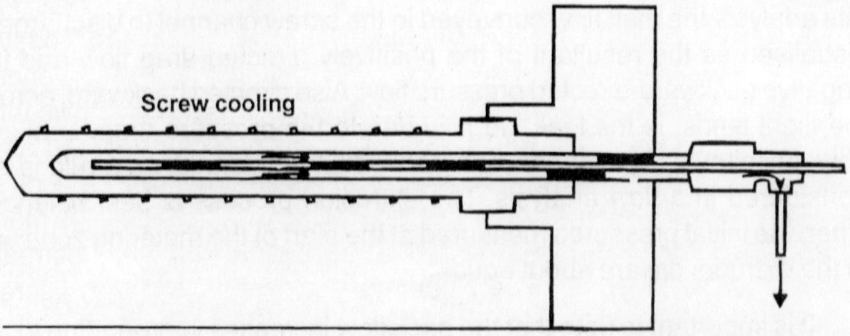

Fig. 6.3 Concept of screw with internal heat or cooling system.

Mixing and Melting

In typical extrusion operations, mixing devices are used in the screws. Many dynamic mixers are used to improve screw performance. Static mixers are sometimes inserted at the screw end or at the end of the barrel. There are also mixing devices that remain independent of the screw.

Proof of the success and reliability of dynamic on-line mixers is shown by their extensive use. Each mixer offers its own advantages and disadvantages with different machines and materials. Unfortunately there is no one system that solves all melting problems. The data available from the different equipment suppliers can be used in comparative studies.

Static mixers are successfully installed in the adapters between the barrel and the die for further thermal homogenisation of the melt after it leaves the screw. This causes transitory fluctuations and temperature variations in the melt to decrease considerably. As a result an increased pressure drop occurs and the heat level increases a few degrees, while temperature peaks disappear. Thus in selecting a static mixer, one should be sure that its resistance to flow is as low as possible.

The dynamic mixing elements should be fitted as near the end of the metering zone as possible. For maximum performance, a standard screw can have the following sectional dimensions in respect to its diameter (D): feed zone = 5D, compression zone = 3D, metering zone = 12 to 13D, and mixing zone 2 to 3D. In principle, any mixing zone, wherever it is located within the metering zone, is more effective in homogenising than the screw threads normally present in that position. Where practical, mixers should be located in a region where the melt viscosity is not too low. Only in the metering zone can the flow phenomenon be explained theoretically. In this analysis the melt flow conveyed in the screw channel to discharge is visualised as the resultant of the positively directed drag flow and the negative backward-directed pressure flow. Also directed backward, across the flight lands, is the leakage flow due to the pressure drop. Leakage flow, despite its significance with non-wetting materials, as a rule is not considered in a flow analysis. The extrusion process is best balanced when the initial pressures measured at the start of the metering zone and in the extruder die are about equal.

It is important to note that the back flow increases in proportion to the third power of the depth of the thread. For this reason, screws with deep cut channels are not the best choice for thermoplastics (but are okay with thermosets). If the speed of single screw extruders is increased, especially in the processing of high molecular weight viscous melts, the extrudate obtained may be rough, unattractive in appearance, and unsalable. Such results also can occur with slower-running machines using relatively deep cut screws in conjunction with extrusion dies of low resistance to flow.

This situation is due to an unstable combination of screw and die, and basically can be related to unsuitable pressure melt variations. Approaches to improving the situation include using longitudinally adjustable (regular mechanical) screws with tapered clearances as throttling sections, independent throttling valves in different positions of the die, and so on. The goal is to eliminate dead spots in which stagnating melt could be thermally degraded; so streamlining is in order, such as that provided by conical screw tips. (6.3).

In-line dynamic mixers, independently driven at optimum speeds, perform distributive mixing with moderate pressure loses, low power requirements, and small heat increases. The use of dynamic mixers mounted on the end of a screw may not be optimum because extruders may have to be driven at slower speeds to avoid problems such as surging; but independently driven mixers can be sized and run at optimum speeds to provide the best mixing. Other benefits of independently driven mixers involve feeding. For example, metering pumps can inject liquid additives directly into the mixer in the exact quantities needed to modify a resin. In fact, an auxiliary extruder can add a secondary melt stream to the mixer, thereby allowing for such techniques as resin alloying while simultaneously colouring or stabilising the resin.

A major and important use of mixers is to ensure minimum exposure of the melt to shear and high heat, so that, with heat-sensitive melts, less stabiliser is needed. With these devices, a moderate pressure drop and melt uniformity are achieved in a short process time. The mixers can be placed adjacent to a die, to provide the least flush time between material changes. All the mixing devices discussed in this section make it possible to achieve better melts by literally breaking up the solid beds. Like an ice cube that more easily melts in water when it is cracked, the plastic "solids" break up, resulting in a better melt.

Venting

During extrusion, as in IM melts must be freed of gaseous components (monomer, moisture, plasticisers, additives, etc.); so a vented screw is used. It is especially difficult to completely remove air from some powdered materials unless the melt is exposed to vacuum venting (a vacuum is connected to the vent's exhaust). The standard machines operate on the principle of melt degassing. The degassing is assisted by a rise in the vapour pressure of volatile constituents, which results from the high melt heat. Only the free surface layer is degassed; the remainder of the plastic can release its volatile content only through diffusion (1-4, 8-9, 96, 100, 143). Diffusion in the non-vented screw is always time-dependent, and long residence times are not possible for melt moving through an extruder. Thus a vented extruder is used.

Most single screw vented extruders have two stages; a few have two vents and three stages. The first stages of the transition and metering sections are often shorter than the sections of a single stage conventional screw. The melt discharges at zero back pressure into the second stage, under vacuum instead of pressure. The first stage extrudate must not be hot enough to become overheated in the second stage. Also, the first stage must not deliver more output per screw revolution at discharge pressure than the second stage can pump through the die under the maximum normal operating pressure, such as might occur just prior to a screen pack change. Usually this requirement means that the second stage metering section must be at least 50 per cent deeper than the first stage. In practice, the best metering section depth ratio (pump ratio) is about 1.8: I. The best ratio depends on factors such as screw design, downstream equipment, feedstock performance, and operating conditions.

With a high compression ratio or metering depth ratio that is a little too low, melt flow through the vent is likely. If this ratio is moderately high, gradual degradation of the output occurs. If the screw channel in the vent area is not filled properly, the self-cleaning action is diminished, and the risk of plateout increases. In any case, sticking or smearing of the melt must be avoided, or degradation will accelerate.

Screen Packs

Melt from the screw usually is forced through a breaker plate with a screen pack. Extra heat develops when melt goes through the screens, so some heat-sensitive materials cannot use a screen pack. The function ofa screen pack initially is to reduce rotary motion of the melt, remove large unmelted particles, and remove other contaminants. This situation can be related to improper screw design, contaminated feedstock, poor control of regrind, and so on. Sometimes screen packs are used to control the operating pressure of extruders. However, there are advantages in processing with matched and controlled back pressure, operating within the required melt pressure, as this can facilitate mixing, effectively balancing out melt heat. (Table 6.1(a) provides a troubleshooting guide to the use of screens).

In operation, the screen pack is backed up by a breaker plate that has a number of passages, usually many round holes ranging from 1/8 to 3/16 in. in diameter. One side of the plate is recessed to accommodate round discs of wire screen cloth, which make up the screen pack (Table 9.2b). Pressure controls should be used on both sides of the breaker plate to ensure that the pressure on the melt stays within the required limits. Based on the processing requirements, manual to highly sophisticated screen changers are used. With limited runs or infrequent changes, manual systems are used. The packs are usually mounted outside the extruder between the head clamp and the die and can be changed via mechanical or hydraulic devices. Continuous screen changes also are used. The more sophisticated the system is, the higher its costs.

The majority of barrels and screws are made from special steels, which are nitrided to a minimum depth by special techniques. Low alloy steels are sometimes used with wear-resistant linears.

ENERGY CONSUMPTION

Like the output capacity, the energy efficiency of an extruder is

TABLE 6.2
TROUBLE SHOOTING GUIDE FOR SCREEN CHANGERS.

Problem : Seal laekage

Possible Causes	Remedy
• Head pressure above maximum set pressure	• Reduce head pressure
• Excessive overhung load	• Support downstream die adapter, etc.
• Seals improperly installed	• Remove, clean, and re-install
• Excessively scored seals or slide plate	• Correct cause of damage (see below) or replace
• Disc spring relaxed	• Replace
• Initial pressure setting of upstream body too low	• see produce for setup in manual

Problem : Excessively scored seals

Possible Causes	Remedy
• Maximum set pressure rating too high	• See procedure for setting U/S body
• Wire strands protruding above face of slide plate	• Ensure correct screen size and installation
• Screen treating out or folding on shift	• Utilize positive screen retention
• Tramp metal caught by screens device	• Utilize hopper magnet or other metal-catching

Problem : No slide ptate movement

Possible Causes	Remedy
• Guards not closed	• close guards
• Pressure ready light not on (w/opt. selenoid valve)	• Check hydraulic power unit
• Limit switches or interlock wiring faulty	• Repair or replace
• Direction control valve not operating	• Repair or replace

Problem : Erractic or slow slide plate movement

Possible Causes	Remedy
• Air in system	Purge air
• Low percharge in accumulator	Recharge accumulator
• Oil viscocity too high	Replace with correct viscocity oil
• Pressure drop across breaker plate too high	Reduce pressure drop
• Polymer viscocity too high	Decreae viscocity
• Initial pressure setting of upstream body too high	Procedure for setting U/S body
• Leakage past the directin control valve or changer cylinder	Repair or replace

Problem : No pressure hydraulic power unit

Possible Causes	Remedy
• Motor not running	• Check disconnects, motor overloads, motor
• Unload selenoid valve not closed	• Replace
• Pump/Shaft damaged	• Replace pump

Problem : Low pressure, motor stops

Possible Causes	Remedy
• Faulty pressure switch	• Replace switch

Problem : Low pressure, motor continues to run

Possible Causes	Remedy
• Low fluid level	• Fill reservoir
• Suction stainer blocked	• Clean or replace
• Oil overheated	• See below
• Air entertained in fluid	• Allow bubbles to subside, use antiform
• Leakage past direction control valve	• Repair or replace
• Leakage past screenchanger cylinder	• Repair or replace
• Pump damaged/worn	• Replace pump

Problem : Normal pressure, does not stop

Possible Causes	Remedy
Faulty pressure switch	Replace switch

Problem : Rapid pump/motor cycling

Possible Causes	Remedy
• Faulty pressure switches	• Replace switch
• Leakage past check valve	• Replace pump
• Pump damaged or worn	• Replace pump
• Leaking past direction control valve or screen changer cylinder	• Repair or replace

Problem : Oil Overheating

Possible Causes	Remedy
• Rapid screenchanger cycling	• Shift less frequently
• Resctricted air movement or high temperature around reservoir	• Assure free movement of air around hydraulic unit
• Fluid bypass through system causing excessivepump up time or rapid pump cycling	• See above.

Table 6.2b : Screens used before the breaker plate to filter out contaminants in the melt[a].

		Wire Mesh		
Contaminant	Metal Fibres	Square weave	Dutch twill[b]	Sintered powder
Gel Captured	5	1	2	3
Contaminant capacity	6	2	3	3
Permeability	4	4	1	2

[a] Range is from poorest (1) to best (6) Multiple screens usually are used; example screen pack has 20-mesh against beaker plate followed by 40-, 60-, and 100-mesh (coarest mesh has lowest mesh number).

[b] Woven in parallel diagonal lines.

dependent on the torque available on the screw, screw RPM, heat control, and material being processed. Unfortunately, costly energy losses can occur, ranging from 3 to 20 per cent and due to various factors, with the major loss occurring in the drive mechanism. The power for screw rotation is supplied by a variable speed motor drive system, and is transmitted through a gear reduction unit, a coupling, and a thrust bearing. Gear reducers impart the final speed and torque to the screw. Most gear reducers use double-reaction helical or herringbone gears for their ruggedness and to hold noise levels within acceptable limits. Worm and pinion gear combinations have been used on smaller extruders. The efficiency of the power transmission gear with the worm is a maximum of 85 per cent; that of the helical gear reaches 95 per cent, and the herringbone 97 per cent.

Thrust bearings absorb the thrust force exerted by the screw as it turns against the material in the barrel. The size or rating of the thrust bearing provides an anticipated number of operating hours (if kept clean). The operating pressure, size of extruder, and operating speed are important factors in selection of a thrust bearing. The motor size must be sufficient to allow for the energy required to melt the plastic and to pump the melt at the desired output condition and rate. For example, higher outputs at higher screw speeds require more power than low outputs. The specific heat of the resin will also be a determining factor. As a guide, simple extrusions usually require 1 HP for every 10 to 15 lb/h output. For high energy or where high heat at low speeds is required, 1 HP may be required for every 3 to 5lb/h. Plastics require different power or running torque on screws, based on the type of plastic and the screw size. Extrusion of rigid PVC requires about twice the power needed for LDPE. Increasing screw diameters could at least double torque requirements for every one inch of diameter increase. As previously observed, in comparing single extruders with intermeshing co-rotating twin screw extruders, the twins provide significant energy conservation and efficiency.

Energy consumption is a major factor in production costs, as well as all equipment efficiency. Many extruders, as well as other equipment, are usually overpowered. This situation may be better than using underpowered equipment; but processes should not waste energy. In an extruder, as in any other machine, the energy output is always equal to the energy input, regardless of the forms into which it may be converted. The energy may be furnished by mechanical or thermal sources. Mechanical energy is supplied by the drive motor; thermal energy is supplied "positively" by electrical heater bands or "negatively" by cooling devices. It is important to evaluate and compare equipment performance in order to minimise energy waste.

GEAR PUMPS

Gear pumps, also called melt or metering pumps, have established themselves in all kinds of extrusion lines. They consist of a pump, a drive for the pump, and pump controls, located between the screen pack (or screw) and the die. Two counter-rotating gears will transport a melt from the pump inlet (extruder output) to the pump discharge outlet (die) as shown in Fig. 6.4. Gear rotation creates a suction that draws the melt into a gap between one tooth and the next. This continuous action, from tooth to tooth, develops surface drag that resists flow; so some inlet pressure is required to fill the cavity.

The inlet pressure requirements vary with material viscosity, pump speed, and mixing requirements. These pressures are usually less than 1,000 psi but cannot go below certain specified pressures such as 300 psi. An extruder specifically designed for use with a pump only has to "mix", with no need to operate at high pressures to move the melt. It only has to generate the low pump inlet pressure; thus it can deliver melt at a lower than usual heat, requiring less energy and often yielding a higher output rate. The positive displacement gear device pumps the melt at a constant rate. It delivers the melt to the die with a very high metering accuracy and efficiency. Pressure differentials as high as 4,000 psi between the pump inlet and discharge are common.

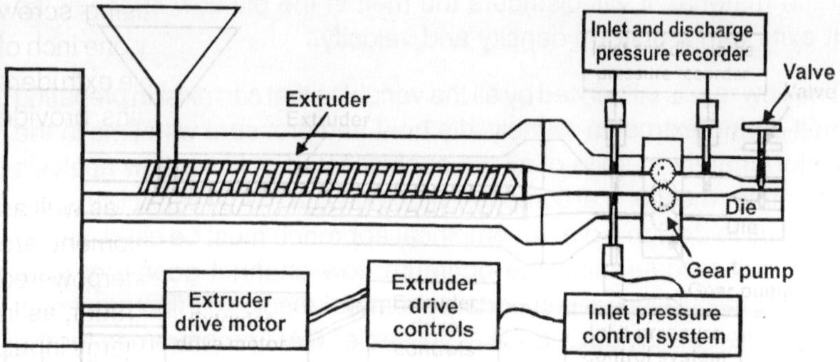

Fig. 6.4 : Schematics of a gear pump used in a typical extrusion system.

Besides improving gauge uniformity, a pump can contribute to product quality by reducing the resin's heat history. This heat reduction can help blown film extruders, particularly those running high viscosity melts such as LLDPE and heat-sensitive melts such as PVC. Heat drops of at least 20 to 30°F will occur. In PS foam sheet extrusion, a cooling of 10 to 15°F occurs in the second extruder as well as a 60 per cent reduction in gauge variation by relief of back pressure. One must be aware that all melts require a minimum heat and back pressure for effective processing.

With pump use, potential energy savings amount to 10 to 20 per cent. Pumps are 50 to 75 per cent energy-efficient, whereas single screw extruders are about 5 to 20 per cent efficient.

Although they can eliminate or significantly improve many processing problems, gear pumps cannot be considered a panacea. However, they are worth examining and could boost productivity and profits very significantly. Their major gains tend to be principally in (i) melt stability; (ii) temperature reduction in the melt; and (iii) increased throughput with tighter tolerances for dimensions and weights.

DIES

The function of a die is to accept the "available" melt from an extruder and deliver it to takeoff equipment as a shaped profile (film, sheet, pipe, filament, etc.) with minimum deviation in cross-sectional dimensions and a uniform output by weight, at the fastest possible rate. A well-designed die should permit colour and compatible resin changes quickly with little off-grade material. It will distribute the melt in the die flow channels so that it exits with a uniform density and velocity.

The flow rate is influenced by all the variables that can exist in preparing the melt during extrusion-namely, die heat and pressure with time in the die. Unfortunately, in spite of all the sophisticated polymer flow analysis and the rather mechanical computer-aided design (CAD) capabilities, it is very difficult to design a die. An empirical approach must be used, as it is quite difficult to determine the optimum flow channel geometry from engineering calculations. It is important to employ rheological flow properties and other melt behaviour via the "applicable" CAD programmes for the type of die required. The most important ingredient is experience, which, for the novice, is properly recorded in a computer programme. Nevertheless, die design has remained more of an art than any other aspect of process design. Design experience can work only if the operator of the processing line has developed the important ability to debug it.

An extrusion die is usually massive. Dies for profiles such as mouldings, counter edging, rods, etc. have an orifice of the approximate shape and size of the required contour, the final shape developing outside the die as the material warps and shrinks or expands. Some comparisons of finished profiles with their corresponding die orifices are shown in Fig. 9.7. For complex profiles it is not possible to design a satisfactory die. A first approximation to the required die shape is made, and then by trial on the extruder the shape of the die orifice is modified as required. The size and shape of an extruded profile can also be changed by altering the extrusion speed and the rate of cooling after the plastic leaves the die.

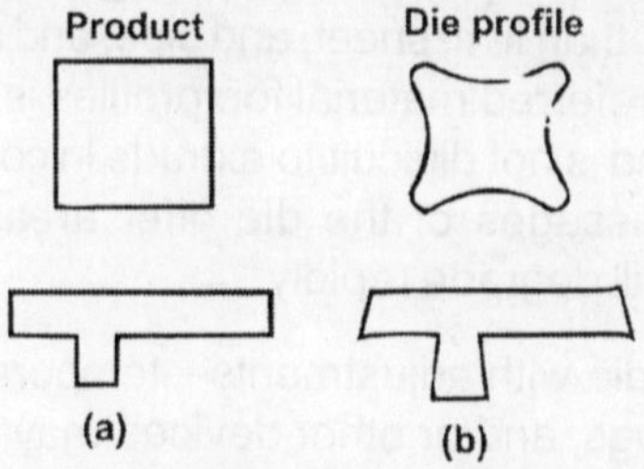

Fig. 6.5 A comparison of two extruded shapes and the die profiles required to produce them

Critical dimensions for a profile die are the percentage die oversize, the land length, and the angle of entry into the land section. The land is the length of constant cross-section measured back from the die opening. (Fig. 6.6). The land is required to provide back pressure for better mixing. Longer lands are used for very fluid polymers, shorter ones for viscous polymers. Usual land lengths are eight to ten times the thickness (vertical dimension) of the die orifice.

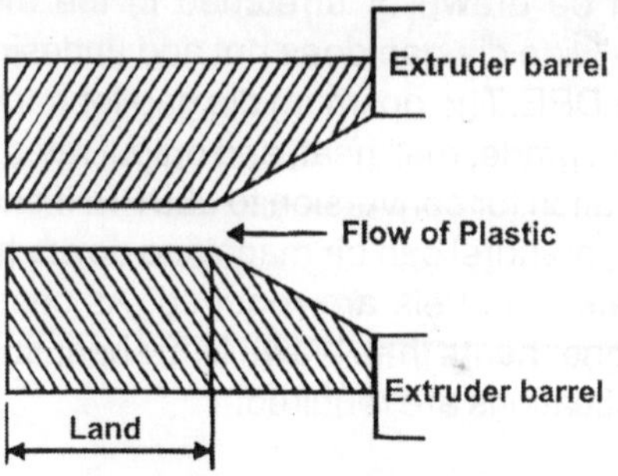

Fig. 6.6 Land of an extrusion die.

Usually the die orifice is made oversize. Tension is needed to pull the plastic away from the die, and this tension reduces the cross-section of the profile. In addition, the polymer shrinks on cooling. At the same time the plastic tends to swell when it leaves the die and is free of the confining pressure within the die. The crystalline plastics such as nylon and high-density polyethylene require about 20 per cent oversize; PS and UPVC require about 10 per cent oversize.

Corners and sharp projections in the contour have a large surface area for cooling and therefore shrink.first when the contour cools, which tends to make them smaller. This tendency is corrected by enlarging the die at these points. This necessary correction explains the curved shape needed to obtain the square profile of Fig. 6.5. Profiles are required in smaller quantities than film, sheet, and pipe, and are usually run on smaller extruders. The preferred material for. profiles is PVC. This thermoplastic is inexpensive and is not difficult to extrude in complex shapes. However, if the internal passages of the die offer areas where the plastic can stagnate, PVC will degrade rapidly.

A well-built die with adjustments—temperature changes, restricter/choker bars, valves, and/or other devices-may be used with a particular group of materials. Usually a die is designed for a specific resin. For example, conventional LDPE blown film dies with 0.030 in. (0.8 mm) die gaps will not process LLDPE satisfactorily at high output rates. The higher-viscosity LLDPE increases back pressure significantly, thereby decreasing the throughput. Also, melt fracture, or sharkskinning, may occur, resulting in a rough surface finish. With its extensional rheology, processors of LLDPE can overcome these problems with wide die gaps in the 0.090 in. (2.3 mm) range. With an increase in the die gap, the head pressure decreases, making possible significant increase in output.

LLDPE can be drawn or stretched in the melt with low induced orientation, so a wide die gap does not add undesirable film stresses for LLDPE as with LDPE. The optimum die gap for each application will vary according to resin grade, melt heat, and output rates. Only the die mandrel requires modification for conversion to LLDPE. If only LLDPE is to be run, then the existing mandrel can be machined down. If both resins are to be run, two separate mandrels are required. As cast film is processed at considerably higher heats than blown film, shear stresses are minimised, and no die modifications are required.

A good PS sheet die usually can run some other resins. The gauge control capability of the die for PS or other resins is determined to a great extent by the flow adjustments. Heavy gauge dies might have a lip land length of 3 to 4 in. and a relatively coarse method of adjusting the massive lips. In contrast, a film die would have a lip land length of 0.75 in. and a lip adjustment capable of extremely fine adjustments. Many film dies and thin gauge sheet dies utilise a flexible lip for extremely close gauge control.

Any analysis of die efficiency must include a careful examination of the compability of the die with the products to be extruded. If a die is designed for sheet thicknesses of 0.150 to 0.375 in., it is extremely difficult to extrude 5 mil (0.005 in.) film. As there is no die design that could be called a "universal" die, it is very inefficient to expect an operator to run a die beyond its capabilities. The result would be poor gauge control, and so forth. If the flow channel geometry is optimised for a resin under a particular set of conditions (heat, flow rate, etc.), a simple change in flow rate or in heat can make the geometry very inefficient. Except for circular dies, it is essentially impossible to obtain a flow channel geometry that can be used for a relatively wide range of resins and a wide range of operating conditions, such as those reviewed for LLDPE and LDPE.

For this reason, adjustment capabilities are provided in the die that basically permit heat and pressure changes. Some dies require that the heat profile be across one direction or in different directions, using individual heating pads, and so on, with appropriate controls. As a guide to film and sheet selection for a die, the following general classification may be helpful: (i) film dies are generally applicable for thicknesses of 0.010 in. or less; (ii) thin-gauge sheet dies normally are designed for thicknesses up to 0.060 in.; (iii) intermediate sheet dies may cover a thickness range of 0.040 to 0.250 in.; and (iv) heavy-gauge sheet dies extrude thicknesses of 0.080 to 0.500 in.

To simplify the processing operation, the die design should consider certain factors if possible. The goals are: to have extrudate (product) of uniform wall thickness (otherwise the heat transfer problem is magnified); to minimise the use of hollow sections; to minimise narrow or small channels; and to use generous radii on all corners, such as a minimum of 0.02 in. (0.5 mm). An "impossible" or difficult process can be designed, but it requires extensive experience (both practical and theoretical), with trial-and-error runs, to make it practical.

Basics of Flow

The non-Newtonian behaviour of a plastic makes its flow through a die somewhat complicated. One plastic characteristic is that when a melt is extruded from the die, there is some swelling. After exiting the die, it is usually stretched or drawn down to a size equal to or smaller than the die opening. The dimensions are reduced proportionally so that in an ideal resin the drawn-down section is the same as the original section but smaller proportionally in each dimension. Because of melt-elasticity effects of the material, it does not draw down in a simple proportional manner; thus the drawdown process is a source of errors in the profile. The errors are significantly reduced in a circular extrudate, such as wire coating. These errors must be corrected by modifying the die and takeoff equipment (Fig. 6.7).

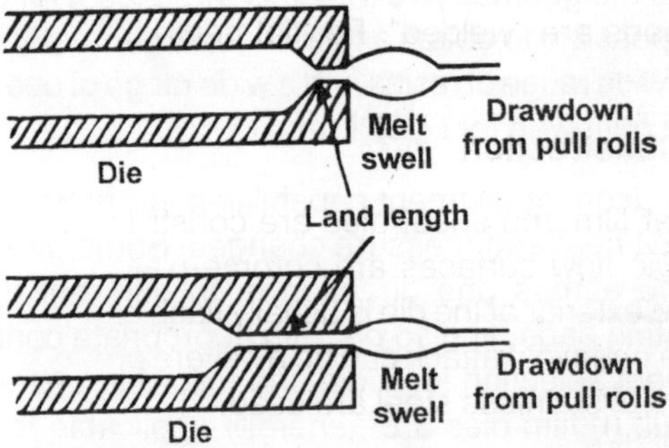

Fig. 6.7 : Effect of land length on swell.

There are substantial influences on the material due to the flow orientation of the molecules; so there are different properties in the flow direction and perpendicular to the flow. These differences have a significant effect on the performance of the part.

Another important characteristic of melts is that they are affected by the orifice shape. The effect it produces is related to the melt condition and the die design (land length, etc.), but a slow cooling rate can have a significant influence, especially with thick parts. Cooling is more rapid at the corners; in fact, a hot centre could cause a part to "blow" outward and/

or include visible or invisible vacuum bubbles. The popular coat hanger die, used for flat sheet and similar products, illustrates an important principle in die design. The melt at the edges of the sheet must travel farther through the die than the melt that goes through the centre of the sheet. Thus. a diagonal melt channel with a triangular dam in the centre is used to restrict the direct flow to some degree. The principle of built-in restrictions is used to adjust the flow in many dies. With blow moulding dies and profile dies, the openings require special attention to provide the proper product shape.

Special Dies

Some special dies produce interesting flow patterns and products such as tubular to flat netting dies. For a circular output, a counter-rotating mandrel and orifice have semi circular shaped slits through which the melt flow emerges. If one part is held stationary, then a rhomboid or elongated pattern is formed; if both parts rotate, then a true rhombic mesh is formed. When the slits overlap, a crossing point is formed where the emerging threads are "welded". For flat netting, the slide is in opposite directions.

Materials of Construction

Usually flat film and sheet dies are constructed of medium carbon alloy steels. Die flow surfaces are chrome-plated to provide corrosion resistance.The exterior of the die is usually flash chrome-plated to prevent rusting.Where chemical attack can be a severe problem (with PVC, etc.), various grades of stainless steel are used.

Profile, pipe, blown film, and wire coating dies generaliy are constructed of hot rolled steel for low pressure melt applications.When high pressure dies are required, 4140 steel is utilised. Chrome plating generally is also applied to the flow surfaces. particularly with EVA Stainless steel is used for any die subject to corrosion.

Maintenance

The die is an expensive and delicate portion of any extrusion line. Great care should be taken in the disassembly and cleaning of components. Disassembly should be attempted only when the die has had sufficient time to heat-soak or at the end of a run. Experience has shown a temperature of 450°F (232°C) to be adequate for cleaning up most non-degradable resins. For degradables, cleanup should begin immediately after shutdown to prevent corrosive action on the flow surfaces. While the heat is left on, all die bolts should be broken loose. The heat should then be turned off, and all electrical and thermocouple connections removed-carefully; then while it is still hot, the equipment is disassembled and thoroughly cleaned with "soft" brass and copper tools.

If the extruded materials tend to cling to the flow surfaces, it is usually best to purge the die prior to cleanup, with a purging compound. During assembly, the die bolts should be just snugged tight until the die heat is in the normal operating range. Once this heat is reached and a sufficient heat soak has been allowed (which could take at least 15—30 min.), all bolts should be tightened to the manufacturer's recommended sequence and torque levels. If the die is stored disassembled, care should be taken in its handling to prevent damage to individual components and to flow surfaces, which can include storage in a vacuum sealed container.

COEXTRUSION

Coextrusion provides multiple molten layers–usually using one or more extruders with melts going through one die–that are bonded together. This technique permits using melt heat to bond the various plastics (Table 6.2), or using the centre layer as an adhesive. Coextrusion is an economical competitor to conventional laminating processes by virtue of reduced materials handling costs, raw materials costs, and machine-time cost. Pinholing is also reduced with coextrusion, even when it uses one extruder and divides the melt into at least a two-layer structure. Other gains include elimination or reduction of delamination and air entrapment (1-12, 33-36, 100, 124, 153-161).

In the past, a processor desiring to enter the field had little choice of equipment, but the increased interest in coextrusion has produced a probiferation of equipment. With rapidly changing market conditions and the endless introduction of useful materials, the design of machines has become much more involved. It is important that the processor have flexibility in making selections, but not at the expense of performance, dependability, or ease of operation. One should provide for the material or layer thickness necessary in product changeover without high scrap rates. The target is to incorporate scrap regrind in the layered construction.

It is very important to be able to control the individual layer distribution across the width of the die. It is normal, as the viscosity ratio, or the thickness ratio, of the polymers being combined increases, for the individual layer distribution(s) of the composite film to become displaced. Viscosity differences influence reduction and saving of materials.

A number of techniques are available for coextrusion, some of them patented and available only under license. Basically three types exist: feed-block, multiple manifold, and a combination of these two.

Table 6.3 Example of compatibility between plastics for coextrusion.

	LDPE	HDPE	PP	Lonomer	Nylon	EVA
LDPE	3	3	2	3	1	3
HDPE	3	3	2	3	1	3
PP	2	2	3	2	1	3
Lonomer	3	3	2	3	3	3
Nylon	1	1	1	3	3	1
EVA	3	3	3	3	1	3

Code : 1 Layers easy to separate.
2. Layers can be separated with moderate effort.
3. Layers difficult to separate

With the feedblock die, different melts are combined just upstream of the die, prior to entering the die via a special adapter. Laminar flow keeps the layers from mixing together so that the layup exists as an integral construction from the die.

A multiple manifold die involves the combination of melts within the die. Each inlet part leads to a separate manifold for the individual layers involved. The layers are combined at or close to the final land of the die, and they exist as an integral construction through a single lip. Although the multi-manifold die can be more costly than the feedblock type, it has the advantage of more precise control of individual layer thickness.

A third approach. combines the feedblock and multi-manifold types, and provides further processing alternatives as the complexities of coextrusion increase. This approach has been used successfully in barrier sheet coextrusions where requirements preclude other alternatives. The feedblock is placed on the manifold or manifolds, permitting the combination of materials of similar flow characteristics in the feedblock while feeding dissimilar materials directly into the die.

Assuming both types have a good manifold design, the multi-manifold can process a broader flow range of resins than the feedblock. No matter which method is used, it is important to maintain melt heat of each layer above the "freezing" temperature of all layers, or poor adhesion results. The heat has to be the most important operating requirement for all resins used.

It is also desirable to be able to vary and control the thickness of the plies. As there are two or more extruders feeding the separate inlet channels, the first step is to calibrate them in terms of output rate vs. screw speed. As previously discussed, gear pumps can be used. The next step is to establish the required width to thickness and takeoff speed, and convert this value into an output rate for each resin. From such output rates and calibration curves, screw speeds are established. When a feedblock is not designed properly, problems such as excessive pressure drops, shear rates, or residence time can affect the quality of the extrudate. The tear-drop shape manifold has proved beneficial for coextrusion.

All extrusion processes require some form of melt transfer from the extruder to the feedblock or die. The transfer device can be short, such as an extruder adapter, or longer, as required in coextrusion piping. The pipe design is integral to coextrusion success; in general, the inside diameter should be large enough to avoid excessive pressure drops, and not so large as to cause extended residence time. Its heavy wall provides maximum thermal stability and heat distribution efficiency. The heat should be uniform to avoid hot and cold spots. Low voltage heaters are desirable, but heater tapes are dangerous because of the possibility of non-uniform heat distribution.

Safety consideration should be the determining factor in the design of piping. Pipes have been known to cold-pack, depending on shutdown procedures. The location of the control thermometer is important. Overheating of a zone, particularly on startup, can cause degradation of the plastic into a gas, creating extremely high pressures.

Tie-Layers

Choosing an adhesive layer is by no means a simple operation; there are many different types, each with specific capabilities, with EVAs forming the bulk. Selection of a material is based on its providing good adhesion and surviving the process. For example, high melt strength in a blown film improves bubble stability. At temperatures above 460°F (238°C), EVAs could suffer from gel formation and decomposition. High melt strength also can help in cast extrusion and thermoforming processes, and the melt draw is important in coextrusion of cast film/sheet or a coating. Good melt draw is required to run higher takeup speeds and/or thinner adhesive layers without causing flow-distribution or edge-weave problems. Effects such as "neck-in" and "edge bead" are also minimised by choosing adhesives with a good draw.

Various processing conditions can require the tie resin to fall into a particular melt index (MI) classification. MI is inversely related to molecular weight (MW); a high-MW adhesive will have a low MI. Most adhesive are available in a range of MIs to meet different requirements. The melt stability or flow is easily influenced by regrind. It is important that the regrind the compatible with the adhesive.

ORIENTATION

Orientation consists of a controlled system of stretching plastic molecules to improve their strength, stiffness, optical, electrical, and other properties. This process has been used for almost a century, and became very prominent during the 1930s for stretching fibres up to ten times; later it was adapted to stretching film/sheet and more recently blow moulded containers. Many other products take advantage of its benefits (tape, pipe, profile, thermoformed parts, etc.). Practically all plastics can undergo orientation, although certain types find it particularly advantageous (PET, PP, PVC, PE, PS, PVDC, PVA, and PC).

In extrusion the most important orienting processes are used for blown film, flat film and sheet, and blow moulding. During blown film processing the blow-up ratio determines the degree of circumferential orientation, and the pull rate of the bubble determines longitudinal orientation (Fig. 6.8).

The optimum stretching heat for amorphous resins (PVC, etc.) is just above the glass transition temperature; for crystalline types (PET, PE, etc.) it is just below the melting point (Table 6.3). During the stretching process, the structure changes because of crystalisation, thus usually necessitating an increase in heat if further deformation is planned. Afterward, the orientation is "frozen-in" by lowering the heat or, with crystalline types, set by increasing the crystalline portion.

With orientation, the thickness is reduced and the surface enlarged. If film is longitudinally stretched in the elastic state, the thickness and the width are reduced in the same ratio. If lateral contraction is prevented, stretching reduces the thickness only.

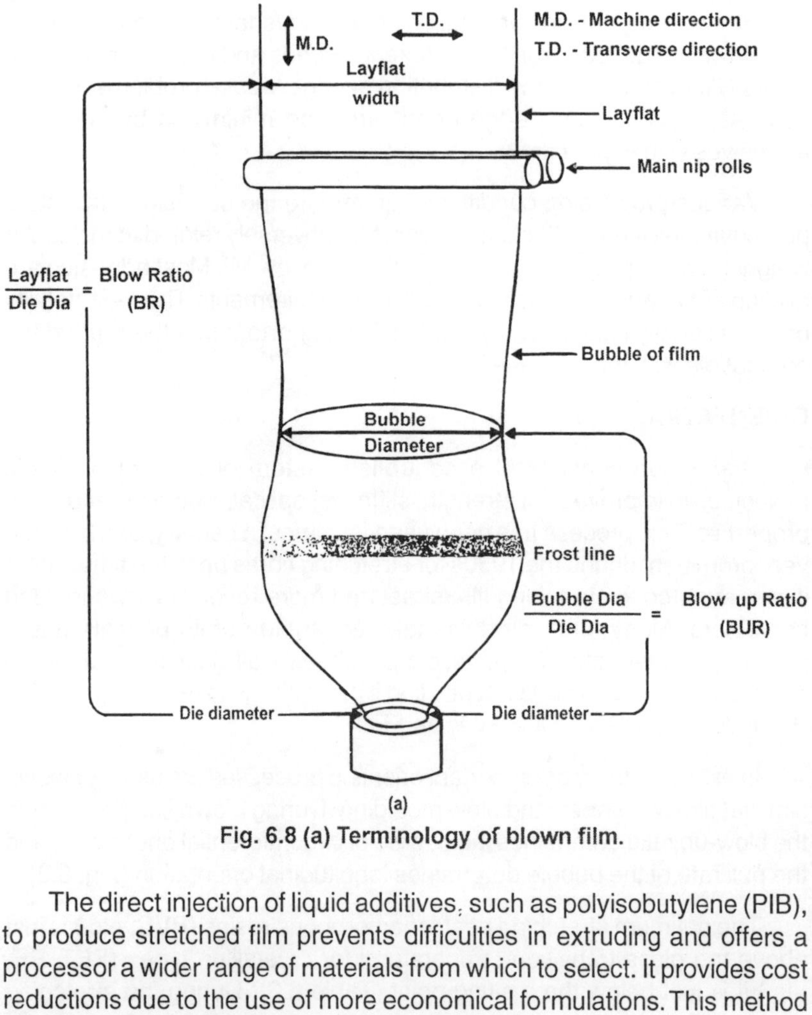

Fig. 6.8 (a) Terminology of blown film.

The direct injection of liquid additives, such as polyisobutylene (PIB), to produce stretched film prevents difficulties in extruding and offers a processor a wider range of materials from which to select. It provides cost reductions due to the use of more economical formulations. This method is suitable for the injection of cross-linking agents, liquid colours, and the like, via the extruder or a gear pump.

In orienting film or sheet the processor uses a tentering frame (typically llsed for many decades in textile weaving), which is enclosed in a heat-controlled oven, with a very accruate and gentle air flow used to hold the oven at the required orienting heat (Fig. 6.9).

The frame has continuous speed control and diverging tracks with holding clamps. As the clamps move apart at prescribed diverging angles,

Table 6.4 Examples of orienting conditions for plastics.

Plastic	Melting temprature (T_m) in °C	Glass transition temprature (T_g) in °C	Modulus of elasticity, MPa x 10^3					Density G/Cm^3
			Biaxially oriented film		Unoriented Film	Oriented fibre		
			Longitudinal	Transferse		Melt spun	Gel spun	
PVC	-	70 to 90	2.5 to 2.7	3 to 3.5	2.2	5.5	-	1.35
HDPE	138	–70 to –110	3 to 4	3 to 4	1.2	5	170	0.96
PP	137	–5 to –20	3 to 4	2 to 3	0.9	5	18	0.90
PA	260	50 to 75	2 to 2.5	2 to 2.5	0.5	4.5	19	1.13
PET	250	70 to 110	4 to 5.7	4.5 to 8.5	1.5	15	28	1.35

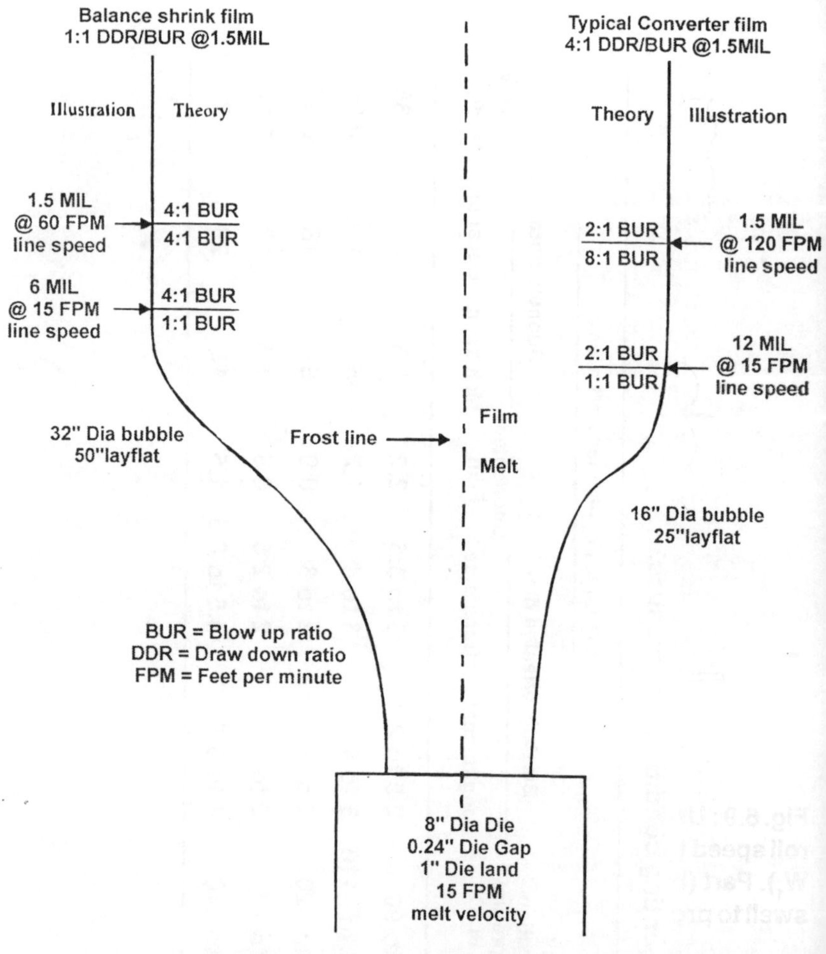

Fig. 6.8 (b) Orientation of blown film.

the hot plastic is stretched in the transverse direction resulting in single orientation (O). To obtain bidirectional orientation (BO) an inline series of heat-controlled rolls are located between the extruder and tender frame.

The rotation of each succeeding roll is increased, based on the longitudental stretched properties desired.

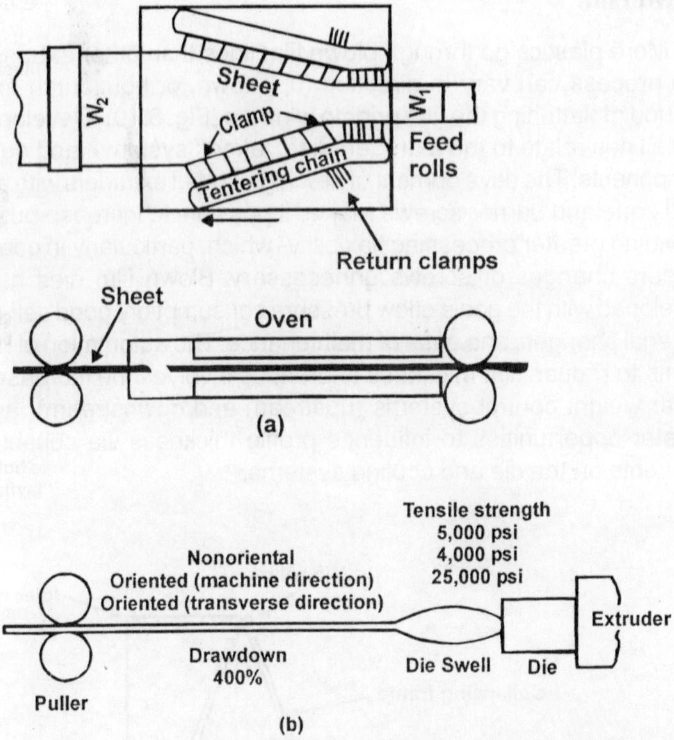

Fig. 6.9 : Use of tender frame to biorient film or sheet. In (a) the feeder roll speed to puller roll speed ratio is 1:4 (the ratio of width W_2 to width W_1). Part (b) is a schematic of the drawdown phenomenon with die swell to produce orientation in the longitudinal (machine) direction

PROCESSING LINES

Each line has inter relating operations, as well as specific line operations, to simplify processability (1-5, 8-11, 85, 122, 124, 163, 165-184). Usually the extruder is followed by some kind of cooling system to remove heat at a controlled rate, to cause plastic solidification. It can be as simple a system as air and/or water cooling, or a cooled roll contact can be used to accelerate the cooling process. Some type of takeoff at the end of the line usually requires an accurate speed control to ensure product precision and/or save on material costs by tightening thickness tolerances. The simplest device might be a pair of pinch rolls or a pair of opposed belts (caterpillar takeoff). A variable speed drive is usually desired to give the required precision.

Blown Film

More plastics go through blown film lines than other extrusion lines. The process can vary in direction (up, down, or horizontal) and in the method of flattening the film prior to wind-up (Fig. 6.10). Developments in these lines relate to the extruder, dies, takeoff systems, and automation components. The development of new high-speed extruders with a grooved feed zone and barrier screws makes it possible to increase output while providing greater processing flexibility–which, particularly in coextrusion, renders changes of screws unnecessary. Blown film dies have been developed with the goals oflow pressure consumption, good self-cleaning, material changes, and ease of maintenance. The automation of blown film plants to reduce film thickness tolerances involves the increased use of linear weight control systems (upstream and downstream), as well as greater opportunities to influence profile thickness via suitable control elements on the die and cooling systems.

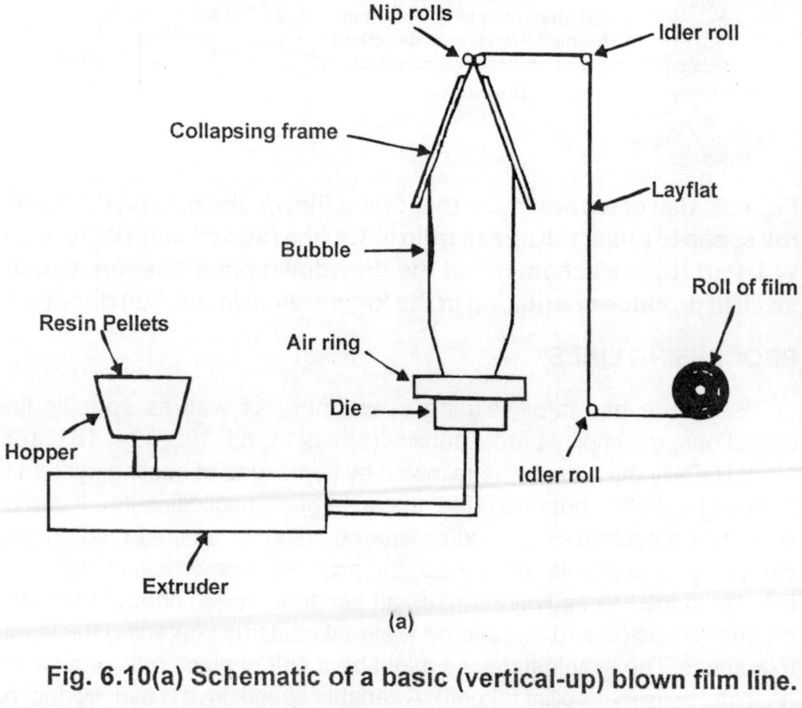

Fig. 6.10(a) Schematic of a basic (vertical-up) blown film line.

Regarding the film direction, horizontal operation entails no overhead installation and a low building height, but requires a larger floor space with probable adverse effects of gravity and uneven cooling. Vertical-down operation has the advantage of start-up without flooding of the annular die gap by exiting hot melt. However, vertical-up operation is the usual method, provided sufficient melt strength exists for an upward start-up, and so on. Special die blow heads are designed, with (usually) a multiple threaded helical mandrel discharging into an expansion space. The tubular melt assumes its final shape in a "smoothing-out" zone, which in all heads is a cylindrical land in a parallel position between the mandrel and the orifice. Its length is about I 0 to 15 times the annular gap width (the lower value applies to thin film and the higher to thick film). The gap width is generally 0.5 to 2.0 mm.

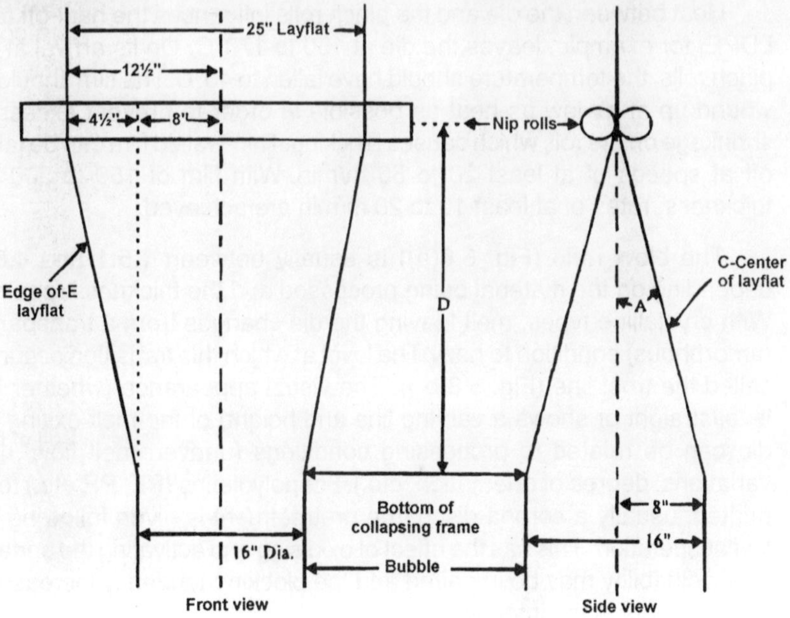

Angle A°	22	11	5½
Distance D in.	20	40	80
Edge E. in	20½	10½	80½
Centre C. in	2 1/2	40 3/4	80/1/2
C>E%	5	1½	5/8

(b)

Fig. 6.10(b). Geometry of collapsing bubble.

Different methods of bubble cooling exist. each with advantages and disadvantages. For example, because of their different extensional rheologies (flow), LLDPE bubbles are less stable than those of LDPE. Proper cooling is very important in obtaining good gauge uniformity. Gentle, very cold air has a better cooling effect than high velocity cool air; the gentle air helps to minimise bubble instability (usual pressure is 150-600 mm water column). Although single-lip air rings have proved adequate for some applications, dual-orifice designs provide enhanced cooling, which effectively stabilises the bubble and speeds up the line. Internal bubble cooling (IBC) with a dual-lip air ring is also effective in increasing bubble stability at high production rates. However, improperly arranged IBc configurations can cause melt fracture due to chilling of the die lip.

Heat between the die and the pinch rolls influences the haul-off rate. LDPE, for example, leaves the die at 150 to 170°C. On its arrival at the pinch rolls, the temperature should have fallen to 40°C. The film should be wound up at as low as heat as possible in order to prevent excessive shrinkage on the roll, which causes blocking. Thin-walled film can be taken off at speeds of at least 20 to 50 m/min. With film of 150 to 300 μm thickness, rates of at least 10 to 20 m/min are achieved.

The blow ratio (Fig. 6.8(a)) is usually between 1.5:1 and 4.0:1, depending on the material being processed and the thickness required. With crystalline types, melt leaving the die changes from a transparent (amorphous) condition to hazy. The level at which this transition occurs is called the frost line (Fig. 6.8(b)). The visual appearance (whether it is level/straight or shows a varying line and height) of the melt exiting the die can be related to processing conditions (uneven melt flow, heat variations, degree of orientation, etc.). For polyolefins (PE, PP, etc.) to be printed, usually a corona discharge pretreatment is given following the layflat operation. This has the effect of oxidising and activating the surface. The weldability may be impaired and the blocking tendency increased if the treatment is too intensive.

A certain degree of variation in thickness is unavoidable. When caused by the tubular film die, these variations always occur at the same position. A local film excess usually appears as a line. This can be countered if the die head, the haul-off and wind-up gear, or, with a vertical extruder, the extruder barrel is rotated or moved from side to side at regular intervals (Fig. 9.13).

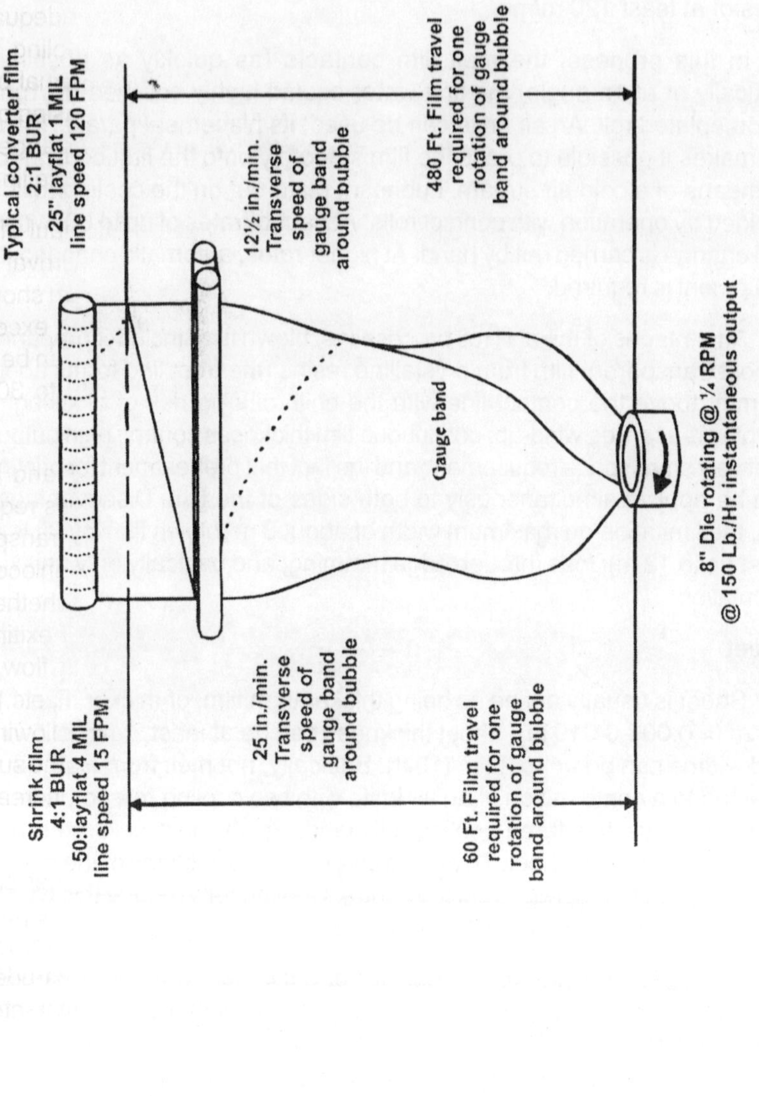

Fig. 6.11 : Example of averaging out thickness changes in blown film by rotating die head.

Flat Film

Flat film processed through slit dies are cooled principally by using chilled rolls. Many different resins are used, with thicknesses ranging from 15 to 200 μm. Alternatively, certain plastics go directly into a water tank, but that creates many technical difficulties in production. Thus, the chill roll process is preferred; and film up to 3 m in width will have output rates of at least 120 m/min.

In this process, the melt film contacts (as quickly as possible, vertically or at an angle) the first water-cooled highly polished (to 1 μm) chromeplated roll. An air knife can be used; its placement parallel to the die makes it possible to press the film smoothly onto the first cooling roll by means of a cold air stream. Lubricant plate-out on the cooling rolls is avoided by operation with contact rolls. At haul-offrates of up to 60 m/min, reel change is carried out by hand. At higher rates, automatic changeover equipment is required.

Advantages of the chill roll process (vs. blown film) include: preparing almost transparent film from crystalline resins (the frost line forms about 50 mm above the contact line with the chill roll); no risk of blocking; a simple crease-free wind-up; continuous film thickness control; high output; relatively small space requirement; and the fact that pretreatment for printing can be applied simultaneously to both sides of the film. Disadvantages are: the limitation on maximum width of about 3 m (blown film layflat is at least up to 12 m); loss through edge trimming; and basically only uniaxial orientation.

Sheet

Sheet is usually define as being thicker than film, or thicker than 1 to 4 mm (≈ 0.003-0.010 in). Sheet thickness can be at least 2 mm (0.5 in.), and widths can be up to 30 m (10 ft). Basically, hot melt from a slit die is directed to a combination of an air knife with two cooling rolls, or, a more popular choice, to a three-cooling-roll stand, which cools, calibrates, and produces a smooth sheet. To aid the chill rolls, end sections of the die are operated at a higher heat than the centre. Cooling rolls require this type of heat control from their ends to the centre.

The operation (as well as design) of a slit die, particularly for wide sheets, requires extensive experience. Its rather high melt pressure can deform the die.

Sheet is produced by extruding the thermoplastic through a long horizontal slit in a sheeting die. The hot sheet is taken through polished metal cooling rolls and then cut to size or coiled (Fig. 6.12).

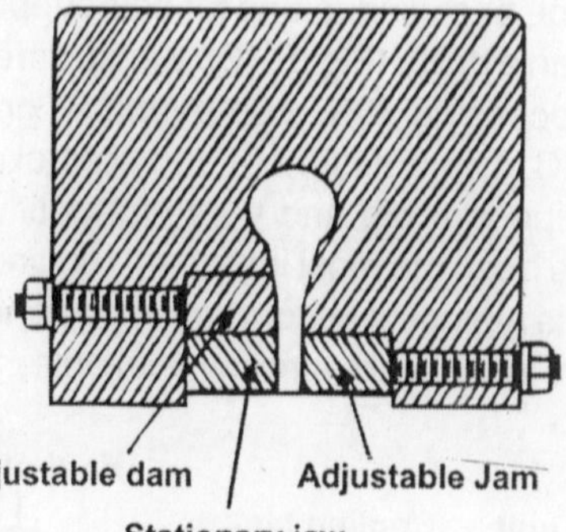

Fig. 6.12 : Cross- section of a sheeting die

Film is considered to be thinner than 0.010 in. Probably the term "sheet" should embrace all flat material extruded from a sheeting die, while "film" should mean flat material blown on film equipment as described below. Narrow strips are slit from wider sheet and film.

Film is produced either as cast film or tubular film. Cast film is, like sheet, extruded through a linear slot die and cooled by contact with a polished metal roll. Most film, however, is blown film.

The plastic is extruded vertically from an annular die in a thickness usually in the range of 0.0 15 to 0.025 in. The tube is closed by pinch rolls located high above the extruder; then air is admitted through the centre of the die mandrel to blow the tube of plastic into a bubble to thin the tube wall to final thickness, after which the tube is slit to make a flat film. The bubble expands the tube to 1.5–3 times the diameter of the die. A lower extrusion temperature is used for blown film than for cast flat film.

Tubular film is generally tougher and stronger than flat film. The tension of the windup rolls orients the film longitudinally, and air pressure provides orientation in the cross-direction. The transparency of polyolefins also improves the blow ratio (ratio of bubble diameter to die diameter). Best gloss and clarity, however, are given by cast film.

Pipe

A typical pipe line consists of a single or a twin screw extruder, a die, equipment for inside and outside calibration. a cooling tank, a wall thickness measuring device, marking equipment, haul-off and automatic cutting and pallet equipment, or a windup unit for self-supporting pipe coils or lengths that are coiled on a drum (Fig. 6.13). Single screw extruders are generally used when processing PYC compound in granule form; twins handle powders of PVC. The adjustment and control of back pressure are very critical. PVC pipe is a big and very competitive market, so quality and profitability have been the most important requirements for years. Improving the equipment is almost of secondary importance because the equipment for good-quality products is already available.

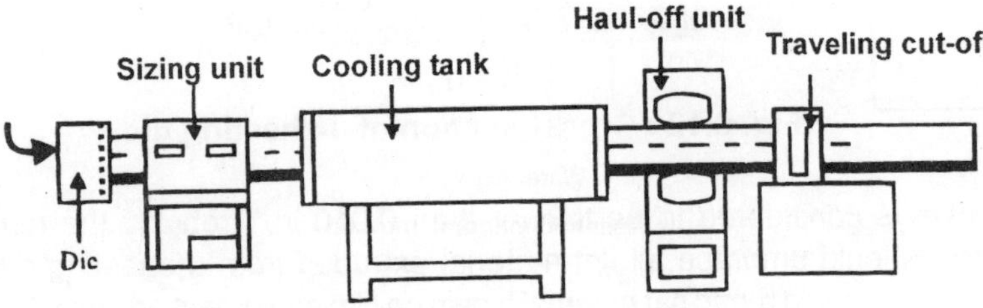

Fig. 6.13 : Example of the important downstream equipment used in pipe and profile extrusion.

The consumption of material, the main cost factor, can be gradually mininised by the use of current measuring the control systems. The goal is always tighter tolerance control to save material. Calibrating discs and pressure calibration methods of many different designs are used to meet various requirements. The operator's expertise in using these calibration systems is as important as controlling the complete line. A system of feedback and control of the extruder by a micro processor is used to control wall thicknes, combining ultrasonic gauging with gravimetric proportioning. Such new technologies are availa le but have to be debugged. Perhaps it can be said that any equipment from the "past" is definitely non-co petitive, based on all the new equipment that has been made available from upstream, through the extruder and downstream. In the last few years, all the equipment has been significantly altered to increase profits.

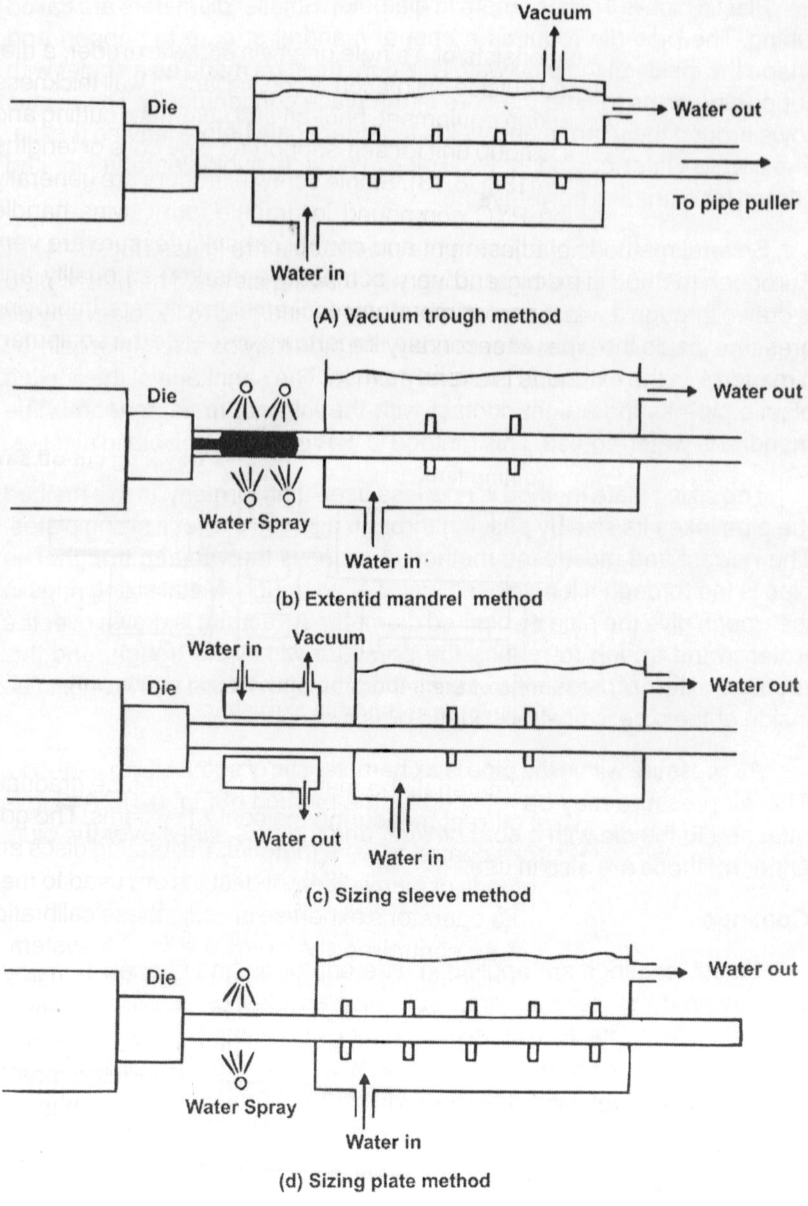

Fig. 6.14 Methods of sizing extruded pipe

Plastic pipe is 1/2 in. or more in diameter. Smaller diameters are called tubing. The pipe die requires a central mandrel or core to support and shape the inside of the pipe wall. This core must be made as a spider with supporting arms to hold the core in the place concentrically. The plastic flows around these arms and welds together again before leaving the die. The core is water-cooled for PVC pipe in order to avoid degradation, and heated for extruding polyethylene.

Several methods of bringing the pipe to size are in use (Fig. 6.14). A European method is external sizing with a sizing sleeve. The plastic pipe is drawn through a water-cooled metal sleeve and held to the sleeve by air pressure inside the pipe. Alternatively, the pipe may be sized internally by a mandrel, in the extended mandrel method. The shrinkage of the cooling plastic pipe keeps a tight contact with the internal metal mandrel. The mandrel is water-cooled. This method is well suited to polyolefin plastics.

The sizing plate method is now less used than formerly. In this method the pipe takes its size by passing through a series of metal sizing plates. The newest and most used method of sizing is the vacuum trough. The pipe is fed through a long closed water-filled trough. Metal sizing rings in the trough give the pipe its desired diameter. A vacuum is drawn over the water in the trough to reduce the pressure within the trough, and this reduced external pressure expands the pipe against the sizing rings. The inside of the pipe is at atmospheric pressure.

Air pressure within the pipe is a characteristic of some sizing methods. This air pressure may be retained by the method of Fig. 6.16. A plug is attached to the die with a cord or wire, and the pipe slides over the plug. Other methods are also in use.

Coatings

Plastic coatings are applied in different forms and shapes on many different products, such as wire, cable, profiles (plastics, wood, aluminium, etc.), films/foils (plastics, aluminium, steel, paper, etc.), rope, and so on. Certain coatings only require snug figs, whereas others require excellent adhesion, usually necessitating cleaning, priming, and/or heating substrates.

Wire Coating

Wire coating is performed by extruding plastic around a wire. This may be accomplished by feeding the wire directly through a hole in the centre of the feed screw, or, by far the more popular method, by using a cross head die through which the wire is fed. Hot melt is extruded over a preheated wire to improve adhesion and reduce shrinkage stresses. Before the wire enters the die, preheating is done by an electric current, radiant heaters, and so on; thick wires or cables can be heated by a gas flame or hot gas. Wire travels at rates up to at least 1,300 m/min (4,000 ft/min). Regardless of the speed, the rate of movement has to be held extremely uniform (or "perfect"). In order to achieve uniformity, all peripheral (expensive) equipment is carefully controlled and monitored, from the wire input drum to the output windup drum.

Wire and cable coating uses a crosshead die, with the wire travelling at right angles to the flow of the polymer, as shown in Fig. 6.15. The uncoated wire is a paid out from a coil and run through a preheater before entering the cross head die. After passing through the die, the covered wire passess through a cooling trough and spark tester.

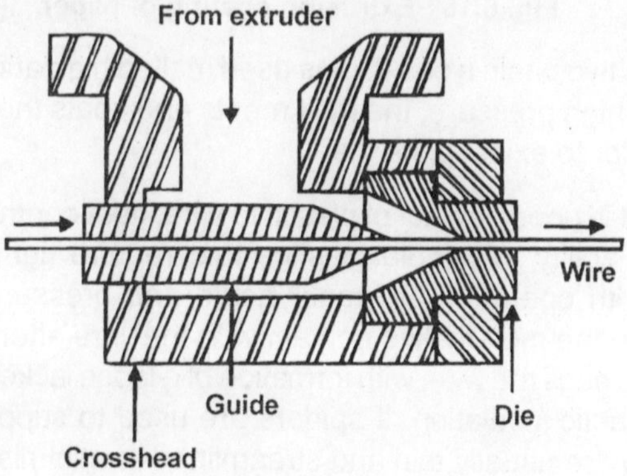

Fig. 6.15 : Wire coated crosshead.

The process for extrusion coating of paper, metal film, or other base stock is illustrated in Fig. 6.16. Adhesion of the plastic coating is promoted by pressure and contact with the chilled metal rolls. To obtain a good bond between the nonadhesive surface of polyethylene and the substrate stock, some oxidation of the PE surface is needed. This is produced by a high melt temperature and adequate distance, and therefore time, between die and contact with the substrate. The substrate material is preheated before coating.

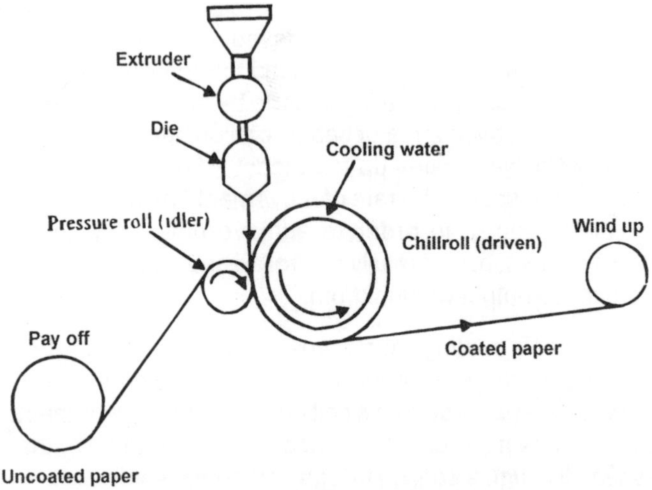

Fig. 6.16 : Extrusion coating of paper.

There are two basic types of dies used, called high and low pressure coaters. With high pressure, the melt meets and coats the wire between the die lips prior to existing the die.

The result is good contact of plastic to wire, tight control of the plastic OD, and the ability to handle plastics that require tight melt control, particularly with operation at "peak" heats and pressures. In the low pressure type, the melt makes contact with the wire after they both exit the die. Plastic hugs the wire, with formation of a loose jacket that facilitates removal of plastic insulation. If spiders are used to support the central mandrel, they are usually thin and streamlined to minimise disruption of the velocity. Adjustment of the wall thickness distribution and concentricity via die centring bolts can be manual or automatic. Automatic control can be achieved with in-line wall thickness measurement probes, and so forth. With high pressure dies, a vacuum can be used in the die just before the wire goes through its snug central support, to obtain an air-free and better bond. With a low pressure die, low air pressure is applied through the centre of the mandrel tube to prevent collapse of the melt tubing on exiting (eliminating melt adherence on the front of the die, which requires down time and cleanup) and to aid in maintaining the plastic ID.

Cooling of the thermoplastic coated wire usually occurs as soon as it leaves the die through water cooling troughs, which may have cascading heated sections. The troughs are usually 20 to 100 ft long. With thermoset plastics or elastomers and natural rubber, the required higher heat of melt solidification is added via hot gas systems, vulcanisation cures, and so forth.

Coating Wood Profiles

Wood, as well as other materials (plastic, aluminium, steel, etc.), can be easily coated in profile shape. Procedures used would be similar to wire coating including possible preheating and cleaning. For non¬continuous profiles, special equipment is available; wood (or other material) filled automatically from a storage-feeding magazine (when required preheated and/or cleaned), through a crosshead die. and finally through a cooling medium of air, water, gas, and so on.

Coating Films/Foils

Extrusion coatings using many different plastics, are applied to film, foil, or sheet substrates of plastic, wood, aluminium, steel, paper, cardboard, and so on. Basically a "curtain" of very hot melt is extruded downward from a slit die (similar to flat film slit dies). As mentioned earlier, preheating and/or cleaning operations may be required. How melt contacts the substrate, which is supported by a large, highly polished chill with a small rubber or metal nip roll. The nip roll applies the required pressure to ensure proper air-free adhesion. As the melt is usually at its maximum heat and pressure, "delicate" operation is required in the equipment and the surrounding area. Changes in air currents and moisture can cause immediate down time; tighter controls may not be necessary if all that is required is not to open a "door"–particularly a large garage door.

With coating (as well as other flat film or sheet processes), upon exiting the die the hot film will shrink across the width. This shrinkage. or "neck-in," is the amount of shrinkage from the die face to the coating width.~ neck-in there is also beading, which is a thickening at both edges of the film. The neck-in and beading influence the performance of a coating (as well as a film/sheet), including wrinkling, sagging, coating breaks near the bead, induced unwanted stresses, and so on. The quality of coated edges is unpredictable and may require more than the usual trimming widths. The amount of neck-in and beading varies for different resins (one should get manufacturers' inputs on minimum amounts, etc.). The processing conditions definitely influence these undesirable effects. (Certain die designs practically eliminate edge bead, but the designs are specific for given resins). One should determine the minimum neck-in and bead size based on processing conditions, and use those observations as control parameters. Sensors of neck-in and beads can be used in automatic process control.

CONTROLS

Controlling extrusion processes takes two types of systems, one on the extruder and another on the finished extruded product. In turn, these controls have to be interfaced. Extruder controls have been reviewed (heats, pressures, hopper feed rate, screw RPM, back pressures, etc.), as have product controls (wall thicknesses, rate of travel. width indicators, weight, etc.). Extensive efforts are continually being made to achieve the maximum in speed and precision.

For products with specific requirements, typically the best approach has always been to control the weight per unit area or the length of output that is directly related to a constant melt throughput, by weight. As reviewed in this chapter (and others), many machine controls and designs are required, such as feed rate of loading, screw design, and so on. In regard to products such as film, thickness gauges were once very popular for adjusting takeoff speeds. However, better control is achieved now with weight control systems. Depending on the given weights per unit length or area and the speed of the line, the melt throughput rates of the extruder are pre–calculated accurately enough to ensure, via a melt throughput control system, that the weight can be kept constant within a tolerance range of at least ± 0.5 per cent. Whereas measurement of takeoff speed using a wheel pulse counter is relatively easy, measurement of melt throughput involves considerable expense.

From a practical standpoint, extrusion lines appear to be relatively simple and compact, with a long operating life; their controls should provide ease of startup and shutdown, and must be easy to service. Of course, the real world is not this simple; the various materials and types of equipment in the lines are not stable, and they all work within rather tight limits. Although all types of very tightly controllable equipment are available, the operator or processor (and others) must recognise that all equipment and all materials have limits, optimum operating conditions, and so on. So to benefit from setting up or operating a line one has to determine what is required, determine the limits of operating materials and equipment, and establish quality control and other requirements.

Acquiring "all this knowledge" takes time and experimentation. One must be aware of potential problems or limitations. As new ones develop, one should accommodate them logically in processes.

This approach provides a means of determining which materials and equipment to purchase or upgrade. One could thus set up an ideal line with so-called interchangeable and controllable features. Given a specification that must be met on a complete line, one must meet the target (or no payment is made). Few processors desire tight specifications. but such responsibility can be managed. one step at a time. The processor should determine as well as is possible what is required to meet product performance (colour, dimensions, strength, etc.), and relate the requirements to material and equipment currently in use. It would be unfortunate if one were to purchase the "best" material and equipment available at a particular time and then determine that it did not perform as needed and learn that another piece of equipment was required. This situation happens all too often, as people hastily, or without full knowledge of an operation, make foolish mistakes.

A processor does not have control of all the steps from basic material to finished product. Material processing capability is limited by what is received and by when inspection is made or required; so selection tests are important and must be subject to change. In turn, the process line has many variables that must be co–ordinated. A practical procedure today, with all closed-loop process control systems, is to subdivided the controls into distinct subsystems (Fig. 6.17). They can then be controlled within single control loops or by simple intermeshed circuits. A single-loop feedback circuit has one input and one output signal; disturbances that affect the process are registered by the controller directly, by an additive term in the value of the controlled parameter. A disturbance is registered by its own sensor and interacts with the control signal with an open-loop controller. When the effect of a disturbing factor on a process is well understood, disturbance control provides a rapid reaction to unpredictable influences.

Additional process control signals can be achieved in a single closed-loop system by having it cascade the signal. Cascade control offers the advantages of faster reaction time, reduced susceptibility to disturbance, and less effect from incorrect settings. As this chapter's review of all the variables that can exist and are controlable would suggest, interrelating them with multi-performing controllers is desirable. In some cases, computer integrated micro–processor control systems can be used; they offer some benefits when properly installed with matching hardware, but cannot do the complete job. A complete package that would properly include all parameters is desirable but at present not very realistic. Computerised integrated controllers are available and used, each for its unique capability. Better complete multi-parameter controllers still need to be designed. One must appreciate that use of a controller, whether simple or highly computerised. necessitates that the operator recognise what parameters require control and the degree of control needed. and correlate these factors. For example, if the output rate has to be increased, is a screw RPM increase satisfactory, or should there be a change in back pressure, resin feed rate, and so on, or combinations of certain controls, to provide a product that is acceptable (according to various criteria)? The possibilities of measuring back pressure in the melt and the melt heat at the screw tip are of particular value in processing. In this manner, it is possible to control the reproducibility of the two most important parameters in every processing method: pressure and heat.

From the processor's point of view, the extruder has the following objectives: (i) high throughput proportional to screw speed and basically independent of back pressure; (i) uniform, pulsation-free delivery, with optimum melt heat (with respect to power consumption and quality of extrudate); (ii) uniform melt heat locally and also throughout the run; (iv) delivery of an orientation-free, relaxed melt; (v) homogeneous mixing of the resin with all its additives; and (vi) a por-free extrudate, free of volatiles, at high output rates for both granular and powder feeds.

With all the varieties of materials available, and their individual grades with many different formulations, it has not yet been possible to design a screw in advance, based on the melt or the rheological/flow physical relationships involved in plastification and conveying. Trial and error, with an observant processor using reliable and reproducible controls, makes the screw perform to its maximum efficiency.

DOWNSTREAM CONTROLS

Downstream product controls can be interconnected with process controllers so that any variation in the product is immediately reflected as a corrective change. A decision is derived from the feedback signal about the kind and extent of adj ustment that should be made to a control variable; in other words, the system has to be matched to the process. A few systems permit the properties of the extrudate to be controlled: (i) pipe

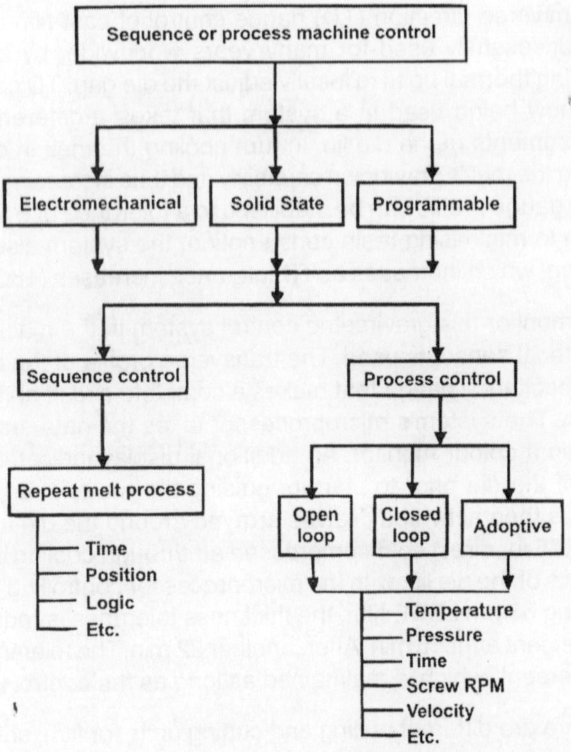

Fig. 6.17 : Simplified overview of process controls for extrusion machine

thickness distribution is controlled by centring of the die either mechanically or thermally, and wall thickness by the haul-off speed; (ii) blown and flat film averaging thickness are controlled by extruder speed and haul-off speed, thickness profile by the die gap restricter bar height (thermal or piezoelectric), film width by the diameter of the calibrator, transverse thickness tolerances by cooling air, and edge shift by side-gusseted triangles; (iii) a profile's dimensional stability (weight per unit volume) is controlled by haul-off speed, screw speed, and recorded melt throughput or a product dimension; and (iv) all products' throughput is controlled by screw speed, and the running length by haul-off speed and screw speed (gravimetric metering).

Transverse direction (TD) gauge control of cast film and sheet has been successfully used for many years worldwide, by automatic dies employing thermal bolts to locally adjust the die gap. TD control of blown film is now being used in a system that takes a different approach; it cools segments of the die lip, in turn cooling the melt in contact with it, reducing the melt's drawdown capability and thus increasing the thickness. The TD gauge profile can be stabilised to a tolerance of ± 1.7 per cent. In addition to minimising resin consumption, the system also reduces film curvature, which increases as TD tolerance increases (180).

To monitor this gravimetric control system in the machine direction, an electrical sensor is used. The transverse profile of the bubble is read by a capacitance gauge that makes a complete circuit of the bubble in 2 to 3 min. The system's microprocessor takes the data and displays the profile on a colour monitor. An additional display indicates the centring status of the die prior to startup, guiding the material adjustment. The system is then activated. Yalves arrayed around the die at a spacing of about 0.75 in. direct cold compressed air through cooling channels onto segments of the die lip, with the microprocessor controlling the operation. In running 53 μm LDPE film, the thickness tolerance is reduced from 3.3 to 2.0 percent after 15 min. After .another 22 min. The tolerance is reduced to 1.7 percent, which is maintained as long as the control is on.

There are different pulling and cutting units for film, sheet, pipe, and so forth. Tube pullers are driven by various methods. Electric drives are available with techometer feedback accuracy ± 0.5 to 1.0 percent. Digital drives can held to ± 0.01 percent.

Automatic slitter/rewinders, for handling blown or cast films such as rigid PVC, PS, and non-uniform-thickness laminates, operate at speeds of 300 to 500 m/min, producing reels up to 3,000 mm in diameter and slit reels up to 1,000 mm in diameter. Film is drawn from an unwind to the slitting/ rewinding stations through a translation bridge equipped with idler rollers that facilitate web feed and prevent the deposition of dust due to static. Rewinding/slitting machines are available that can handle highly tension-sensitive materials such as PP and PET, video film, magnetic tape, and heavy gauge laminates, with working widths of 2,500 to 3,000 mm and finished-reel diameters of up to 600 mm for PP and PET. They operate at 600 m/min and produce slit widths of 100 mm and above. Rewind units are also available that operate on single and twin spindle roll-slitting principles. Units incorporate high-accuracy scissor slitting, crush cutting for non-brittle materials, and razor-blade slitting for materials such as cellophane, PE, PP, PVC, and thin aluminium foils.

Machines for automatic winding of blown and cast film, which includes winding and slitting, are available; they handle all types, widths, and thickness, and different winding characteristics, produce different reel diameters on various core sizes, and divide film webs into different lane widths during production. Reel changes are automatic, and reel production can continue for one or two shifts without operator intervention, because of the incorporation of a reel-bar storage system.

Lines produce reels in widths of 900, 1,200, and 1,600 mm and permit winding of all film types on various cores with reel diameters of up to 600 mm. They also provide automatic shaft changes at a predetermined film length and gap winding that is steplessly adjustable from 1 to 10 mm. Jumbo reels run up to 2,000 mm in diameter and weigh up to 3 tonnes in other systems.

Developments in web tension control systems are providing increased capability and function to eliminate problems. They include ultrasonic roll diameter sensors, pneumatic pressure gauge tension monitors, capston-Mt. Hope tension systems, and so on. As an example, replacement of a web-tensioning system's conventional electro-mechanical drive with an ordinary A/c motor enables processors to lower system cost and improve web consistency, as has been done for many years. A vector control system uses a belt and pulley arrangement to remotely couple an encoder to the shaft of the Ale induction motor.

This approach provides closed-loop feedback, without requiring that one modify the relatively inexpensive motor by installing a special feedback device on it.

7

Blown Film Extrusion

A Cool Mix of Water and Air

Today outputs in the blown film extrusion branch are not limited by the extruder capacity but by the stability of the bubble and the capacity to cool down the film in the shortest distance possible. A revolutionary cooling system combines water and air so intelligently that the previous limits in cooling can be extended, thus leading to an increase of output but also an optimization of film quality. This technology is based on the improvement of heat dissipation inside the bubble through symmetrical contactless water cooling of the blown film.

Blown film extrusion works as follows: the melt is distributed in the die head and is then inflated into a bubble with air. The bubble needs intensive cooling in the bubble forming zone (between the outlet of the die head and the frost line). There, convective cooling takes place, that is to say the heat transfer from the bubble to the environmental air, the dominant mechanism of heat transfer. In this zone, heat transfer through contact cooling doesn't play a big role and heat radiation can also be ignored. In addition to the differentiation of the cooling mechanisms, the difference of cooling relative to the outer and inner surface of the film is significant. One distinguishes:

- Outer Cooling
- Inner Cooling

Fig. 7.1 : Perfect Cool in Action : high output combined with high bubble stability in blown film extrusion

Cooling Ring Design

The single air ring is the oldest process of bubble cooling. Such a cooling ring distributes a cool air flow homogenously over the circumference of the bubble. This cooling air is guided through a gap in the extrusion direction on the outer circumference of the film. Today, double gap air rings are used for the outer cooling of blown film. The air flow that goes through the upper gap has a high velocity in comparison with the lower gap. The venturi effect is thus used, which allows the bubble to nestle–up against the outline of the air ring and by doing so increase the middle stream velocity improving heat transfer.

Independent of the cooling ring put design, the air flow coming from the cooling ring decreases in the bubble drawing direction near the film, while its temperature increases constantly. Hence, the cooling effect of the air stream decreases with a longer cooling distance, that is bubble height.

Inner Cooling

One possibility to enhance the bubble cooling in blown film extrusion is the use of a so called IBC system (Inner Bubble Cooling). These devices create an air circulation inside the bubble through an IBC stack and consequently improve heat dissipation. However, heat dissipation through the inner peripheral film surface is limited. The ratio between the dissipated heat quantity through the inside in comparison with the outside peripheral surface reflect this: the ratio generally lies between 75 : 25% up to 80 : 20%. The predominance of heat dissipation over the outer peripheral surface can be attributed to the limited capacity of conventional inner cooling systems to dissipate the heat from the inner peripheral surface. This is due on the one hand to the in comparison little and rather undirected cooling air volume flow inside the bubble and on the other hand to the above described heating of the air and the associated bad heat dissipation from the inner peripheral surface to the ambient air as well as its little heat absorption capacity.

With double air rings that have been available on the market for a few years, the ratio of dissipated heat through the outer in comparison with the inner peripheral surface of the bubble has moved to 90: 10 %. These systems improve the heat transfer through the 3x graduated air stream and at the same time the supporting effect of the bubble is also improved

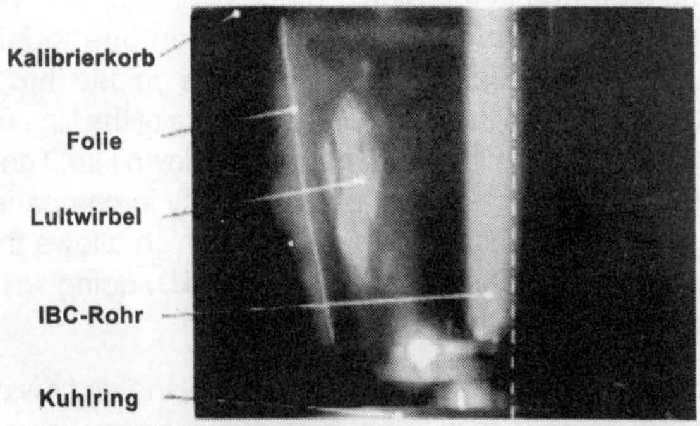

Fig. 7.2 The air supply of a conventional IBC system contains particles which appears green under laser light. One can clearly notice the presence of a twirl and the absence of a targeted air flow, which would dissipate heat efficiently

whereas the unequal distribution of the film cooling (inside: outside) is actually increased.

Water Instead of Air

A lot of work has been done in the past few years to overcome the limits of conventional bubble cooling processes. One starting point is to obtain better cooling through the use of water. Water as a cooling medium is more efficient than air, as the data below shows:

Table 7.1 : Thermal Data of air and water

	Air	Water
Heat conductivity λWL [W/mK]	0,026	0,604
Heat Capacity cp [kJ/KgK]	1,00	4,2
Density ρ [kg/m^3]	1,15	998

The higher heat conductivity of water in comparison with air allows better heat transfer from the film to water. Moreover, due to its higher density and heat capacity, the heat absorption capacity of water is higher than from air. All systems available on the market up today present individual advantages - above all, they enable better cooling of the bubble - however, they usually present increased technical complexity. Further, they do not bring any solution for the second factor, which has an impact on the output of the line, that is the stability of the bubble.

Stability and Cooling

In the frame of R & D projects, KIEFEL Extrusion GmbH in Worms worked on this issue, which resulted in the development of the ECP (Enhanced Cooling Package) and PERFECT COOL cooling systems. Both cooling systems combine the elements air and water intelligently, almost perfectly. PERFECT COOL is the big brother of the ECP system, which was first used for the production of heavy duty shipping sacks. Both systems are based on the same idea, that is stability and cooling. After the development of a system exclusively for die diameters smaller than 200 mm, KIEFEL developed PERFECT COOL, an inner cooling system for die diameters bigger than 200 mm.

The heart of both cooling systems is the cooling device installed inside the bubble, the surface of which is cooled from the inside through a closed water circuit. The geometry of the cooling device as well as its surface are designed so that the air flow forces between the film and the cooling device are kept in balance and the bubble thus remains stable. The surface geometry also leads to a turbulent yet tractive air flow between the bubble and cooling device surface, which ensures a good heat transfer from air to cooling surface without contact with the bubble. The air is hence maintained at a low temperature up to frost line and consequently improves the inner cooling of the bubble. The system ensures that the film never comes in contact with the cooling medium water or with the surface of the cooling device.

The outer cooling is done with a double lip cooling ring, using the acknowledged concept of laminary air flow. The cooling ring lips are adapted to the new cooling systems, to ensure a good balance between turbulent inner air and outer air.

Whereas with conventional lines the inner air retains a high temperature after contact with the hot bubble, with systems including an inner cooling device, its surface is cooled down the whole way in the extrusion direction from the bubble forming zone on. The heat is transferred from air to water inside the cooling device. Moreover, in comparison with conventional IBC systems, with ECP and PERFECT COOL, the whole inner air flow is guided along the film, which ensures an optimal heat dissipation from the film.

Output and Quality Improvement

These two aspects - cool and targeted air flow along the cooling device - are the main reasons for the high potential of ECP and PERFECT COOL systems for transporting heat away from the inner peripheral surface of the bubble. The controlled impact of cooling on the inner and outer peripheral surfaces also allows achieving 50% cooling through the inner side. In addition to higher outputs which can thus be achieved, the homogeneous cooling of the film has a positive influence on product characteristics (for instance decrease of edge break), and it also helps reduce the risk of blocking of the film and hence higher outputs are possible.

The enhanced output R & D projects at KIEFEL Extrusion did not focus on the ECP and PERFECT COOL systems only. In the frame of the projects, the whole blown film line was taken into consideration. In addition to die head and cooling ring, particular attention was given to the development of extruder screws. Only such an overall approach enables the best potential for output increase through better cooling and optimization of film quality.

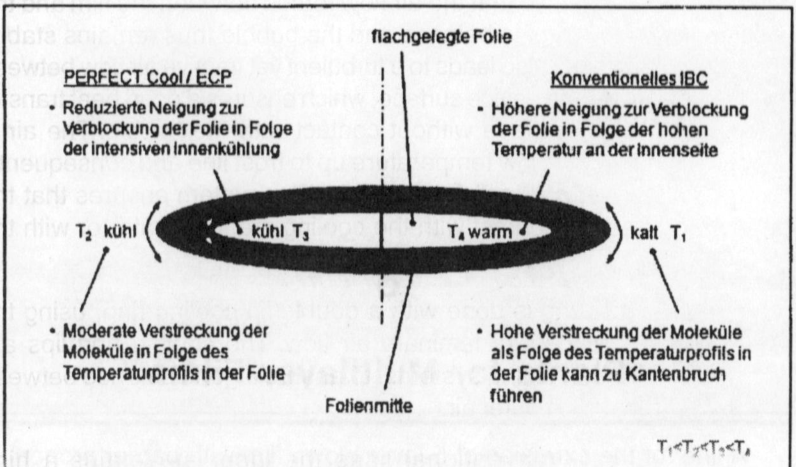

Fig. 7.3 Improvement of film quality through good heat disipation via the inner peripherel surface of the bubble.

8

Plants for Multilayer Films

A line for the extrusion of 5-layer blown film with barrier properties has recently been developed by DOL EXTRUSION which paid particular attention to the "heart" of the line, that is to say the new a coextrusion head.

This is the "pancake" type and represents an evolution of the Multisplit version with direct lateral feed and twin melt flow paths, the difference lying in the spiral section with horizontal rather than conical-vertical arrangement.

The new head is based on a design that provides for distribution and division of each layer on spiral shaped paths intersected on horizontal plane which force the melt to flow towards the centre of the head on cylindrical surface with upward movement.

Each layer has cross section and path length optimized according to the polymer processed (barrier, binder, structural layers), and overlaps the subsequent one.

As for the central barrier layer, melt path and residence time inside the head are shorter than in a conventional head. The plant also offers the option of individual temperature-controlled areas and process, temperature adjustment of each single layer within a range of 40°C.

The head also permits the melt coming from a single extruder to be split into 2 channels with the effect of further laminating a layer when the flow (and/or related speed) is very different from the al average value of the other 4 layers.

The plant is fitted with 5 suitably-sized extruders, each equipped with torque motors and extremely-short head-connection necks. The dual flow external cooling ring features an under-ring which automatically controls the film profile keeping it constantly within a 4% tolerance threshold. The area where the bubble is formed is protected by an external transparent screen and is provided with a "no-contact" IBC unit. The reading head connected to the automatic thickness control installed on the scanner is also of cushion" no-contact" type.

The oscillating haul-off unit is of traditional and horizontal type with diverging rollers, whilst the automatic winder with axial contact has a face-to face structure for the additional application of a central robotized system for reel unloading and removal.

Finally, the line is equipped with a multi-component metering and gravimetric feed system as well as a supervisor for storing and recalling previous process parameters.

CMG (COSTRUZIONI MECCANICHE GALLIA) has recently presented the Innoex Coex 3 line designed for producing 3-layer agricultural stretch film.

Developed for an important German processor, the line features direct polyisobutylene (PIB) injection through the extruder screws. PIB is stored in a 7 m^3 tank and then distributed to each of the 3 extruders (75-100-75 mm) via individual metering pumps.

Fig. 8.1

Each extruder is equipped with 6-component gravimetric blending to control raw material usage and manage the PIB delivered to each extruder screw. This is achieved by constant monitoring and control of screw speed in combination with the metering pumps to maintain the required preset percentage (between 2 and 8% depending on the required tack level).

This design has demonstrated excellent behaviour in both the production of 25-micron (agriculture) and 12-micron (industrial) stretch film. The line includes the latest generation of coextrusion head, designed with axial symmetric distribution to reduce the physical mass resulting in very short residence times.

Fig. 8.2

The cooling ring, together with an automatic thickness control system, has achieved thickness tolerances of less than 2% when producing the agricultural film and below 3 % for the industrial one. The die can be configured with inserts ranging from 400 to 650 mm. For the production of agricultural film the die was fitted with 550-mm inserts.

The design features of the Innoex Coex 3 line include, for example, a non-contact sensor for thickness measurement, collapsing blow tables with carbon rollers, water cooled haul off rollers, special coating of the nip rolls, intermediate nip rolls and various other devices to improve web separation whilst maintaining the correct winding tension.

The winding system is equipped with three winders (face-to-face and back to-back) that allows the tack or elastic layers to be wound inside or outside the reel.

Ghioldi has recently delivered to a Scandinavian processor the world's largest plant for processing Mater-Bi, a biodegradable polymer derived from maize starch, whose main agricultural application is in the production of mulching film.

The plant in question is able to coextrude a 3-layer film with a width of 3,200 mm and thickness of 10 micron reaching a hourly production of 300 kg. The construction of the system was based on a high performance polyethylene plant.

The main components of the line are two extruders (65 and 80 mm respectively), a 3-layer coextrusion head with internal bubble cooling, an oscillating haul-off and an automatic dual winder with a system for handling the finished reel.

The plant incorporates specific systems for assuring and maintaining product quality, such as the bubble methacrylate protections which generates a sort of micro–environment shielded from external interference, or the flattening frames with carbon rollers for preventing any defects due to contact.

Interest in technologies for the production of environmentally friendly products such as Mater-Bi continues to grow, notwithstanding the higher cost of these compared with the processing of traditional materials. However it should also be noted that the higher investment cost is quickly recouped by savings in energy - also achieved through the adoption of low-power consumption and low-noise torque motors.

9

Lamination

Lamination process can be defined as the process in which one side or both sides of the item, are coated by a film. The coating film and the material to be coated are brought into contact with each other with the help of the roller. A permanent bond is formed between the materials by the application of heat or pressure or both. The heating process in lamination is most critical and it is done either at the roller assembly or before the roller assembly. The single integrated material produced after the lamination is called as laminate. Hence a laminate can be a combination of clearly different plastic film materials or plastic with materials like paper, aluminium foil, cellophane etc. The minimum limit to the possible number of layers in lamination is two and one of the material between these two must be a thermoplastic. The lamination process has many advantages such as :

(1) The finished product consists of luster or gloss.

(2) The laminated sheets can be protected by many types of damages, smudges and finger prints.

(3) Due to lamination the sheet can become stiff, resistant to elongation and deformation, easy for printability, durable, as good as new for many years and can stand straight.

(4) Laminated structures have good moisture barrier proof, excellent cohesive and adhesive and tear proof properties.

(5) In some cases it increases the constrast and colour of the laminate.

6) We can give a laminated paper as a gift without any frame or support.

Menus, identification cards, the paper which is printed by instructions etc. can get advantage from lamination process.

Few variations of this lamination process are as follows :

(1) Adhesive lamination

(2) Thermal or Fusion lamination

(3) Hot melt lamination (Wax lamination)

(4) Extrusion lamination

(5) Dry paint transfer-lamination.

(1) Adhesive Lamination

In this process one layer is coated with adhesive and it is then combined with another layer by applying heat or pressure or both. Adhesive lamination can be classified into two types depending on the type of adhesive used for bonding purposes :

(i) Dry Lamination.

(ii) Wet Lamination.

(i) *Dry Lamination* :— The dry lamination process consists of applying the adhesive to the inner face of one web or both webs. These two webs which are used for bonding purpose may be impenetrable. The plastic film can be laminated to other substrates successfully by this method.

In this case, the laminating adhesive is firstly applied to one web in exact amount. This web is passed through the drying open to remove either water or solvent from the laminating adhesive. This web is then combined with another web with the help of pressure rollers. These pressure rollers can be heated in some cases.

The factors which influence the success of this lamination include control of tension, regular and uniform adhesive application, nip pressure and temperature control of drying and roll storage etc.

(ii) *Wet Lamination* : - This method is used when one or more substrates is permeable to the passage of coating solvents.

In this process of lamination, one layer is coated by adhesive on the adhesive applicator. The two layers are combined under nip heated chamber. The laminated web is passed through the drying chamber. This web releases the water vapour which is present in the adhesive. One component of the web is porous in nature. The water vapour escapes through one of the component. If anyone component of the laminated web is not porous then the water vapour will remain entrapped between the layers and hence good quality laminate will not produce.

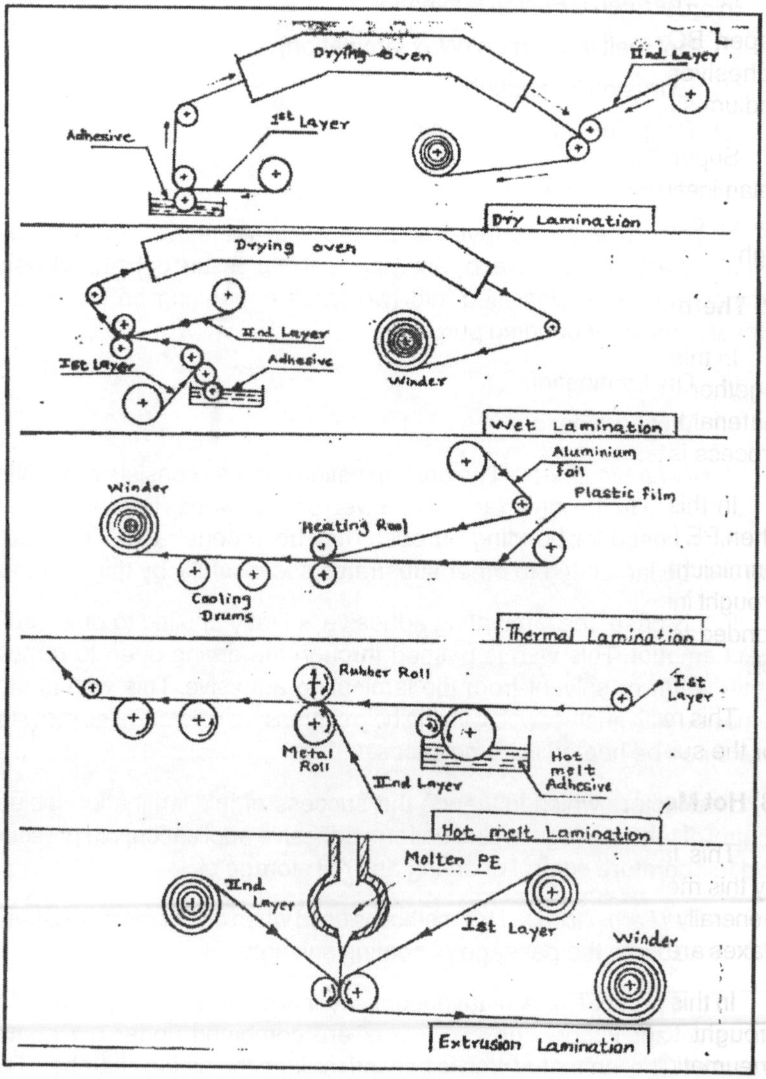

Fig. 9.1

Wet lamination requires water based adhesive. The cost of the water based adhesive is lower than the cost of the adhesive which is used for the dry lamination purpose. The machine has to run in slow speed to provide time required for the water to evaporate, permeate and escape. Hence this process is slow than the other lamination processes.

In order to produce laminates of polyester/paper, polypropylene film/paper, BOPP film/paper, this method can be successfully used. The adhesives which are used for wet lamination purpose are casein, sodium silicate, starch, polyvinyl alcohol, dextrin etc.

Superior bond strengths are possible with adhesive lamination but delamination is a constant fear with adhesive lamination. But delamination can be controlled. Also production speed of adhesive lamination is quite high.

(2) Thermal or Heat or Fusion Lamination

In this method the coated materials are combined by passing them together between rollers in which one roller is heated. The laminated material has great durability and the process is very economical. This process is normally used for lamination of aluminium foil with PE.

In this process the aluminium foil is passed over a heated drum. Then PE film is brought into contact with this heated aluminium foil. The aluminium foil is good conductor of heat. Hence when two webs are brought into contact with each other under nip pressure the two webs get bonded to form the laminate. This laminate is then passed over a chill roll.

This method is quite fast and economical. This method is not efficient for the substrates other than aluminium foil and PE.

(3) Hot Melt Lamination

This lamination technique can also be called as Wax lamination. By this method film/wax/ foil or film/wax/film materials can be produced. Generally waxes are used for the laminating purpose but polymers without waxes are also available as adhesives.

In this process, one of the web is coated with hot melt. Two webs are brought together at the nip between the two rolls one of which is pneumatically loaded and other is fixed roll. The laminate is then wound up after passing through the cooling section. One most important advantage of hot melt lamination is no solvent drying or recovery is required. The laminate has also good properties such as water proof and cohesive and adhesive properties.

(4) Extrusion Lamination

In extrusion coating, the resins such as PE, PP, nylons are used as adhesives between two substrates. In the actual process, a flat die extruder releases a molten curtain of resin at the nip between the two webs to be laminated. By passing the laminated sheet in the oven, the heated adhesive gets cooled. The care must be taken that the flow of the polymer from the die should be uniform and the polymer should not degrade. Extrusion coating process is more economical than the other lamination techniques for long production runs. Also the production speed of the extrusion lamination is high.

Extrusion coated laminates are genenrally softer and more flexible than adhesive laminates and are more economical.

(5) Dry Paint Transfer - Lamination Process

In this process, a temporary flexible casting sheet is coated with colour coat and then coated with exterior clear coat and the film is dried. Then a high gloss surface is transferred to the clear coat. Then with the help of dry paint transfer-laminating technique the coat of a paint is transferred to the semi-flexible thermoformable plastic backing sheet. The laminate is then thermoformed and bonded to the plastic material by injection cladding technique, to form a finished article. The finished article consists of a high gloss, defect free paint coat. This technique is used for making exterior body panel of a car.

From the above discussion we can say that lamination is a process of making laminate in which different plastic films or non-plastic materials can be combined together by the application of heat or pressure or both. Laminates are more expensive than the sum of individual constituents cost. But they do a particular job of achievement of balance of properties at a lower cost.

10

High Speed Production of Thin CPP Films

Producers of CPP films are driven by falling margins and rising demands for quality. A means of enhancing productivity is to increase the line output in order to reduce labour and machine costs. A higher melt output can be handled in two ways: Increasing the width of a liner or increasing the extrusion speed for a given product increasing the speed offers serveral advantages: lower melt residence times , shorter change-over times, less start-up waste, reduced space requirements, lower investment costs, no different film sizes etc. Now a days CPP films can be processed at speeds up to 350 m/min and more. In order to be able to run such high speeds several challenges in terms of machine and process technology have to be met.

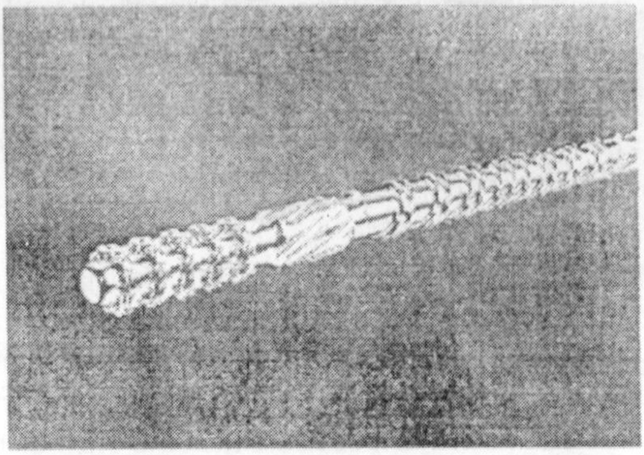

Figure 10.1 : Windmöller & Hölscher cross hole and maddock elements.

Process Stability

The higher the extrusion speed the higher the risk that the process will become unstable. A very important requirement for a stable process is a very homogeneous melt quality. Even small inhomogeneities such as unmolten resin particles or gel spots could lead to a break of the melt in the area between die outlet and melt contact with the chill roll due to the high forces at high speed extrusion. An excellent melt quality can be achieved by combining barrier screws with highly sophisicated

The fixation of the web on the chill roller also contributes to process stability. A secure fixation of the edges can be achieved by electrostatic and pneumatic pinning. Additionally, the whole web will be fixed on the chill roller by using a proper combination of vacuum box, air knife or soft box. To provide optimum process stability, both the the loading angle of the die to the chill roll and the whole system, i.e. die and chill roll unit, have to be optimised. An example of a design for high speed CPP processing -can be found in figure 10.2.

Fig. 10.2 Chill roll unit for high speed cpp production.

Film Quality

As a matter of course the quality of the film has to meet the film producers specifications at all extrusion speeds. To ensure this it is important to provide for intensive and precisely controlled cooling. Another important factor for process stability is web guidance. It is necessary to choose a proper web flow path, especially in the chill roll unit, to create controlled cooling conditions and avoid uncontrolled movements of the web.

Two of the most important film properties are optical and mechanical values. W & H has run various tests to evaluate the influence of extrusion speed on film properties. In Figure 10.3 the results of clarity measurements of three different 20μm 3-layer CPP films (Coex 1-3) extruded at speeds between 200 m/min and 350 m/min show no influence of the extrusion speed. The most important factor for the optical properties is the choice of resins and additives such as anti block agents.

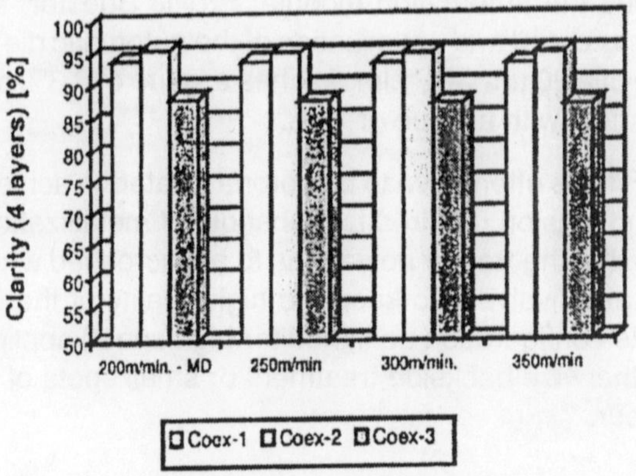

Fig. 10.3 Clarity of different CPP films (20mm)

Also as far as the mechanical properties are concerned, no significant influence of the extrusion speed could be found.

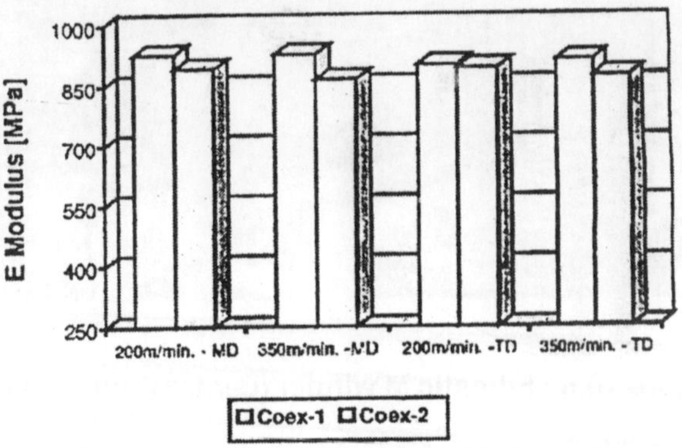

Fig. 10.4 E-Modulus of different CPP Films (20μm)

Figure 10.4 shows the E-Modulus of films land 2 extruded at 200 and 350 m/min in machine and transverse direction (MD and TD). Slightly different values are to be found in the range of the accuracy of the E-Modulus measurements. Similar results can be found for the tensile strength. Especially on a high speed line it is very important to achieve the specifications in very short period of time after start-up in order to produce as little waste as possible. For this reason Windmöller & Hölscher developed the automation module "Profile Booster" to accelerate film thickness control and optimisation of the automatic die at start-up. The 2 μr value of a 20 μm CPP film reaches a value of 3.3% only 3: 15 minutes after starting with a value of 18%.

CPP films often have to be corona treated to achieve a certain level of wetting tension required for subsequent metallization or printing. It is obvious that the treater power has to be increased when high extrusion speeds are involved. To keep the high quality of the film, treaters with electrode configuration designed for high speed applications should be used, otherwise backside treatment or small spots of burned materials may occur.

Figure 10.5 : Filmatic M winder (centre driven, gap/contact).

Last but not least the film has to be wound and the reel quality must stay at a high level independent of the extrusion speed. Especially for CPP it is important to have the right amount of air in the reel to compensate for post crystallization. Therefore the winder of the cast line should be able to control the amount of air in dependence upon the extrusion speed. The W & H Filmatic M winder figure 10.5 is able to wind in-either gap or contact mode with an additional soft "ironing" roller being loaded to the reel. A very low contact pressure allows for sensitive adjustment for reel quality at speeds up to 400 m/min.

11

Linear Low Density Polyethylene Mulch Film

Business with plasticulture

Linear Low Density Polyethylene Mulch film, one more product to the business of polyethylene film brings in a product which results into higher productivity(yield) of fruits such as strawberries. Panchgani and Mahableshwar in Maharashtra wherein rows of strawberries are grown in parallel rows wherein Linear Low Density Polyethylene Mulch Film is laid and strawberries grown at intervals in this film helps farmers in retaining the moisture levels in the soil for a higher produetivity (yield) of strawberries. Strawberries as fruit, in ice-creams, in jams etc brings more number of end uses and end users in the country. Strawberries, a delighte for children brings in a delighteful fruit jam and ice-cream for children. The example of strawberries wherein Linear Low Density Polyethylene Mulch film is used in high quantities also exists for other fruits and vegetables.

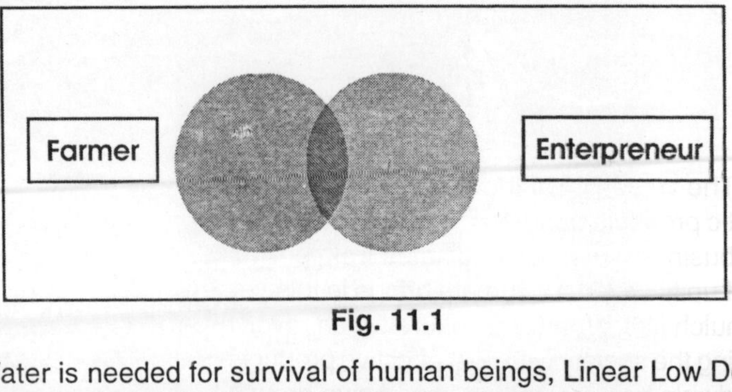

Fig. 11.1

Water is needed for survival of human beings, Linear Low Density Polyethylene Mulch film is needed for the growth of plants. Retaining moisture levels in soil thus becomes a need for achieving a higher productivity of plants for both fruits and vegetables.

Black colour mulch film with addition of carbon black is amongst the most common film used which prevents the film from ultra-violet degradation. Achieving higher quality film with a longer shelf-life with virgin material offers a quality product to the farmers helping in creating a brand for each farmer.

UV stabilised mulch film with addition of carbon black is used for the growth of plants.

Controlled moisture levels in the soil improving the crop productivity is needed bringing in the use of plastic products such as mulch film.

The term "mulch film" means films which are laid on the soil to retain moisture levels in the soil for proper growth of plants. This mulch film is made up oflinear low density polyethylene, a polymer.

Fig. 11.2

The versatility of the polymer capable of producing a wide range of plastic products brings in more and more number of plastic products into this business. Plastics originates from polymer. Polymer which is made up of units called monomers brings in this versatile plastic product such as mulch film. World is a sphere which revolves around plastic products helping the society with cost effective products. Polymer which originated worldwide has created an impressive growth bringing in a boost to the industrial growth as well as economic growth of each country. Polymer a growing plant towards fruition of plastic products brings in a growth to plastic industry.

The plastic processing industry which revolves around manufacturing of plastic products starts with the polymer and ends with the plastic product. The origin of polymer begins with applications which are used in household, with a chain of monomers propagating to infrastructure, agriculture, automotive, packaging. Polymer which has led to the growth of the plastic processing industry bringing in more number of entrepreneurs in the country brings in multi-farious plastic products, numerous enduses and multiple endusers.

Plastics, a key to success for entrepreneurs brings in more and more money for entrepreneurs with a major axis of achieving money leads to success for entrepreneurs which involves multiple processes, multiple machines, multiple end uses and multiple endusers brings in multiple products leading to monetary gains to entrepreneurs.

Plastics, a key to one's pocket helping entrepreneurs to make money with an unbound horizon and unlimited boundaries has unlocked doors for entrepreneurs bringing in more and more money.

One would start thinking about this versatile polymer and versatile plastic product which has helped farmers with a product which offers higher productivity (yield) of plants.

India being No.1 producer of fruits(India accounts for 32 million tons out of 370 million tons of fruits production in the world) & No. 2 producer of vegetables (India's share is 71 million tons out of the 473 million tons of vegetables produced in the world) (Year 2007), in the world, a huge potential exists for plastic products related to agriculture. (Source:http://www.punebds.com/tl.asp., http://www.punebds/tl.asp)

India being No.1 & No.2 producer of fruits and vegetables in the world would bring in a high potential for plastics related to agriculture with a major axis of monetary gains both, to farmers and entrepreneurs would lead to a growth in Agriculture sector and Indian Industry. Entrepreneurs in the country who possess a good business acumen, dynamism and dexterity possessing the capability of achieving high monetary gains needs to look at plastic products related to agriculture which has a high potential in the country. One such product is Linear Low Density Polyethylene

Plastic mulch layer implement   Black plastic mulch in the field

Planting plants into plastics   Water Melons grown on plasticulture

Fig. 11.3

Mulch film which involves a process of film extrusion which involves a high volume business leading to a higher net profitability,

Net profitability involving a major axis of high market potential of plastic products in the country with plastic products in a nascent stage would lead to more and more new entrants into this business. Business means money which involves dynamism of entrepreneurs to market these plastic products with commission agents who possess a competency and capability to market these products helping this business to achieve a faster market penetration.

Versatility of polyethylene films which initially was perceived and referred to carry bags now brings more and more number of new applications and enduses which benefits the society.

Versatile products made up of plastics brings in versatility of farmers in achieving higher productivity (yield) of plants helping these farmers to achieve higher monetary gains.

Agriculture sector which involves farmers who possess knowledge about each variety of fruit & vegetable, knowledge about plastic products related to agriculture needs to be endowed to these farmers. Farming with plastic products, a business which involves money, perseverance and patience to reap in fruits (rewards) helps these farmers in achieving higher productivity (yield) leading into higher monetary gains resulting into a growth in agriculture sector and thus economic growth of the country.

Expanding horizons of business, which an entrepreneur aims at, helping him achieve a higher net profitability bringing in more business would lead to a faster growth of a business, This business can fructify with more and more number of products added by each entrepreneur into his business.

Business revolves around a higher product mix leading to higher capacity utilizations, higher value addition and distribution pattern, Distribution pattern of a business lies on the dynamism of an entrepreneur. Entrepreneur with a good business acumen and dynamism in marketing brings in more business.

Marketing of products for products which have a high market potential in the country needs to be marketed parallely through commission agents, dealers and persons with qualification in agriculture. Shelving out high commissions to the commission agents who are the local people and who know the local language and whom the farmers trust would be able to market these products at a faster pace.

Parallely marketing through dealers who market other products related to agriculture helping entrepreneurs to eliminate one step of business would lead to more business. Students related to agriculture who possess the knowledge of the benefits of the plastic products related to agriculture would be able to communicate the farmers more effectively leading to a faster growth.

Another factor for a faster growth of a business is a high product mix leading to a high capacity utilization of the machinery. Existing processors of multilayer film can look at Linear Low Density Polyethylene Mulch film helping them to add one more product into their business.

This business also offers the flexibility to the existing processors of monolayer film and multilayer film to add one more product to their business without any additional investment. Without additional investment this product would help in increasing the product mix would lead to a higher net profitability.

Business means money and monetary gains of an entrepreneur increases with a higher product mix. Multilayer/Monolayer polyethylene film manufacturers can produce LLDPE Garbage bags, PE Multilayer film for flexible packaging laminates, PE Multilayer film for milk, edible oil, LLDPE Stretch & Cling film, LLDPE Carry bags, LLDPE Nursery bags, LD/LLDPE Liners, LLDPE Perforated film for fruits and vegetables and LLDPE Mulch film on the same film extruder.

Agribusiness - India

- India is the largest producer of milk, fruits, pulses, cashew nuts, coconuts and tea in the world.
- Second largest producer of rice and wheat in the world, and fourth largest coarse grains.

Fig. 11.4

- India is amongst the top 3 producers in the world - Poultry products-Fruits and Vegetables - Spices.
- One of the largest producer of-Cotton-Sugar, Sugarcane - Peanuts.
- 25% of GDP.
- 64% Employments.
- 18% of India's exports.

Fig. 11.5

Plastics in Agro Industry

India ranks 1st in world in fruits & 2nd in world in vegetables.

- Increase in population.
- Higher rate of urbanization.
- Dual Income families & Economic Liberalization.
- Economic Growth.
- Fruits prevents diseases sch as heart diabetes & cancer.

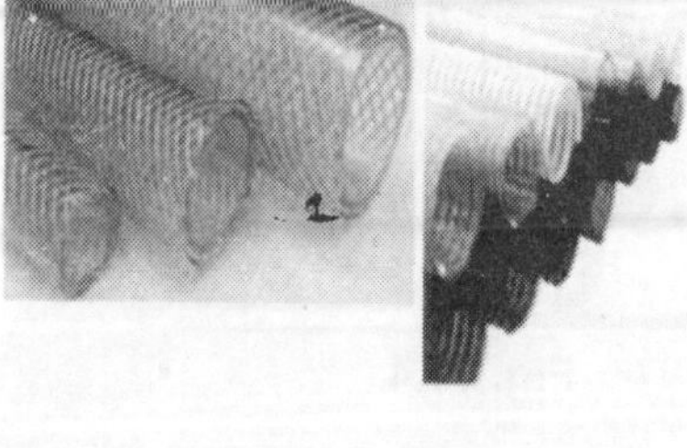

Fig. 11.6

Fig. 11.7

Plasticulture

The need for increasing food production to meet the needs of expanding population by use of reducing resource base of cultivable land and water & hence effective and efficient use of these resources is a must.

Fig. 11.8

Growth in agricultural production will have to be based on productivity improvement by application of technologies like drip Irrigation, Plasticulture

Fig. 11.9

But the increase in agricultural yield has to keep pace with the growing population. To remain self-sufficient in food grains, we need another green revolution, or rather, a greener, revolution.

What is Plasticulture?

Plasticulture is the use of plastics in Agriculture, horticulture, water Management, food grains storage and related areas :

- Plasticulture in water management.
- Drip Irrigation.
- Controlled Environment Agriculture.
- LDPE Film Mulching.

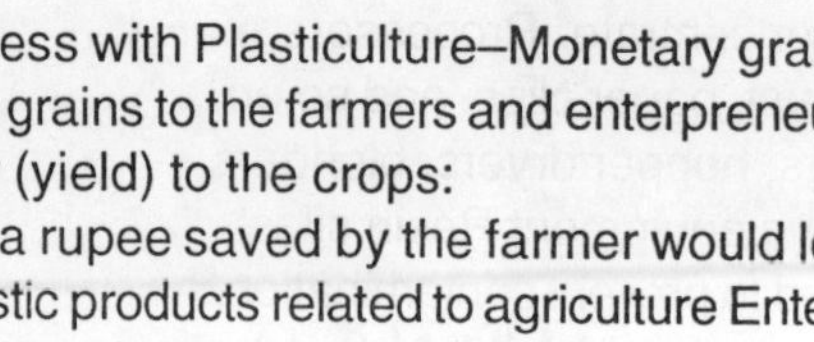

Fig. 11.10

- Business with Plasticulture–Monetary grains to the farmers and enterpreneurs grains to the farmers and enterpreneurs Farmers–Increase in productivity (yield) to the crops:
  - Even a rupee saved by the farmer would lead to a higher usage of plastic products related to agriculture Enterpreneurs-High Value added products.
  - High Flexibility of High Product Mix.
  - High Capacity Utilisation.
  - High Net Profitability.
  - Low Payback Period.

12

Extruder Operation

This section summarises what has been reviewed in this chapter. Machine operation takes place in three stages. The first stage covers the running of a machine and its peripheral equipment. The next involves setting processing conditions to a prescribed number of parameters for a specific material, with a specific die, and in a specific line. The final stage is devoted to problem solving and fine-tuning of the operation, which will lead to meeting product performance requirements at the lowest cost of operation. A successful operation requires close attention to many details, such as the quality and flow of feed material, a heat profile adequate to melt but not degrade the material, and a startup and shutdown that will not degrade the plastic. Processors must become familiar with a trouble shooting guide.

Care should be taken to prevent conditions that promote surface condensation of moisture on the resin and moisture absorption by the pigments in colour concentrate. Processors must avoid contamination from other plastics, dust, paper clips, and so on, and take special care in cleaning feed hoppers, hopper dryers, blenders, scrap granulators, and other material handling equipment Resin silos, containers, and hoppers should be kept covered to prevent contamination. Also, certain established procedures for startup should be followed to prevent contamination, overheating, and excessive pressures.

It is important to provide safe operating conditions for personnel and equipment. One must realise that high production rates cannot be achieved until all parts of the extrusion system reach the optimum operating conditions. This condition is best achieved by gradually increasing heat and rates until desired optimum conditions are reached.

Prior to startup one must take certain precautions: (i) Unless the same resin is already in the machine from a previous run, the entire machine should be cleaned or purged, including the hopper, barrel, screw, breaker plate, die, and downstream equipment. If a resin was left in the barrel for a while, with heats off, the processor must determine if the material is subject to shrink and could cause moisture entrapment from the surrounding area, resulting in contamination that would require cleanup (this situation could also be a source of corrosion in the barrel/screw). One must (ii) check heater bands and electrical connections, handling electrical connections carefully; and (iii) check thermo couples, pressure transducers, and their connections carefully. Also the processor should: (iv) be sure the flow path through the extruder is not blocked; (v) have a bucket or drum, half filled with water, to catch extrudate whenever purging or processing plastics that have contaminating gaseous byproducts; and (vi) inspect all machine ventilation systems to ensure adequate air flow.

Startup procedures also involve precautions: (i) Starting with the front and rear zones (die and feed section), one should set heat controllers slightly above the resin melt point and turn on the heaters. Heat-up should be gradual from the ends into the centre of the barrel to prevent pressure buildup from possible melt degradation. One should: (ii) increase all heaters gradually, checking for deviations that might indicate burned-out or run-away heaters by slightly raising and lowering the controller set point to check ifpower goes on and off; and (iii) after the controllers show that all heaters are slightly above the melt point, adjust the settings to the desired operating heats, based on experience and/or the resin manufacturer's recommendation, checking to ensure that the heat increase is gradual, particularly in the front/crosshead. (iv) the time required to reach temperature equilibrium may be 1/2 to 2 hours, depending on the size of the extruder. Overshooting is usually observed with on/off controllers. (v) Hot melts can behave many different ways, so no one should stand in front of the extruder during startup, and one should never look into the feed hopper because of the potential for blowback due to previous melt degrading; and so on. (vi) After set heats have been reached, one puts the resin in the hopper and starts the screw at a low speed such as 2 to 5 RPM. (vii) The processor should observe the amperage required to turn the screw, stop the screw if the amperage is too high, and wait a few minutes prior to restart; (viii) In working with a melt requiring high pressure, the extruder barrel pressure should not exceed 7 MPa (1,000 psi) during the startup period; (ix) One should let the machine run of a few minutes, and purge until a good-quality extrudate is attained usually (experience teaches what it should look like; a certain size and amount of bubble or fumes may be optimum for a particular melt, based on one's experience after setting up all controls). If resin was left in the extruder, a longer purging time may be required to remove any slightly degraded resin. (x) For uniform output, it is essential that all of the resin be melted prior to entering its metering zone, and that this section run full. (When time permits, after running for a while, the processor should stop the machine, let it start cooling, and remove the screw to evaluate how the resin performance from the start of feeding to end of metering. Thus one can see if the melt is progressive and can relate it to screw performance and product performance. (xi) One then turns up the screw to the required RPM, checking to see that maximum pressure and amps are not exceeded; and (xii) adjusts the die with the controls it contains, if required, at the desired running speed. Once the extruder is running at maximum performance, the processor sets up controls for takeoff equipment, which may require more precision settings, if required. One may get into a balancing act of interrelating extruder and downstream equipment.

In regard to shutdown, the procedures vary slightly, depending on whether or not the machine is to be cleaned out or just stopped for a brief time period. If the same type of resin is to be run again, cleanout generally is not required. The goal is to avoid degradation by reducing exposure of the resin to high heat. If cleanout is required, because a different type of resin is to be processed, it is necessary to disassemble the equipment at a heat high enough to allow cleanout prior to material solidification.

The procedure for shutdown without cleanout is as follows: (i) one should empty the hopper as well as possible; (ii) if coating, one should take the action required to remove the substrate (with wire coating, one removes the wire from the croshead die; in coating paper, film, etc., usually the extruder is on a track and can be withdrawn from the substrate; etc.); (iii) one reduces all heat settings to the melt heat; (iv) one reduces the screw speed to 2 to 5 RPM, purging the resin, if required, into a water bucket or drum prior to reducing the heat to melt heat; (v) when the screw appears to be empty, one stops the screw, and shuts off the heaters and the main power switch (however, steps (iv) and (v) must be completed before the melt heat drops significantly, or a premature shutdown will occur with material remaining in the barrel); and (vi) if a screen pack with breaker plate is used, one disconnects the crosshead from the extruder and removes the breaker plate and screen. If necessary, appropriate action is taken to clean them.

For cleanout of the extruder at shutdown, the first three steps are the same as steps (i), (ii), and (iv) in the preceding paragraph. The procedure then is: (iv) When the extruder appears to be empty, one stops the screw, and (v) shuts off and disconnects the crosshead heaters. One then reduces other heaters to about 170 to 330°C (400 to 625°F), depending on the resin temperature at the melt point. (vi) The processor disassembles the crosshead and cleans it while still hot. One removes the die, and the gear pump if used, and removes as much resin as possible by scraping with a copper spatula or brushing with a copper wire brush. One removes all heaters, thermocouples, pressure transducers, and so on. One should consider using an exhaust duct system (elephant trunk) above the disassembly and cleaning area, even if the resin is not a contaminating type; it keeps the area clean and safe. (vii) One pushes the screw out gradually while cleaning with a copper wire brush and copper wool. Care should be exercised if a torch is used to burn and remove resin; tempered steel, such as Hastelloy, may be altered, and the screw distorted or weakened, and subjected to excessive wear, corrosion, or even failure (broken). (xiii) After screw removal, one conti nus the cleaning, if necessary, and (ix) turns off heaters and the main power switch.

Final cleaning of parts, particularly disassembled parts, is best done manually, or, much better, in ventilated burn-out ovens, if available, at 540°C (1,000°F) for about 1½ h. For certain parts, with certain resins, the useful life could be shortened by corrosion. One should check with the part manufacturer. After burn-out, one removes any grit that is present with a soft, clean cloth. If water is used, one can air-blast to dry. With precision machined parts, water cleaning could be damaging, because of potential corrosion when certain metals are used.

TROUBLE SHOOTING

To do the best job of eliminating or reducing problems, one must understand the complete process, and there is no substitute for experience. Only through hands-on problem solving can an operator, or even management, really begin to understand the comploxity of oxtorsion and know how to handle the wide variety of problems that invariably occllr. An excellent summary of troubleshooting is given in Table 12.1.

TABLE 12.1:
Trouble shooting guide : common extrusion problems and how to solve, them.

Problem	Cause(s)	Solutions(s)
General Considerations		
Surging	Resin bridging in hopper	Eliminate bridging
	Incorrect melt temperature	Correct melt temperature
	Improper screw design	Check design
	Rear barrel temperature too low or high	Increase or decrease rear temperature
	Low back pressure	Increase screen pack
	Improper metering length	Use proper screw design
Gels (Contaminants that look like small specks or bubbles)	Melt temperature too high	Lower melt temperature
	Not enough progression in screw	Use new screw
	Bad resin	Check resin quality
	Melt temperature too high	Check melt temperature
Melt fracture (Rough surface finish, also called "Shark-skin")	Melt temperature too low	Increase melt temperature
	Die gaps too narrow	Heat die lips
		Use processing aids
Bad colour	Colour concentration incompatible	Ensure melt index of concentrate base with resin material of close to melt index of resin
Bubbles	Wet material	Dry thoroughly
	Overheating	Decrease temperature; check thermocouples
	Shallow metering section	Use proper compression ratio screw
Overheating	Improper screw design	Use lower compression screw
	Restriction to flow	check die for restrictions
	Barrel Temperature too low	Increase temperature.

Die lines	Scratched die	Refinish die surface
	Contamination	Clean head and die
	Cold polymer	Check for dead spots in head;adjust barrel and head temperature to prevent freezing
Flow Lines	Overhead material	Decrease temperature
	Poor mixing	Use correct screw design
	Contamination	Clean system
	Improper temperature profile	Adjust profile
Blown Film		
Wrinkles	Dirty collapsing frame	Clean frame
	Too much web tension	Adjust tension
	Improperly designed air ring	Use new air ring
	Gauge variations	See gauge variations
	Insufficient cooling	Use refrigerated air
		Increase flow of air
		Reduce output
	Misalignment between nip rolls and die	Check alignment
Folds, creases	Excessive stretching between nip and roller	Reduce winding speed
	Nip assembly drive not constant	Adjust or replace drive
Blocking	Inadequate cooling	Use better cooling method
	Excessive winding tension	Adjust tension
	Excessive pressure on nip rolls	Adjust pressure
	Bad resin	Check resin

Port Lines	Melt temperature too low	Increase melt temperature
	Die too cold or too hot in	Adjust die temperature relation to melt temperature
Splitting	Excessive orientation in machine	Increase blwo up ratio direction
	Die lines	See die lines
	Degraded resin	Reduce melt temperature
	Poor resin choice	Ensure resin is suitable
Die lines	Nick on die lip	Change die
	Dirty die	Clean die
	inadequate purging	Increase purging time between resin changes
Gauge variations (Machine direction	Surging	Check temperature
		Check hopper for bridging
	Inconsistent take-up speed	Check take-up speeds
Gauge variations (Trnasverse direction)	Non-uniform die gap	Adjust gap
		Centre air ring on gap
Printing Problems	Insufficient treatment	Use properly treated film
	Additives interfering with ink	Use resins no interfereing additives
		Erratic treatment
		Reduce slip level to about 600 ppm for water based inks

Sheet

Note : Most of the problems covered under blown film also relevant to sheet extrusion.

Problem	***Cause(s)***	***Solution(s)***
Poor gauge uniformity	Melt flow is not stable	User gear pump to stabilise flow
Viscosity not stable	Poor mixing	Use static mixer
Streaks	Contaminated system	Clean hopper Check screw and die; clean if necessary
Total discolouration	Excessive regrind	Check amount of regrind used
Discontinuous lines	Too much moisture	Increase resin drying Use hot regrind

Pipe and tubing

Note : this data pertains to extrusion lines using water filled vacuum sizing tanks

Poor output	***Improper die or screw design***	***Ensure die and screw are designed for desired output***
Inside diameter :		
Blisters	Insufficient vacuum	Increase vacuum
	Excessive moisture	Maintain normal % of moisture in compound
	Gases entrapped	Reduce temperature
	Water inside pipe	Stop sater access

Burn streaks	Mandrel heat too high	Check mandrel heat
	Stock temperature too high	Reduce temperature slowly
Grooves	Mandrel is coated with material	Clean mandrel
Wavy surface	Screw clearance set improperly	Adjust clearance
	Puller drive slipping	Adjust or replace puller drive
Outside diameter :		
Burn streaks	Material hangup die	Clean die
	Temperature too high	Reduce temperature slowly
Uneven circumference	Too much air pressure on puller	Reduce air pressure
	Insufficient air pressure	Check air pressure and all connections
Discoloured	Stabilizer level too low	Check stabilizer level
Pock marks	Air bubbles adhering to pipe in floation tank	Install wiper in tank
	Improper adjustment of spray rings that surround water tank	Readjust spray rings
Oversized	Air spray too high	Adjust air supply
	insufficient water supply	Increase water supply
	Pipe hot when measured	Allow pipe to cool before measuring
Wall too thick	Misadjusted die bushing	Adjust die bushing to achieve uniform thickness
	Wrong die set-up	Use correct set-up

Table 12.2 presents a troubleshooting guide for plastic form film. One must be aware that causes of problems are not always obvious; for example, Fig. 12.1 shows contamination in the die presenting a problem that is almost impossible to resolve by equipment controls.

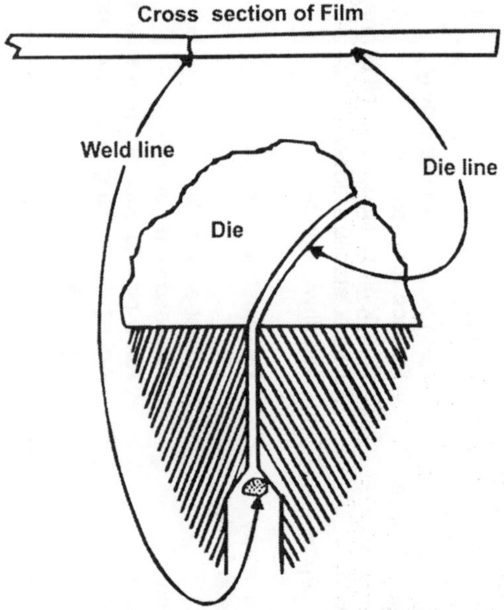

Weld line in film from dirt hangup below die lands
Die line from damaged die mandrel

Fig. 12.1: Example of a contaminated die and a troubleshooting problem.

To determine the source of a problem, it is necessary to understand the basics of a process and apply them to problem solution. For example, with film and sheet dies, tip adjustments only control the uniformity of the transverse thickness. To control the average thickness a proper relationship between the extruder pumping rate and the speed of roll-up is required. Closing the die lip opening has very little effect on the extrusion rate and does not make the entire sheet thinner.

Regarding surges, any variation of the extrusion rate with time originates in the extruder and thus must be corrected in the extruder. This could be the most common and most difficult problem to correct, as it has many interrelated sources, none of which are in the die. A surge can be due to

Table 12.2 : Troubleshooting guide for plastic foam film

Problem	*Probable cause(s)*	*Correction*
Ramdom poor cell structure	Low melt pressure.	Increase screw-speed Reduce die-lip temp. Decrease gauge of screen packs. Use resin of lower melt index. Reduce die gap.
	Hangup in die.	Reduce land length. clean die.
	Stagnant low-pressure areas in head.	Increase screw speed.
	Irregular cells in spider area or opposite die-ring feed.	Use bottom-fed sprial die. Increase head pressure.
Poor skin formation	Too much blowing agent.	Reduce blown agent level.
	Linear skin speed to low.	Increase screw speed.
	Loss of melt pressure in die land.	Reduce land length. Increase L/D ratio. Increase screw speed.
	Die block temperature too low	Increase temperature.
Pinholes in film or bubble burst on surface	Too much blowing agent	Reduce blowing agent level
	Die temperaure too high.	Reduce die temperature
	Resin melt index too high.	Decrease resin melt index. Reduce processing temperature.
	Blowing agent decomposing too soon.	Reduce processing temperature

Problem	*Probable cause(s)*	*Correction*
		Increase screw speed.
		Reduce blowing agent level.
	Poor flow within polymer skin.	Improve flow in head and die.
Cells collapsing	Resin melt index too high	Decrease melt index.
		Reduce processing temperature.
	Cooling too fast.	Reduce cooling rate.

inconsistent feed from the hopper to the barrel, varying frictional forces in the barrel feed zone, improper screw design, and other causes.

Melts basically move in laminar flow in the die, where no mixing action takes place; so poor mixing and incomplete thermal homogenisation must be corrected prior to melt flow in the die. In regard to melt heat, because they are generally very efficient heat insulators, melts are in the dies for only a few seconds. It is possible to alter frictional effects on the melt skin through changes in the die heat, but there is usually a better chance to produce an even heat in the extruder.

Die adjustments do not significantly influence the extrusion rate; the lip opening restrictor bar clearance, die heat, and overall die design have small to moderate effects on the back pressure. However, the extrusion rate is only slightly affected by substantial changes in back pressure. Thus attempts to open the lip or increase the die heat to increase the extrusion output rate can be exercises in futility, as well as the sources of many additional problems.

13

Details of Processing Equipments

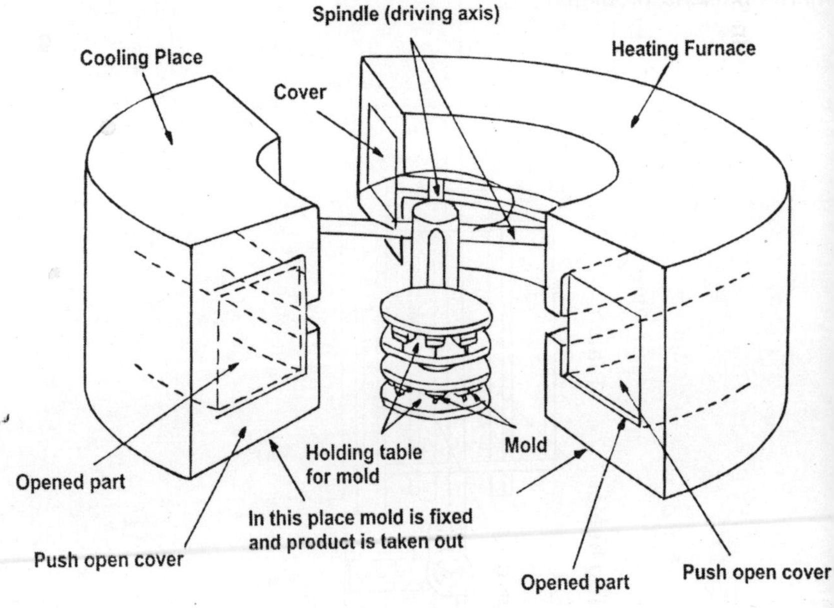

Fig. 13.1 :
Multi-axis (4 AXES) votomoulding machine.

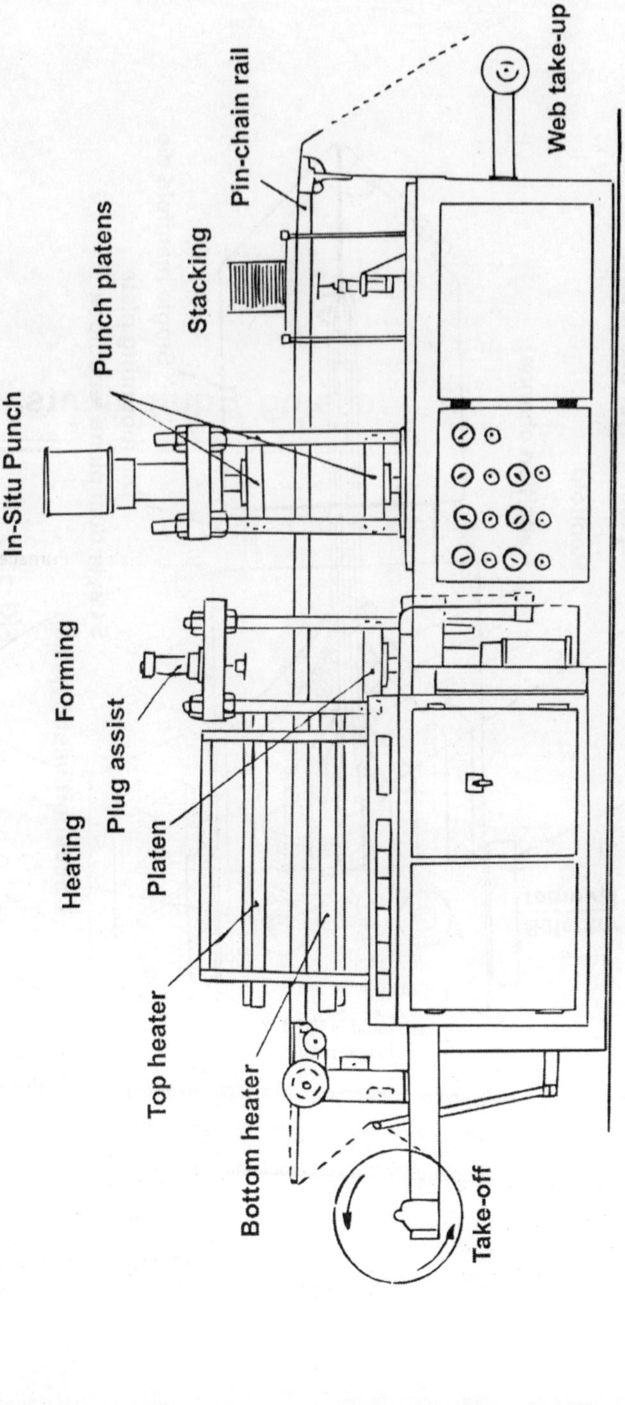

FIG. 13.2 :
Thin-guage Roll-fed Thermoformer (kiefel)

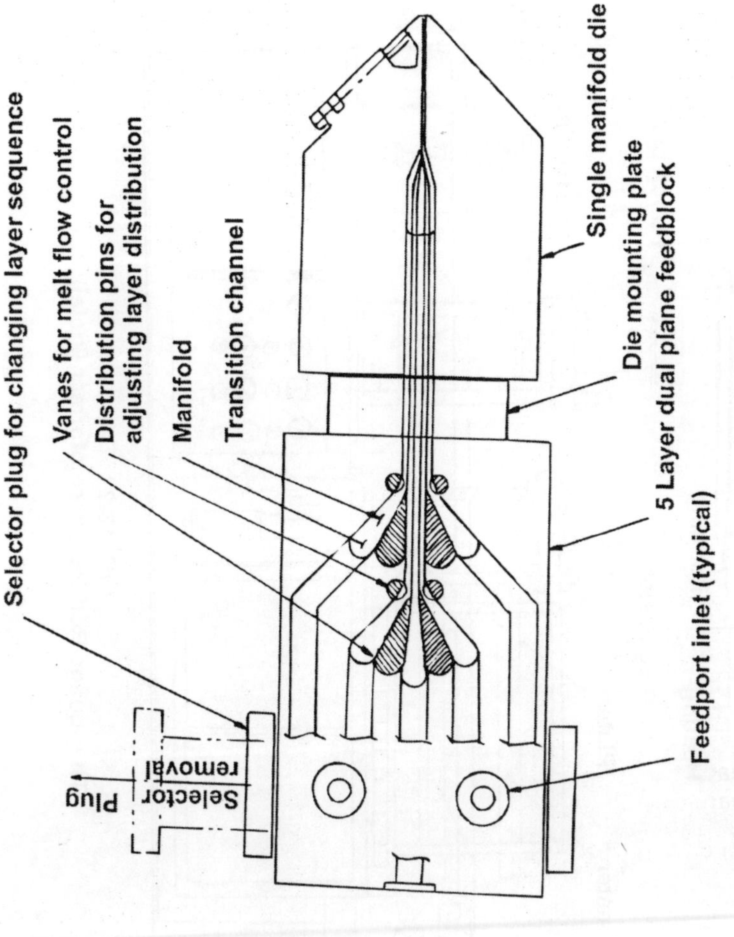

FIG. 13.3 :
Five Layer Cloeren Feedblock

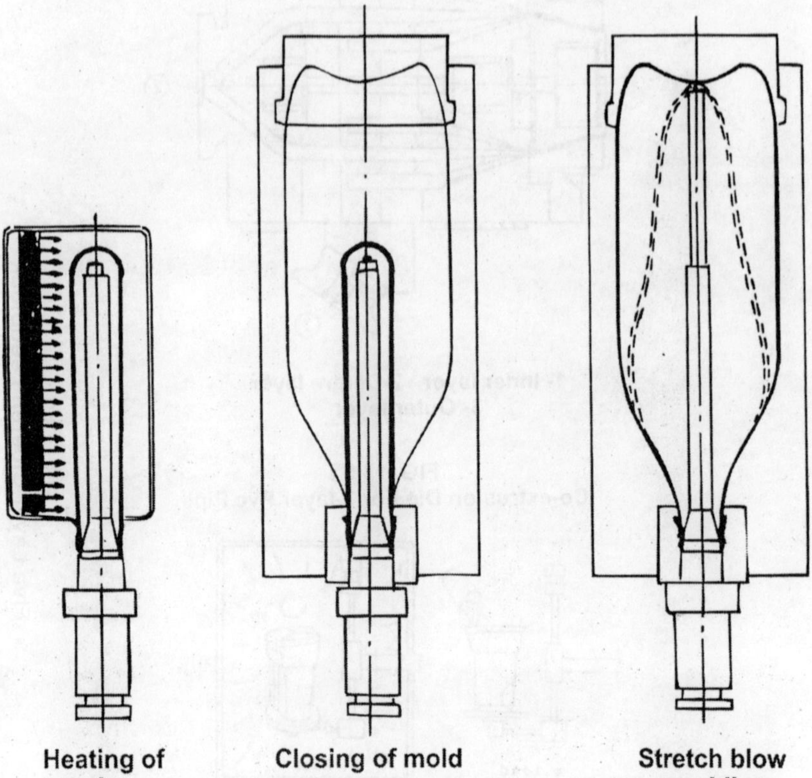

Fig. 13.4 :
Biaxially Stretch Blow Moulding Of Cold Parison Made By Injection Moulding

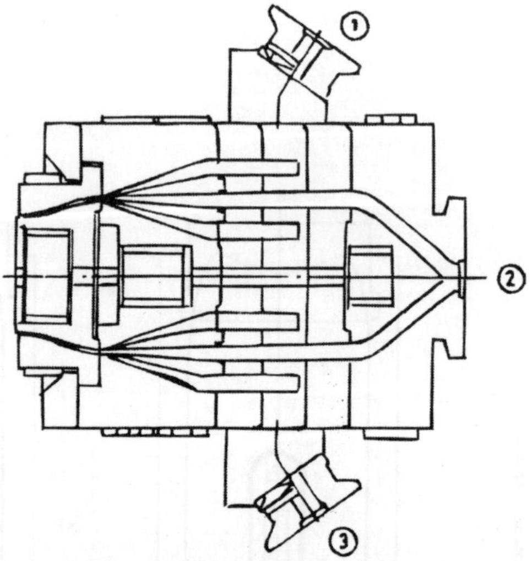

1- Inner layer 2-Centre layer
3- Outer layer

FIG. 13.5 :
Co-extrusion Die For 3-layer Pvc Pipe

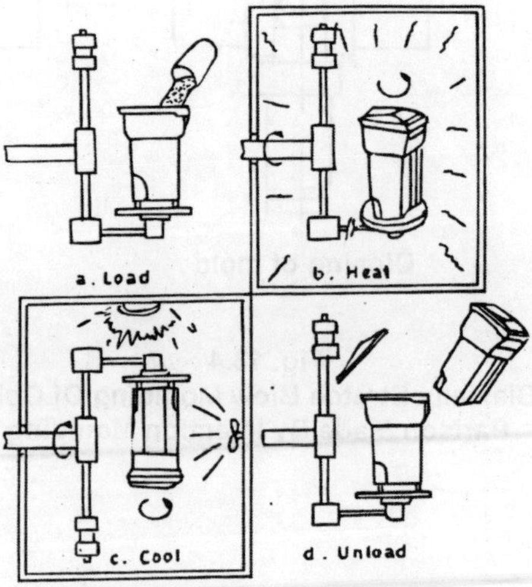

a) Load plastic into mould, b) Heat mould and plastic,
c) Cool mould and plastic, d) Remove the moulded part

FIG. 13.6 :
Four Steps Of Rotational Moulding Process

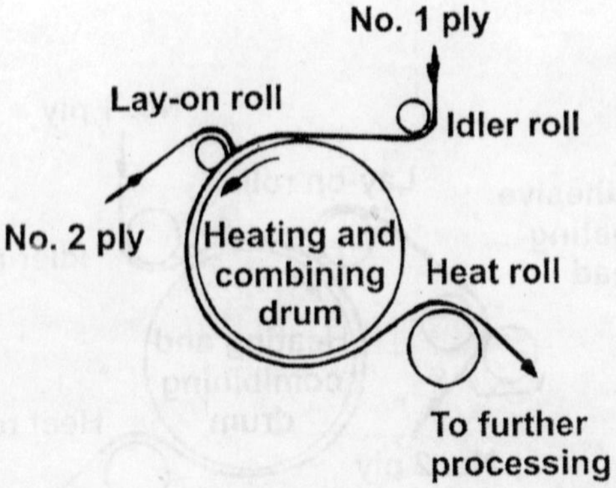

Fig. 13.7 :
Typical Two-ply Lamination By Fusion

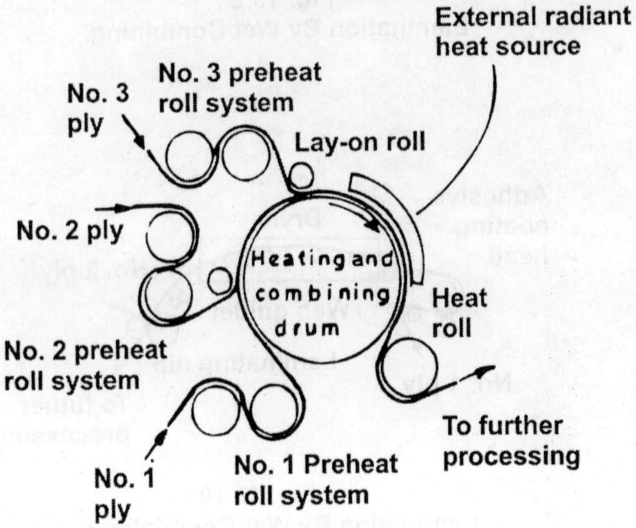

Fig. 13.8 :
Three-ply Fusion Lamination

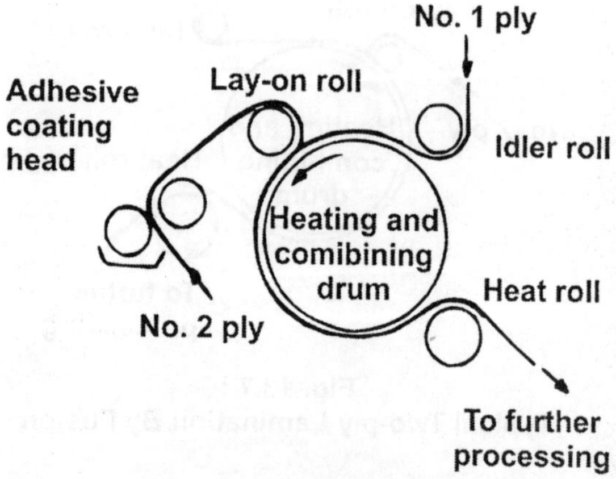

Fig. 13.9 :
Lamination By Wet Combining.

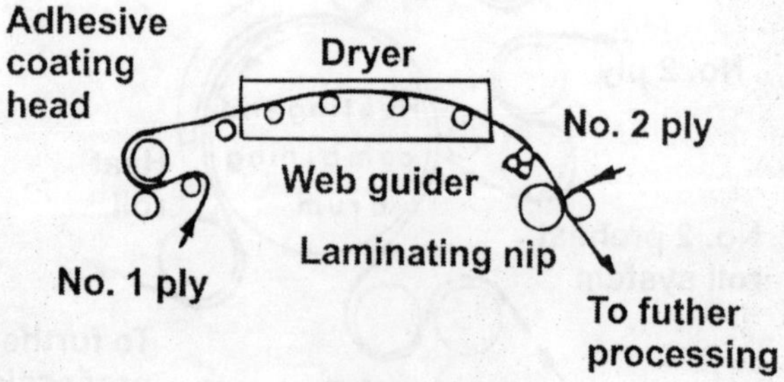

Fig. 13.10 :
Lamination By Wet Combining When Water Or Solvent Is Present.

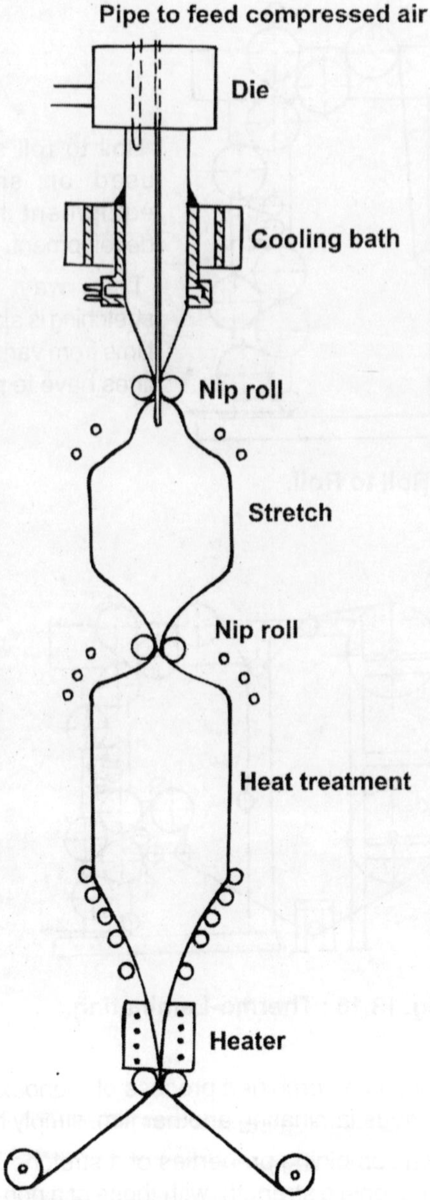

Fig. 13.11 :
Apparatus For Manufacturing Of Biaxially Oriented Film (tubular Method)

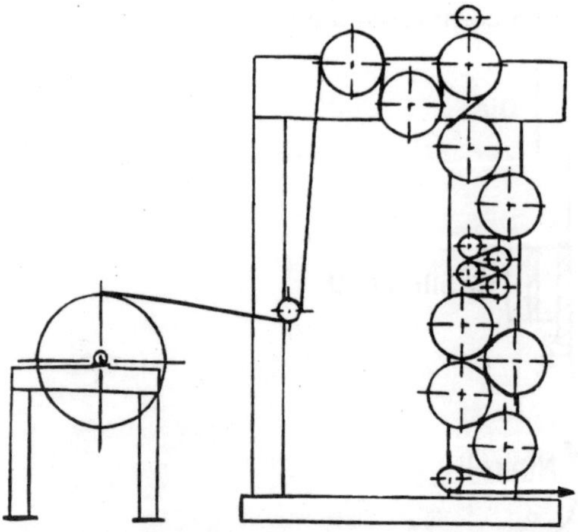

Roll to roll stretching is used on smaller size equipment for process development.

This way of off-line stretching is also used when films from various extrusion lines have to processed.

Fig. 13.12 : Roll to Roll.

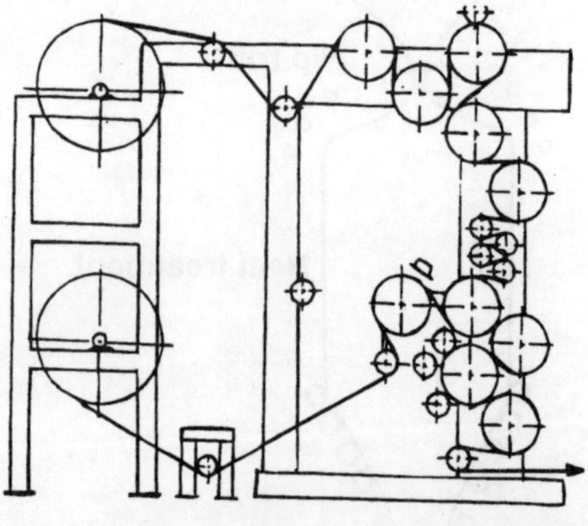

Fig. 13.13 : Thermo-Laminating.

Thermo Laminating is a combined process of monoaxial stretching one film and simultaneous laminating another film, simply by heat.

The result is a film combining properties of a stretched product, like increased stiffness and tensile strength, with those of a non oriented film, providing for instance superb heat sealing.

The unstretched bottom web might also be printed roll shock.

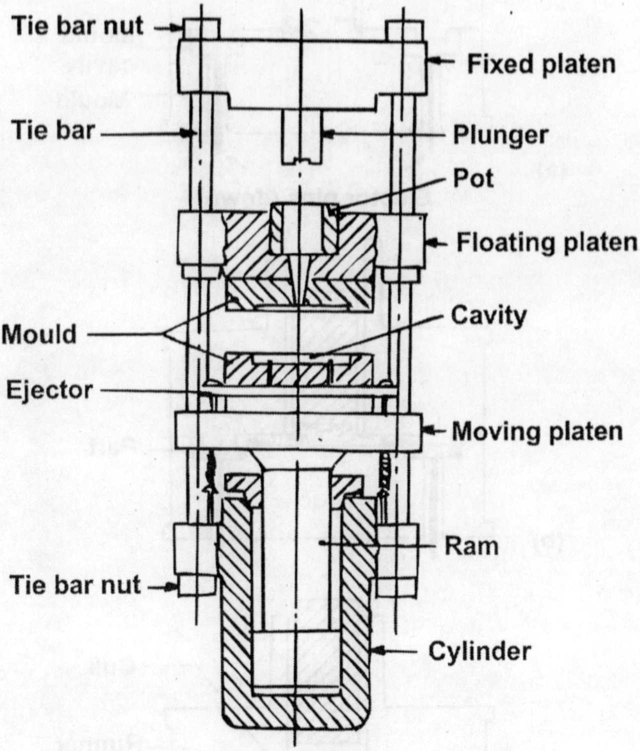

Fig. 13.14 :
Pot Type (up Stroke Type).

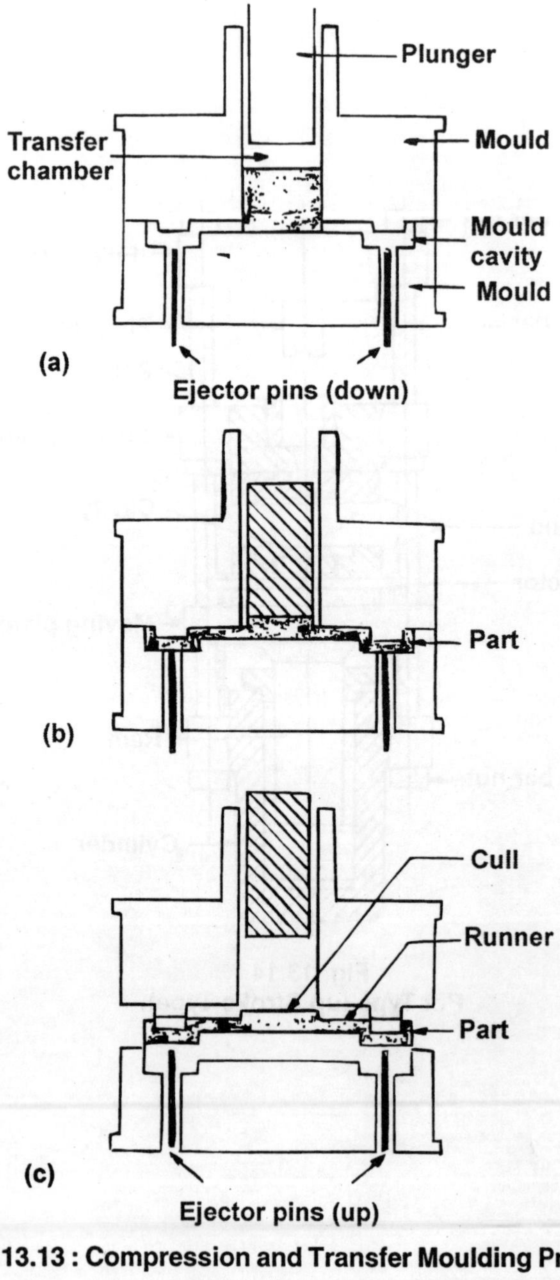

Fig. 13.13 : Compression and Transfer Moulding Process.

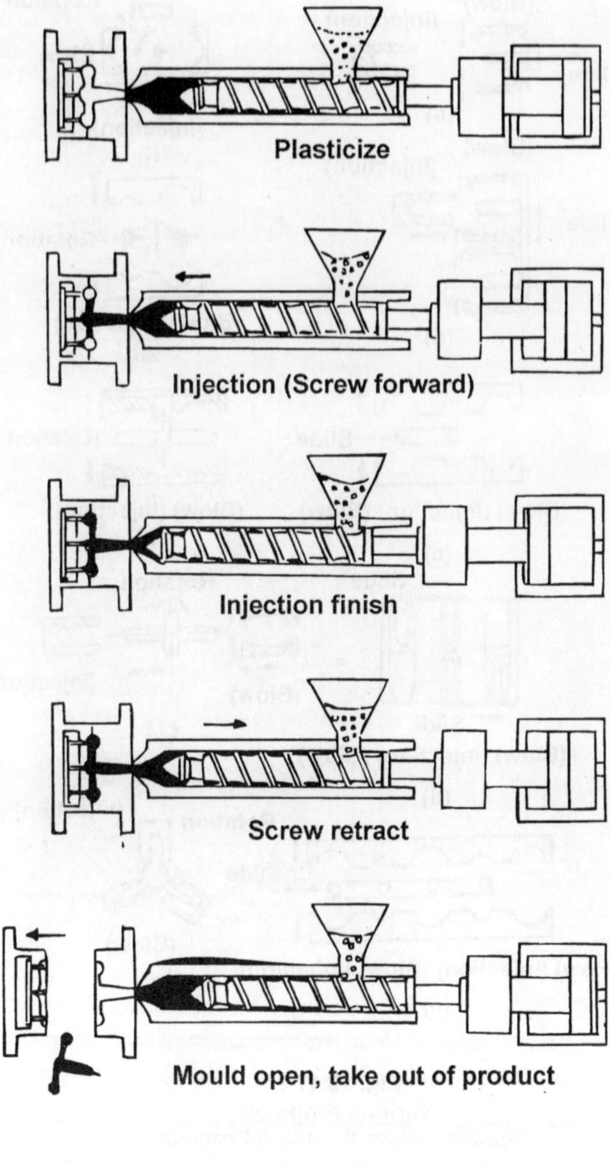

Fig. 13.16 : Injection Moudling Process.

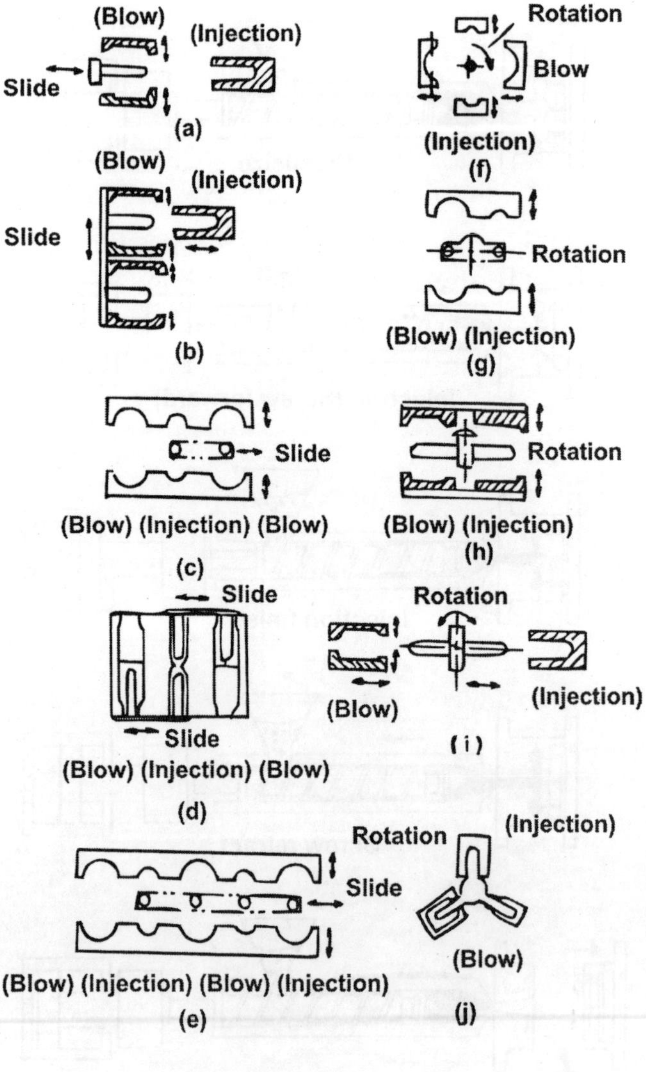

Fig. 13.17 :
Various Kinds of
Injection Blow Moulding Process.

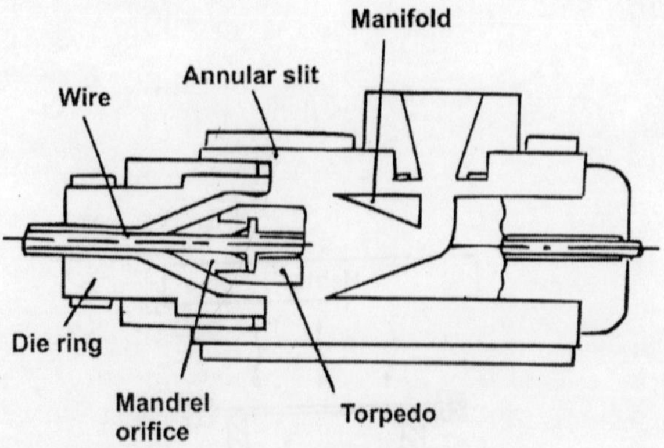

Fig. 13.18 : Wire Coating Process.

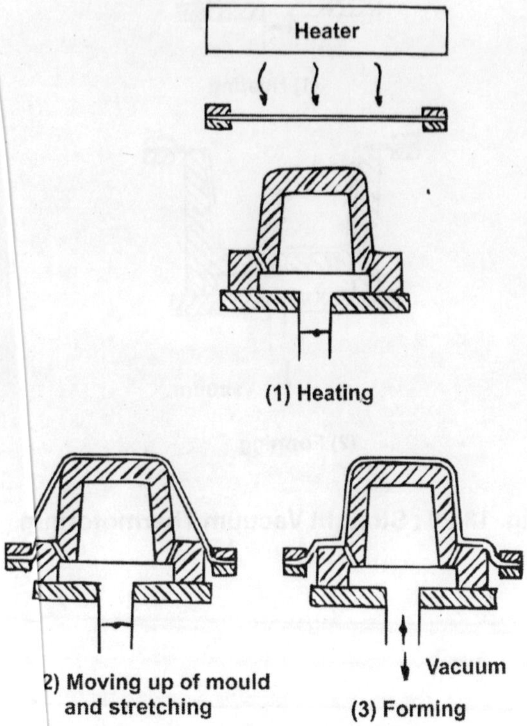

Fig. 13.19 :
Drape Vacuum Thermoforming
(one Of The Several Methods).

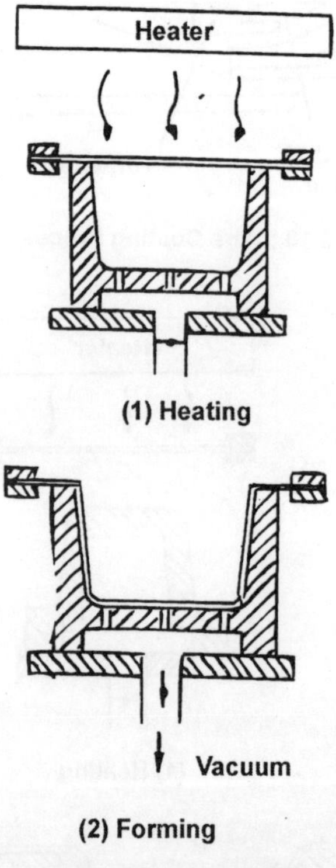

Fig. 13.20 : Straight Vacuum Thermoforming.

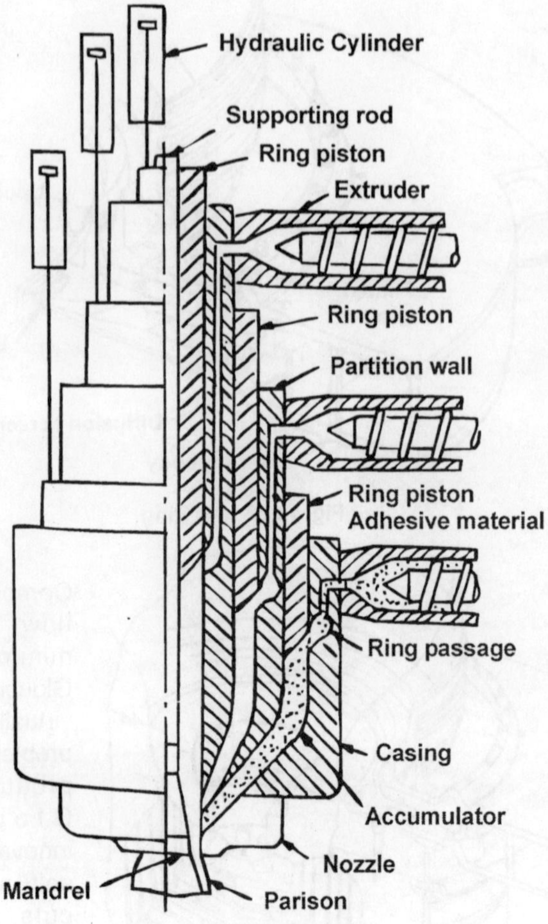

Fig. 13.21 : Construction of Die for Multi-layer blow moulding.

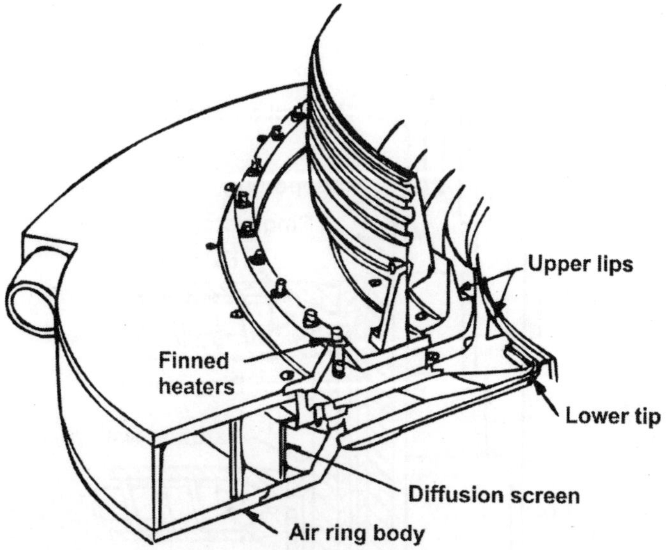

Fig. 13.22 : Air Ring

Fig. 13.23 : 7 Layer Optiflow Blown Film Die.

Computer designed flow channels minimise polymer Gloucester Dies. This virtually eliminates gel problems and speeds product changes. Gloucester's innovative taper lock self, aligning design cuts downtime by permitting simple die cleaning at the processor's plant. The easy to reach non-rotating dies minimise string-up and adjustment time.

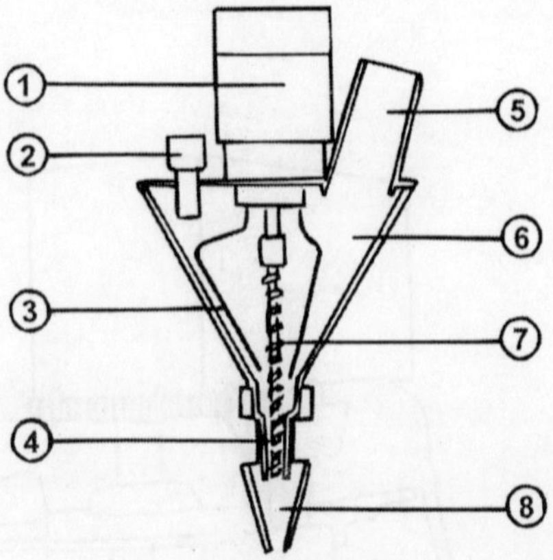

1. Drive mechanism. 2. Level control. 3. Stirrer. 4. Filling tube. 5. Product inlet. 6. Hopper. 7. Filling Screw. 8. Discharge funnel.

Fig. 13.24 : Filling Systems (auger-filler).

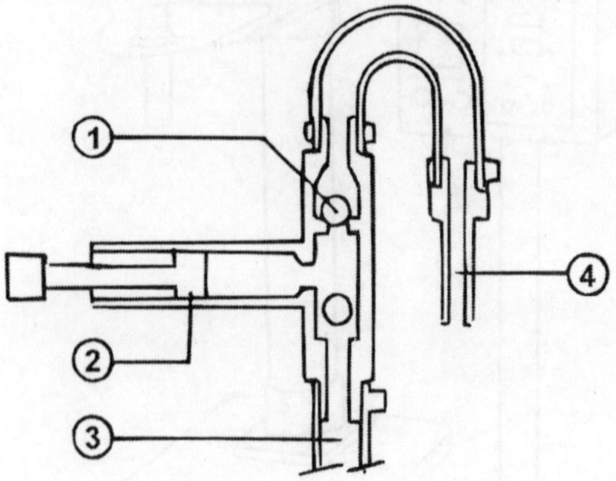

1. Ball valves. 2. Filling piston. 3. Inlet pipe. 4. Outlet pipe.

Fig. 13.25 : Filler For Liquids.

Auger Filler is a versatile power filling machine for dosing free flowing as well as non free flowing powders, like Pharmaceutical powder, Chemical powders, Talcum powder, Pesticide powder, Ground spices, ground coffee, flours, Milk powders etc.

The machine operates on the principle of positive displacement Screw operating under constant head.

The precisely designed Auger displaces the product through funnel into the pouch container held under the funnel. The filling cycle is controlled by an Electromegnatic Clutch/Brake unit and Photoelectric sensor.

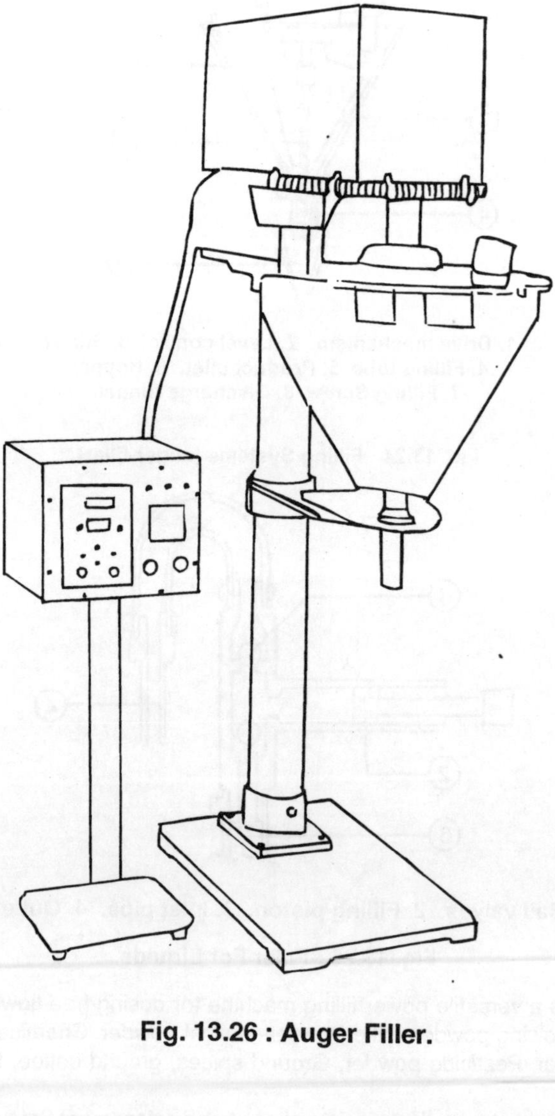

Fig. 13.26 : Auger Filler.

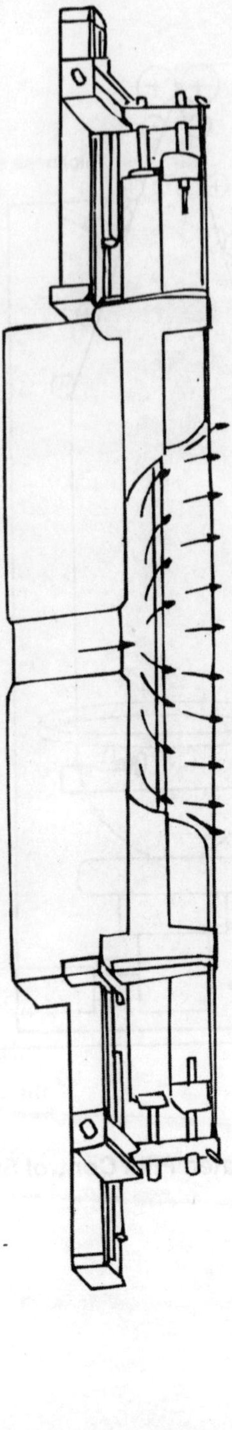

Fig. 13.27 : Extrusion Die For Edge Bead Reduced/beadless Estrusion In The Extrusion Coating And Lamination Processes.

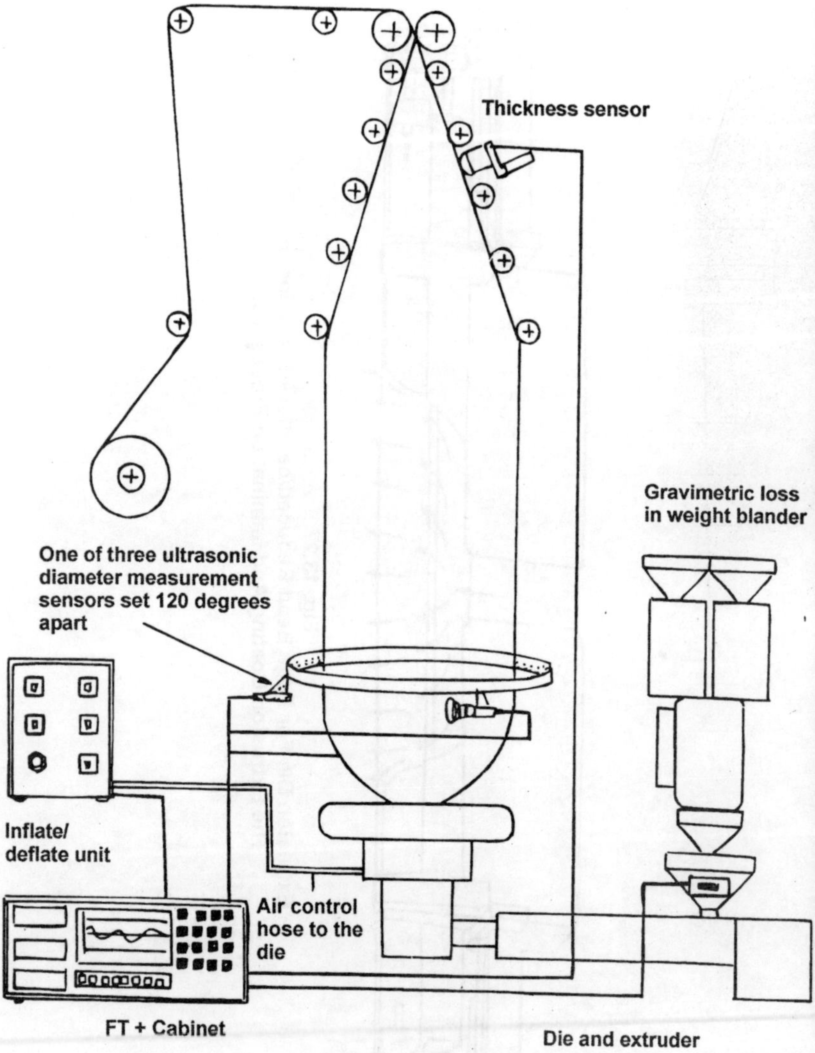

Fig. 13.28 : Integrated Film Control System.

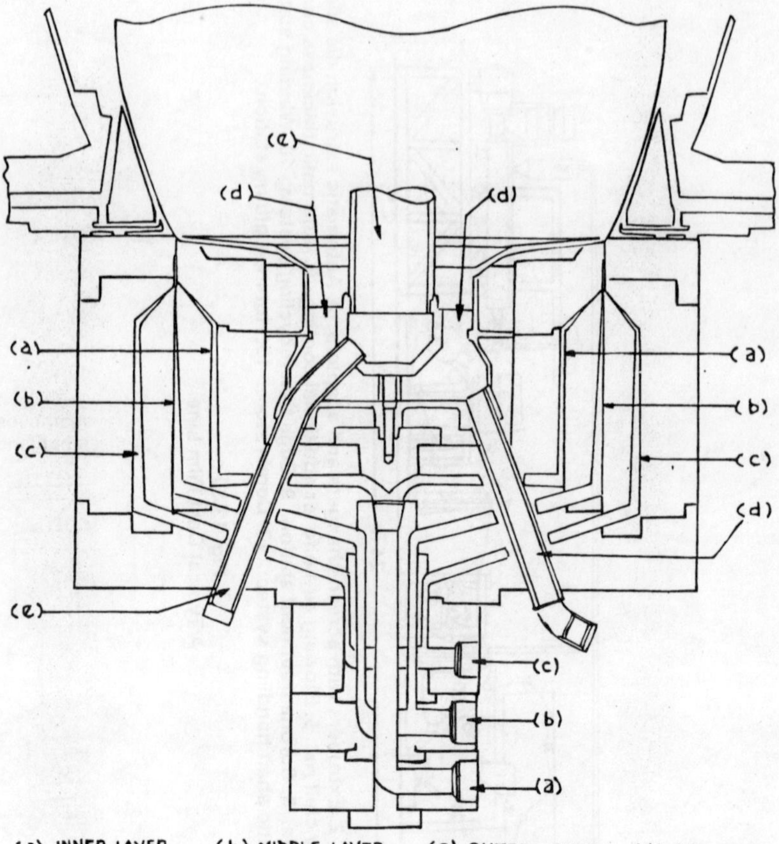

(a) INNER LAYER (b) MIDDLE LAYER (c) OUTER LAYER (d) AIR-INLET
(e) AIR-OUTLET

Fig. 13.29 : A Five layer co-extrusion die hard.

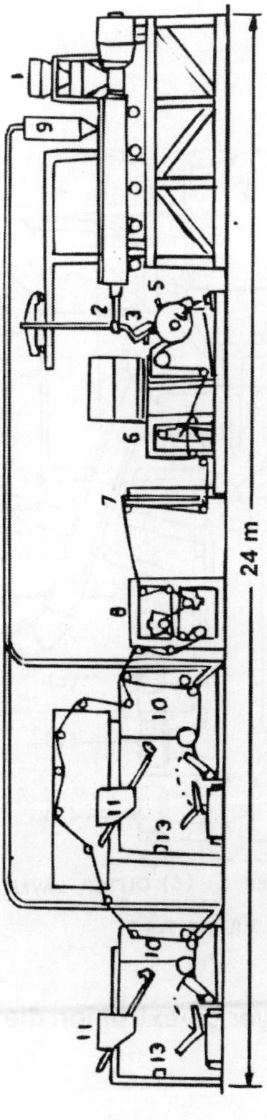

1. Gravimetric feeding system. 2. Extruders with screen changers and adapters. 3. Automatic extrusion die and feed block. 4. High cooling capacity chill roll. 5. Blowing air-knife for additional cooling. 6. Automatic thickness control. 7. Oscillating web-guide. 8. Corona treatment station. 9. Edge trim recycling system. 10. Winding station. 11. Automatic shaft handling system. 13. Core's store. 13. Hot-melt gluing station.

Fig. 13.30 :
A Typical Cast Film Line.

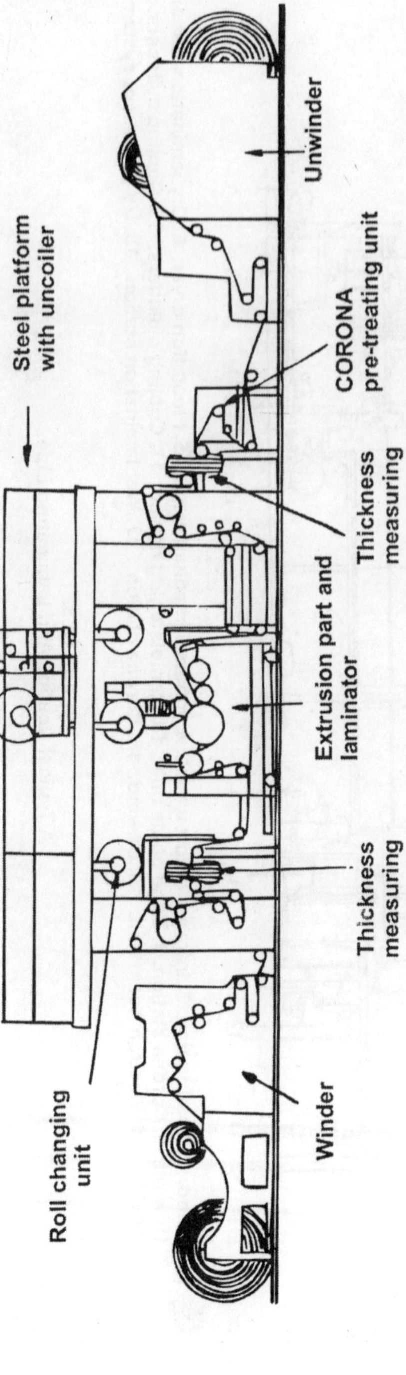

Fig. 13.31 : Extrusion Coating Line.

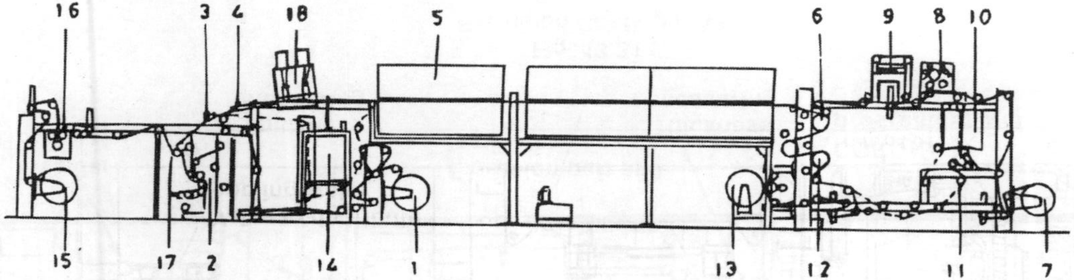

1. Unwind. 2. Coating unit. 3. Infrared (short wave). 4. infrared (medium wave). 5. Floatation dryer. 6. Dry lamination station. 7. Unwind. 8. Corona station. 9. Edge guide unit. 10. Remoistening device. 11. Cooling cylinders. 12. Cooling cylinders. 13. Rewind. 14. Electron beam unit. 15. Unwind. 16. Corona station. 17. Wet lamination station. 18. UV processor system.

Fig. 13.32 :
A Typical Coating And Laminating Line.

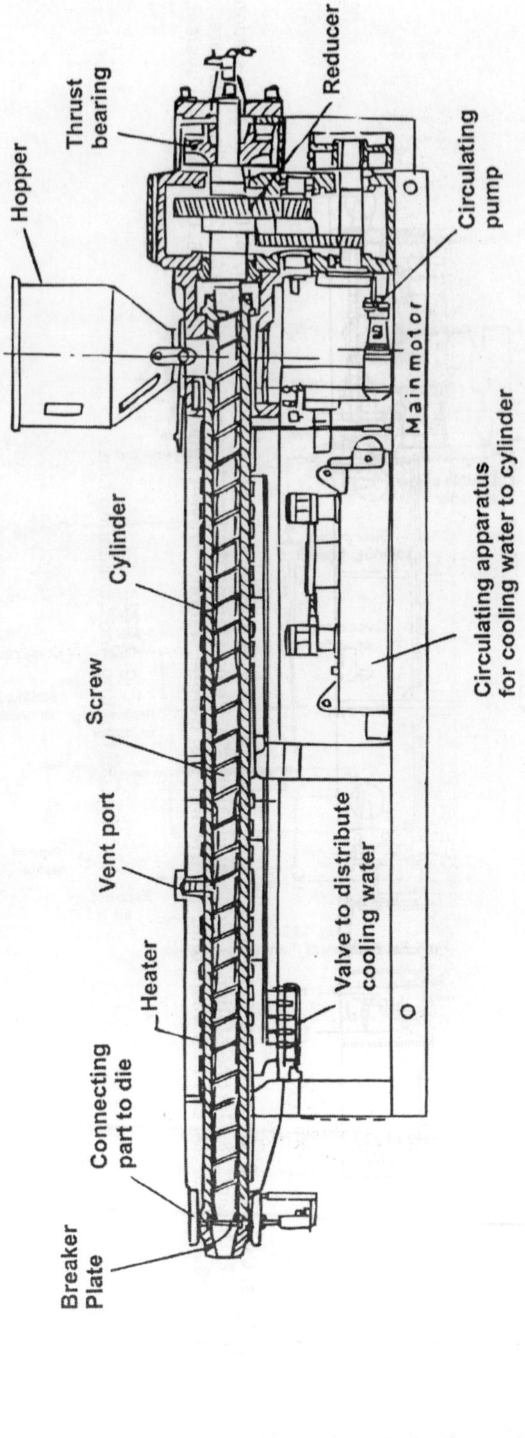

Fig. 13.33 :
Single Screw Extruder (vent Type).

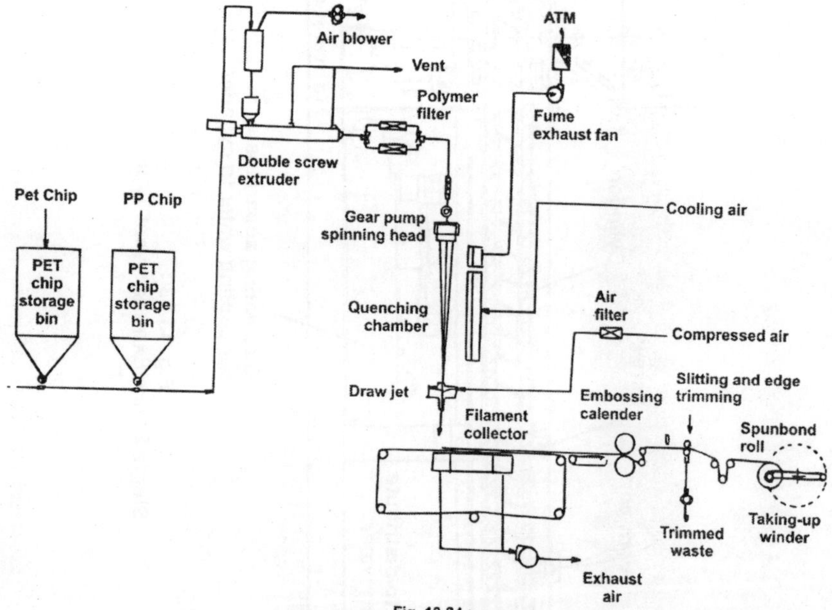

Fig. 13.34 :
Pp & Pet Spunbond Plant (non-wovens).

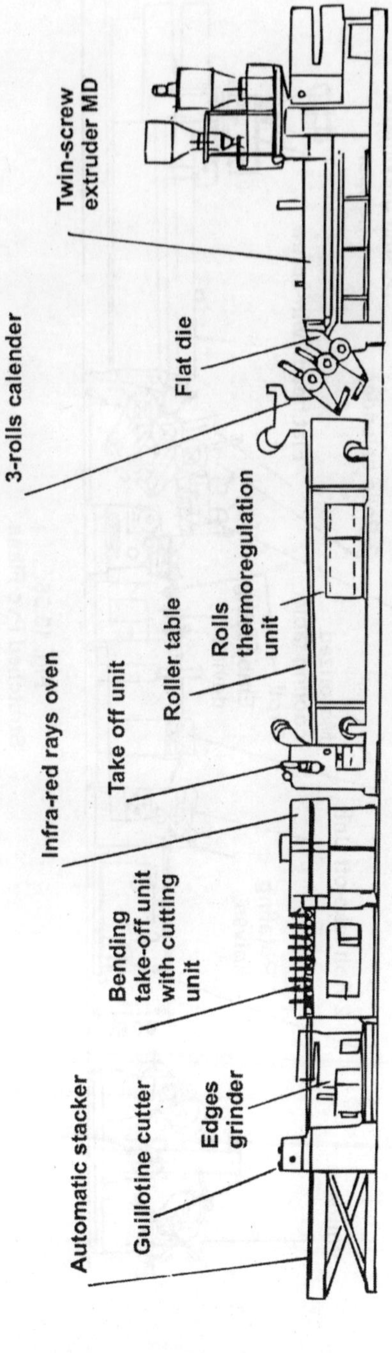

Fig. 13.35 : Corrugated Sheet (pp).

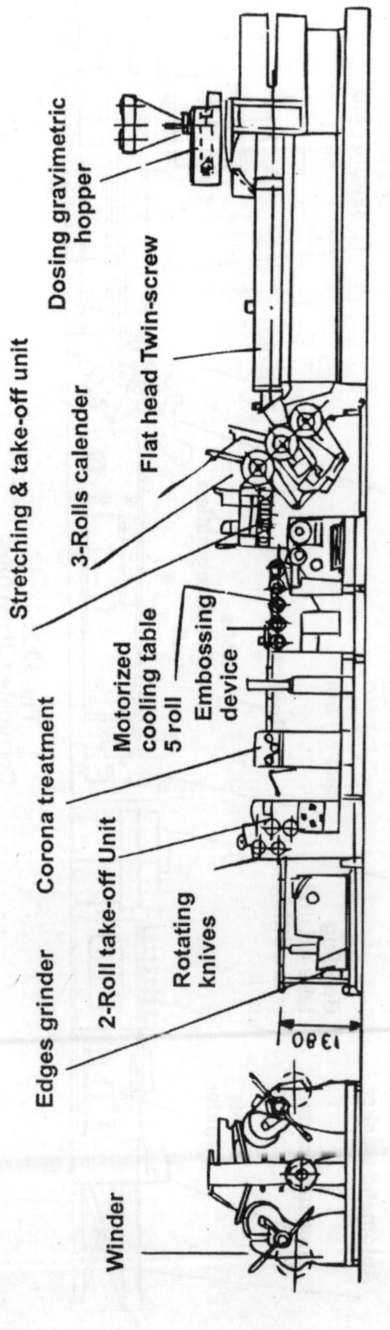

Fig. 13.36.
Stretched Pvc Films.

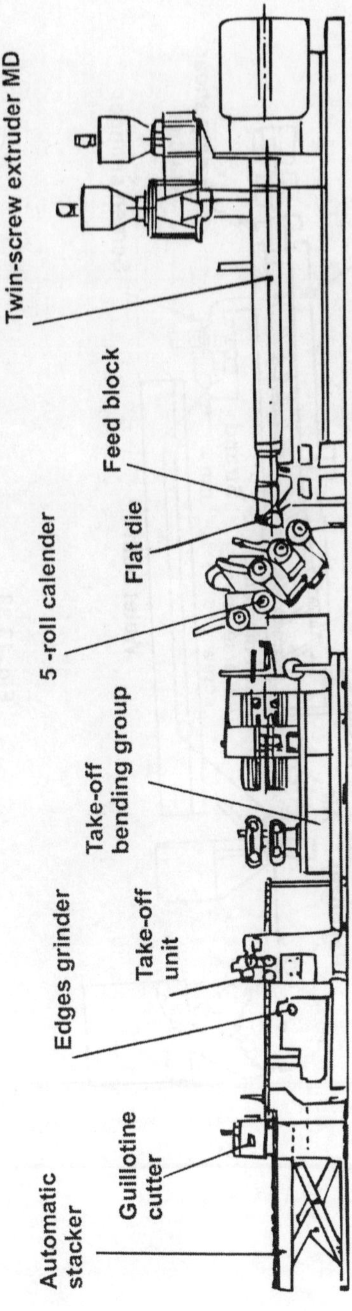

Fig. 13.37.
Edge Board Profiles Unit For Packaging.

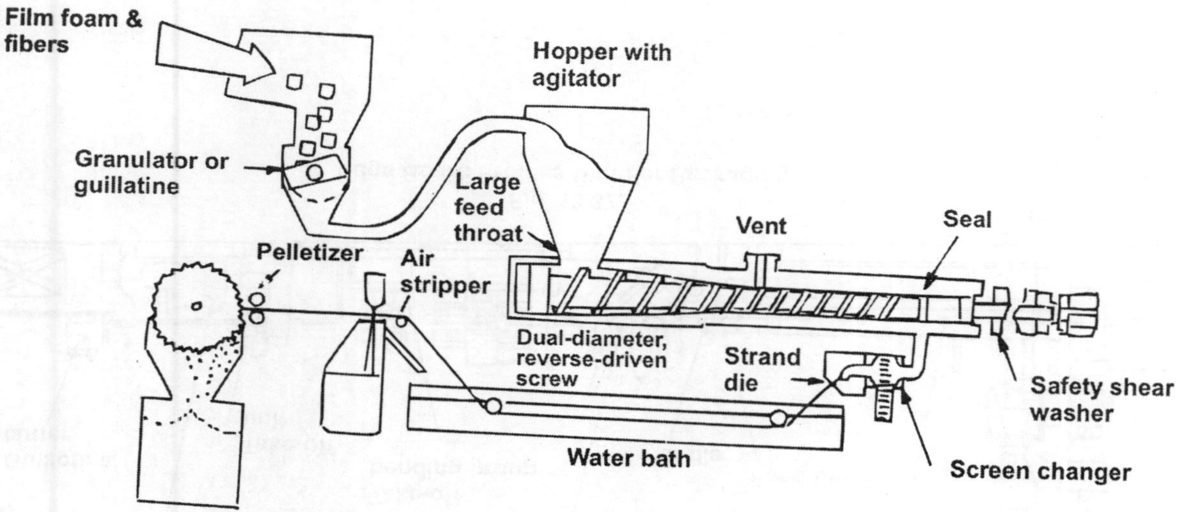

Fig. 13.38 :
Extrusion System Geared For Reclaim.

Flow low bulk density scrap, this system has dual-diameter screw driven from the discharge end. This allows 72 : 1 compression ratios and eliminates ram suffers. The extruder's is available is output of 300-3,000 lbs/Hr

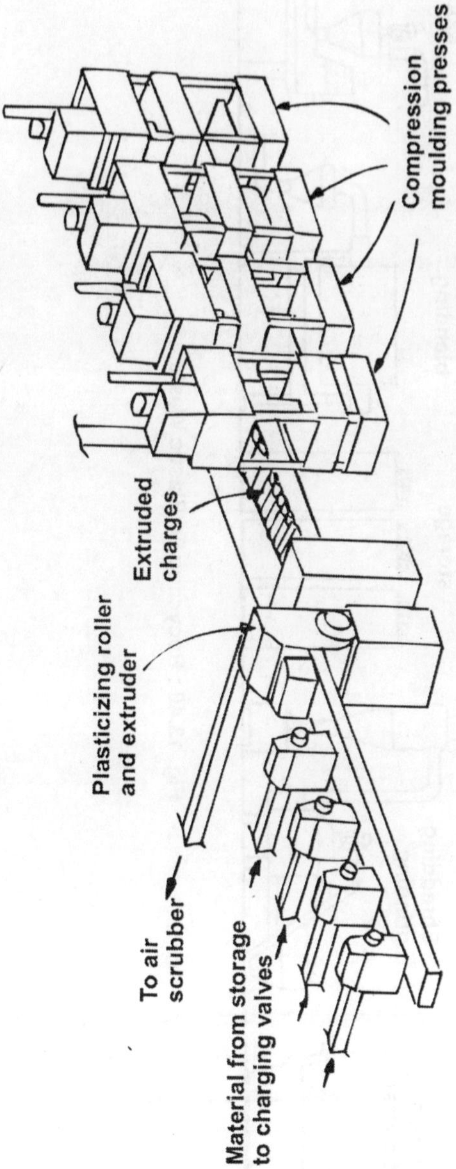

Fig. 13.39 :
Recycloplast Reduces Sheet Using 50% Scrap.

This system granulates commingled scrap and plasticates it with a 50% PE or PVC resin carrier. Continuously extruded charges are fed to compression moulding presses that produce sheet. This technology can be licenced through innovative Plastics Products, Inc., Atlanta Ga.

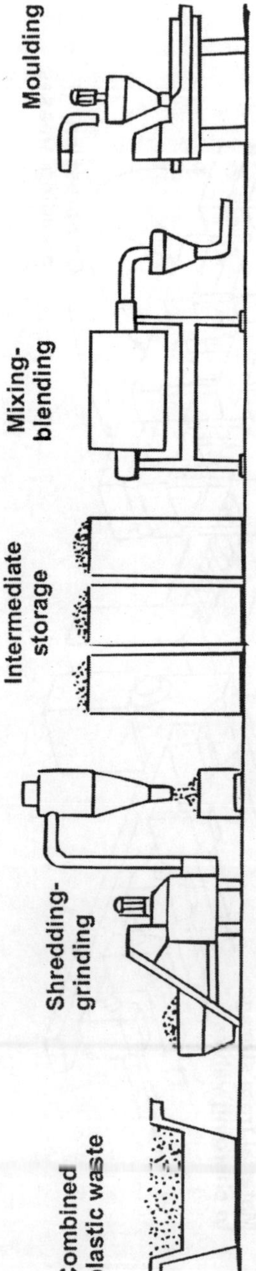

Fig. 13.40 : Recycling Of Plastic Waste.

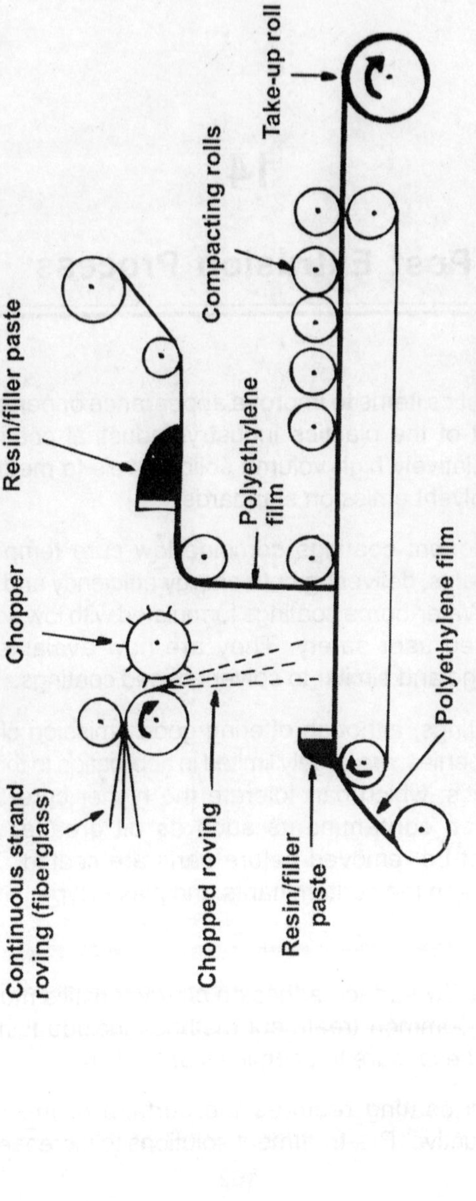

Fig. 13.41 : Manufacture Of SMC.

14

Post Extrusion Process

PAINTING

Painting plastics items to improve appearance or performance is an established part of the plastics industry. Industrial coatings are now available with relatively high volume solids levels to meet increasingly stringent EPA solvent emission standards.

Plural-component coatings combine low cure temperatures and low-solvent contents, delivering both energy efficiency and low emission characteristics. Water-borne coatings formulated with low solvent content provide increased user safety. They are now avaiable with curing temperature range and similar to solvent based coatings.

Powder coatings, although offering good emission characteristics and superior properties, are largely limited in application to those materials, such as phenolics, which can tolerate the higher cure temperatures required. Surface contaminants such as oil grease, and release compounds must be removed before parts are coated. The cleaning process depends on the contaminants and plastic type.

Pre-treatment

Plastics with low surface adhesion characteristics must be treated prior to coating Common treatment methods include flame oxidation, acid etching, and exposure to chemicals or UV light.

Electrostatic coating requires the surface of the plastic to be electrically conductive. Pre-treatment solutions to increase conductivity can be sprayed on, or the part can be dipped. Spraying is preferred; dipping is more expensive, less efficient, and more sensitive to labor costs. The use of conductive compounds in the plastic formulation can eliminate the need for pre-treatment.

Application Methods

Dipping flow coating roller coating, curtain coating, and spraying are the more conventional application methods.

Conventional air spray painting is by far the most widespread coating method in use. It is fast, versatile, and properly controlled, can produce a finish of un-matchable quality. Equipment can range from a single air atomizing spray gun used to manually apply a coating to large multiple-gun systems or painting robots.

Some types of spray equipment can be relatively inefficient for certain tasks, such as coating very small or open parts like grilles, louvers, etc. Over-spray results in considerable waste of coating materials and potential violations of proposed Environment Standards. This is particularly true of conventional air-atomized spray equipment Airless spraying equipment is generally more efficient in this regard and is usually employed when the process requires high delivery rate.

The current economic and environmental concerns are causing a shift to electrostatic application and it is already the method of choice in such high-volume industries as automotive, office machinery, computer and athletic and recreation equipment. Applying the electrostatic principle greatly increase the coating transfer efficiency. Over-spray is reduced, resulting in lower material costs, fewer rejects, and easier compliance with Environment regulations.

The very high transfer efficiency of the electrostatic system derives from the fact that opposite charges attract. a d.c. voltage of 60 or 120 kv. is applied to the atomizer with the part to be coated at ground. When the coating is atomized, it is charged, and the particles are drawn to the grounded part. The attraction of the coating particles to the part is so strong that it creates a wrap-around effect: the charged, atomized particles can turn corners to deposit on the sides and rear of the object being coated. Over-spray is subsequently reduced to a minimum.

The latest generation of electrostatic equipment uses a disk of bell-shaped metal atomizer rotating at very high speed to atomize the coating. The centrifugal force of a bell rotating at 10,000 to 60,000 r.p.m. spins the coating outward in a cone-shaped pattern that can be as much as 48 in. wide. Atomization is much finer than either air or airless processes, and transfer efficiency. is even higher than conventional air atomizing electrostatic equipment. Fluid delivery rates can be very high resulting in increased production capability.

Automated-finishing

High production rates and consistent quality are difficult to achieve using purely manual coating methods. Even plants producing relatively small quantities of identical or similar parts can be at least partially automated and the payback on a properly designed system can be fast.

In the past-automated finishing has consisted primarily of transverse and reciprocating type machines equipped either with conventional of electrostatic spray equipment. Many finishing lines have never been fully automated as manual reintorcement has been required in recess areas. This is typically true of the plastics industry, as today's molding processes produce not only parts, but whole units, with a wide variety of shapes and sizes and many recess areas.

The answer to today's plastic finishing needs is robotics. Robots (Of the painting variety) have been in existence in the U.S. for approximately ten years and in the last several years have gained considerable popularity. The robots can be equipped either with conventional of electrostatic spray equipment with the latter capable of being used as both. This capability is important because the electrostatic charge can be controlled by the robot alternately charging and uncharging the paint so that high transfer effi-ciency can be achievd on large surface areas while recess areas can be coated duting the same sequence.

Robots are being used in the plastics industry to coat such items as shutters, computer components, bumper fascias, etc. Applications such as texture coating of computer terminals also have seen a recent surge of interest. The advantage of using a robot for these types of applications is quality and repeatability along with high transfer efficiency.

Printing

In the plastics industry, various printing methods are used for applying functional information and/or decorations to products. For lay-flat film products such as bags, packaging materials, wrapping papers, etc., gravure and flexographic printing presses are most commonly used. For three-dimensional objects. silk screening and jet printing are used or traditional printing is first done on labels, decais, or hear-transfer webs and then applied to the product.

Most of the processes for printing on paper also apply to printing methods for plastics are flexography and gravure Other methods like screen printing, jet printing or modifications of gravure also are used but account for a small market share

Letterpress is by far the oldest method of printing flat plastic substrates. However, its use is rapidly giving way to such process as gravure and flexography which contribute higher quality reproduction and faster line speeds.

<u>Gravure</u> (also called rotogravure) transfers ink from cells etched or engraved on a copper and chrome-plated cylinder to the material being printed. The cylinder rotates in an ink fountain and the cells pick up the liquid ink. A doctor blade then wipes excess ink from the roller, leaving ink only in the cells.

As the plastic substrate moves between the cylinder and the impression roll ink is transferred from the cells onto the substrate in the form of the etching of image. The number and volume of the cell controls the amount of ink applied to the plastic substrate.

For colours which appear to be solid to the eye, cells of a uniform size are used various shades are created by controlling the size and volume of the cells. The gravure process is capable of reproducing fine tone and process-colour graphics.

The low viscosity liquid inks used in the process contain volatile solvents for rapid drying. A series of printing units with driers in tandem are used to apply a layer of colour and dty it before the next colour is applied.

Gravure is used when designs require good continuity of sharp pattern details and rich colour effects. It is a high-speed process often used for printing quality packaging films, plastic-based wall coverings and other products run in high volumes. However it can be expensive for shorter runs because of the high cost of the gravure cylinders.

<u>Flexography</u> is a widely used method for printing short to medium runs but also adaptable to long runs. Flexography prints by transforming

images from a flexible raised printing plate directly to the material.

A uniform film of ink is applied to the raised portion of the printing plate by bringing it in contact with the anilox cylinder (form roller). The plate continues to rotate until it contacts the substrate and transfers the image to the plastic substrate. Individual colours applied by a series of separate decks (printing stations).

Fast-drying liquid inks and general reliability of this method make it a prime choice for printing on packaging films cartons labels, and plastic-based wall coverings.

Improvements in photopolymer printing plates and inks. along with the upgrading of the press themselves have given flexography high-quality capabilities. Although not yet able to match the color effects possible with gravures, flexographic presses are narrowing the gap.

Printing press manufacturers in recent years have combined gravure and flexography systems in single presses. These hybrids can create patterns and images that blend the best of gravure and flexography in a single run. Quick automatic changes can be made on some models from one process to the other to give better production flexibility.

The combination presses also avoid the diffculties that can be encountered in transferring partially printed rolls of film from one press to another.

Screen Printing was originally known as silk screen printing, but in recent years other supporting materials for the stencil image have replaced silk. Most commercial screen printing is now accomplished with stainless sleel mesh with openings much finer than those possible with silk or other textiles; and stencils are now made by photographic processes.

In screen printing ink is forced through the stencil screen onto the plastic surface by a squeegee made of a flexible material such vinyl. Printing from flat bed or rotary systems makes is possible to decorate large or complex parts. However despite the richness of colour attained as a result of the thick film of ink that is applied. only one colour can be applied per pass through the system. Another factor is that image sharpness is of lower quality than with other processes.

The major uses for screen printing have been for short-run applications on molded products with complex contours on flat substrates, or in order or achieve special colour effects.

Jet printing needs no printing plates; ink in droplet form is impinged onto the substrate at high speeds. The electrically charged ink droplets pass from a series of nozzles through an area that is flanked with plates of the opposite charge. The intensity of charge on tile ink determines its deflection which controls the nature of the character printed. Electronic circuitry provides the information from which the image is formed.

Pad transfer printing is a gravure-like process offering versatility for printing on a variety of shapes and surfaces. Unlike gravure, the image is not transferred to an etched plate directly to a substrate but to a special silicone pad instead. The pad is very soft and flexible and conforms itself to almost any shape to be printed. The transfer properties of the pad are such that all of the ink is released to the surface to be printed, and the pad is clean and ready for the next printing cycle. Multiple colours are applied one at a time, drying is not usually required.

Besides high speed, this new method offers extremely accurate control of images. The equipment is highly specialized but promises much for the future.

Web printing in web printing which is th largest volume process, the choice between gravure and flexography may be decided by specific features of the printing equipment. For example the choice may be one of having printing done on presses in stacked, in-line of common impression arrangement.

Each of these designs has features that affect printing capability. The stacked arrangement has printing decks arranged one on top of the other with space between it is less flexible than in-line systems that allow quick changes from flexography to gravure back again. The in-line presses have printing decks arranged in a horizontal sequence that gives better access to modular printing sections. Common impression systems have printing decks arranged around a large single cylinder that supports the web and is expecially suited for thin plastics.

Selection Factors

The primary considerations for the converter or product manufacturer are the substrate (material) quantity or volume, graphics product form and cost. Plastics normally require a pre-treatment for ink adhesion and special inks are used. Some plastics are sensitive to drying temperatures, so there may be a restriction on which inks may be applied.

The number of parts or web footage will have a direct effect, on the method of printing and the printing press chosen. It is sometimes necessary for economic reasons to switch from one process to another as volume increase. Thus screen printing may be practical at first but with increasing volume flexography, or even gravure may show an advantage.

The cost of a particular graphic treatment depends on a variety of factors including the colour effects desired, volume of the run, and size of the surface to be printed. Halftones will only be possible with certain methods, and methods that do not yield sharp register of the tiny dot patterns will detract from the overall effect.

Flexographic printing quality is improving in its ability to reproduce halftones, or often it can be teamed up with gravure providing the sharp background colours, with gravure providing the sharp pattern detail screen printing, especially where low volumes are involved can impart heavy opaque colour over solid colours to produce rich, bright effects.

Printing of molded shapes requires radically different equipment than printing on web stock. Screen printing normally is applied to injection molded and bloe molded shapes; gravure and flexography are the choices for web stock; however, there are also rotary screen techniques for web printing.

Quality may be the prime factor along with volume, lead time, and special production costs related to the printing method employed. It is sometimes possible to bring cost in line with market requirements by compromising high graphic standards to achieve a lower-cost final product. for example flexography sometimes is a more attractive method than the higher quality gravure systems because of the lower costs, especially in low- to medium volume runs.

POST-MOULDING PROCESSES

Hot Stamping

In hot stamping, decoration from a hot brass die is generally transferred to the package surface by heat and pressure through a coated hot-stamp foil made of 12 to 25 micron thick polyester film. Hot stamping is a dry process and no wet ink or pre-treatment is required. The most commonly used colour is gold for attractive appearance, such as for lipstick and cosmetic containers.

In-mould decoration

The system utilizes a paper or a reverse printed plastics film lable with a heat activated coating on the reverse side. The label is placed in the mould and the plasticized material on the parison, in case of blow moulding, is introduced into the mould cavity. The label is held in position by vacuum suction. The label thus gets attached to the moulded surface.

Ultrasonic Welding

The sealing of two plastic parts or metal inserts to plastic parts by the application of vibratory mechanical pressure at ultrasonic frequencies.

Electroplating

The disposition of metal on to plastic for finish purposes.

15

Vacuum Metallizing

Vacuum metallizing is the application of a metal onto a substrate in a vacuum. Traditionally, this has meant the large-scale decorative application of thermally evaporated aluminum onto a plastic substrate. The plastic is usually, but not always, ABS and the metallized layer is supported by two organic coating layers - a basecoat and a topcoat.The primary function of the basecoat is to produce a smooth surface on molded plastic parts so that the metallizing layer will have a maximum luster. The basecoat constituting a clean new surface, maximizes the adhesion of the metal to the plastic workpiece.The primary function of the topcoat is to protect the metal layer from physical or chemical deterioration.

Equipment and Processing for Batch Systems.

For decorative metallizing three pieces of equipment are required : (1) a vacuum metallizing system, (2) a coatings application system and (3) a drying system.

The vacuum metallizing system most used in large-capacity industrial applications cylindrical in shape, horizontally positioned and operated in the batch mode. Commercially available vacuum chambers range in size from small laboratoty models (e.g, 24 in. diameter by 24 in. long) to very large (84 in. diameter by 110 in. long) production models. Large horizontal chambers are also used for semi-continuous operation. The chamber is pumped down to firing pressure by a series of vacuum pumps. The firing pressure for aluminum usually is 0.5 micron or 5 x 10 Torr.

Batch metallizing is usually limited to the use of a bank of tungsten filaments that are sourced with aluminum "stables" or "canes". The actual time of firing is approximately 15 to 30 sec., after which the chamber is repressurized and the metallized product removed. The door-to door cycle time of batch metallizing is on the order of 12 to 15 min.

The coating applications system can be as simple as a hand sprayer with spray booth to an elaborate automated flow coater. Although dipping, spraying, and flow coating are all viable coating techniques the majority of installations use the flow coater. A flow coater has an array of nozzles that eject a continuous/stream of coating onto a rotating reel. The reel continuously rotates after the spray period therby flowing the resulting material in an even distribution about the fixtured workpieces. The same flow coater may be used for both basecoats and topcoats in many applications.

The third system is the drying installation. Typically the coatings are dried in a bank of convection ovens at approximately 150 F. However because of the continuing increase in energy costs many firms have gone to IR or UV drying. The present market trend is to UV drying where applicable because the associated coatings are 100% solids. The utilization of these types of coatings not only eliminates the solvent emission problem but also reduces the drying time from the order of 1 hr. to approximately 1 min. Throughput is then only limited by the evaporation cycle.

Applications

Decorative merallizing adds beauty to components of the automotive, appliance toy and packaging industries. Increasingly, the trend is from decorative to functional use. Some of the latest developments have been in the following areas :

Electronics: Evaporated conductive and barrier metal layers are being applied in computer and microwave circuit technology.

EMI : An electronics market has developed because of FCC regulations for shielding plastic 'computer and radio housing. The two major evaporated materials that have been used thus far have been aluminum and copper.

Video Disks : Aluminum is being metallized on plastic recording disks for both the video and audio markets.

Solar technology: Metal layers are being applied in the manufacture of large-area solar cells.

Semi-continuous Processing

The two major characteristics that differentiate semi-continuous metallizing from batch processing are: 1) the length of processing and 2) the form of the substrate The semicontinuous process time is normally between 1/2 and 2 hr. and the substrate is usually a roll of plastic film. Present equipment is capable of coating roll widths from 40 to 84 in. Roll width and length are determined primarily by economic considerations. The dominant coating metal is aluminum. The vacuum level and metal thickness are on the order of 0.5 micron and 2 micro in., respectively Because the vacuum level is the same as in batch metallizing, both technologies require similar types of vacuum pumping equipment. From atmospheric to about 100 microns pressure a mechanical booster is used. After this rough pumping cycle is concluded, the pumping manifold is switched to the fine pumping assembly that includes a diffusion pump together with its associated hold pump.

The semicontinuous process (Fig 15.1) has the following structures that differentiate It from the more common batch process :

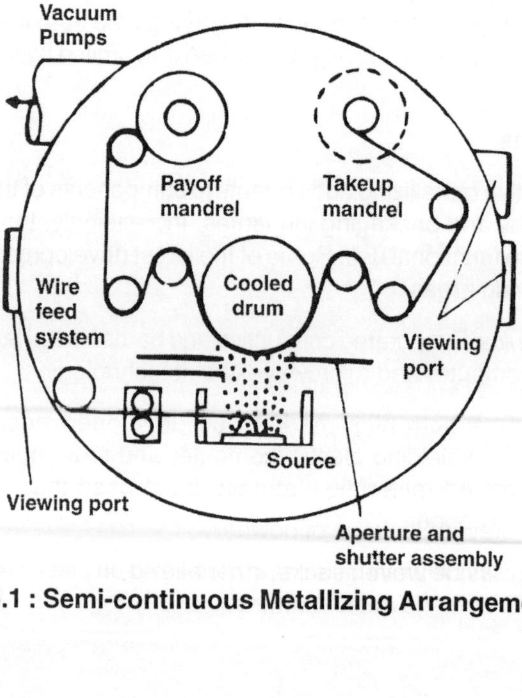

Fig. 15.1 : Semi-continuous Metallizing Arrangement.

1) Feed/takeup reel assembly for the film substrate.
2) Sooled plating drum, required because of the radiant hear produced by the source holder during the extended plating time.
3) Wire feed assembly for continuous soruce replenishment.
4) Source holder configuration and material type Normal configuration is a shallow boat made of boron nitride alone or with titanium diboride.
5) Shutter assembly for exact startup and termination of deposition, as well as a film shield while roll is not in motion.

Semi-continuous Operating Cycle

A typical metallizing cycle includes the following steps:

1) Load substrate roll onto feed shaft and interlace about feed, coating and takeup rolls. Test-wind a small section.
2) Clean and load evaporation feed assembly.
3) Evacuate chamber and heat source holders to temperature.
4) Start feed roll and remove shutter to begin evaporation.
5) Close shutter and decelerate feed roll to terminate evaporation.
6) Coli sources, vent chamber, and remove coated roll.

Applications

Metallized plastic and paper film products are used in a wide variety of industries for decorative and functional applications. The majority of uses for semi-continuous. The majority of uses for semicontinuous products are functional, with the packaging industry being the major end user. Many types of food products (particularly processed foods) are packaged in metallized films. Other functional uses include capacitors. reflective insulation tobacco products, and solar control products. Some of the typical decorative products being merallized include wrapping papers and commercial and residential laminations for housewares.

<u>Purpose of Extrusion Coating with LDPE &. PP</u>

1. To provide protection from moisture water and dust.
2. To prevent leakage of powdery products from woven sacks.
3. To provide woven sacks, inner heat-sealable layer.

Purpose of Lamination with LDPE &. LLDPE Films

1. To provide inner heat-sealable layer to substrates which are otherwise not sealable
2. To provide additional protection from moisture, water and dust.

IMPORTANT LAMINATES & THE APPLICATIONS

Structure	End-use Applications
(I) EXTRUSION COATING:	
* HDPE Woven Fabric/LDPE	Packing of fertilisers, pharmaceutical &. chemicals.
* HDPE Woven/fabric/LDPE Kraft Paper	Packing of polymers, Pharmaceuticals etc.
* White Poster Paper/LDPE HDPE Woven	Packaing of white cement.
* Jute fabric/LDPE	Packing of Foodgrains
* Glassine paper/LDPE	Pharmaceutical tablet packing
* Poster paper/LDPE	Packing of detergent cakes and powder.
* Paper/LDPE/Al. Foil/LDPE	Packing of Biscuits, Confectionary, Coffee, Electral, Powder etc.
II. HEAT PRESSURE LAMINATION :	
* Aluminium Foil/LDPE	Packing of pharmaceutical tablets and capsules
(III) ADHESIVE LAMINATION :-	
* Polyester (pet)/ Adhesive/LDPE and PET/Adh./LLDPE PET / Adh./LDPE/LLDPE PET / Adh./LDPE/HDPE	Packing of Biscuits, Tea, Spices Powders, Instant Food powder, Potato Chips, Pan Masala, Hybrid seeds, Shampoo, Lubricating oil etc.
* BOPP/Adhesive/LDPE/ Al Foil/LDPE and PET/Adhesive/LDPE Al Foil/LDPE	Packing of Coffee, Confectionary Shampoo etc.

Simple Extrusion Coating Process

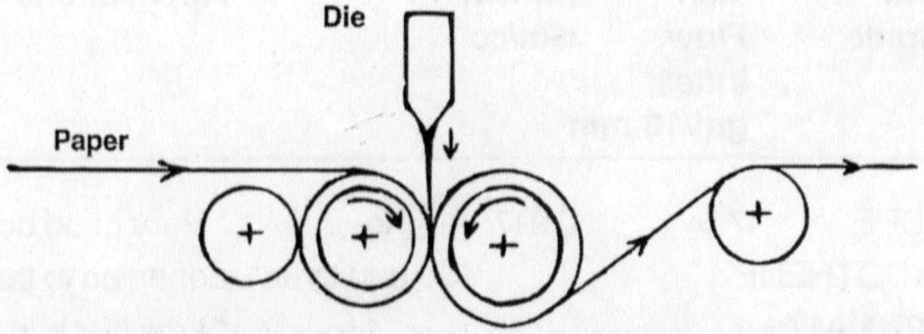

Sandwich Extrusion Coating Process

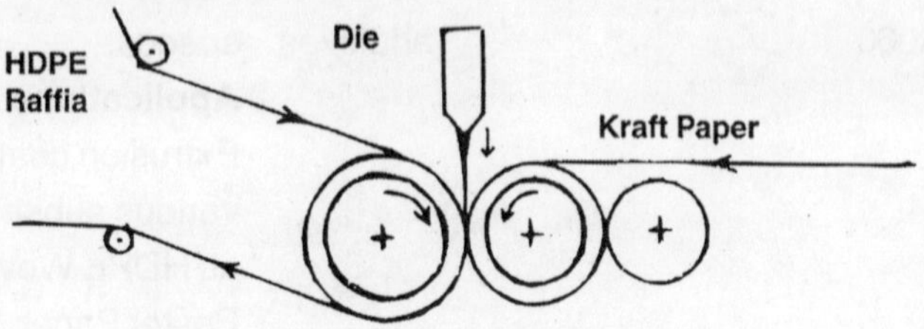

Heat Pressure Lamination Process

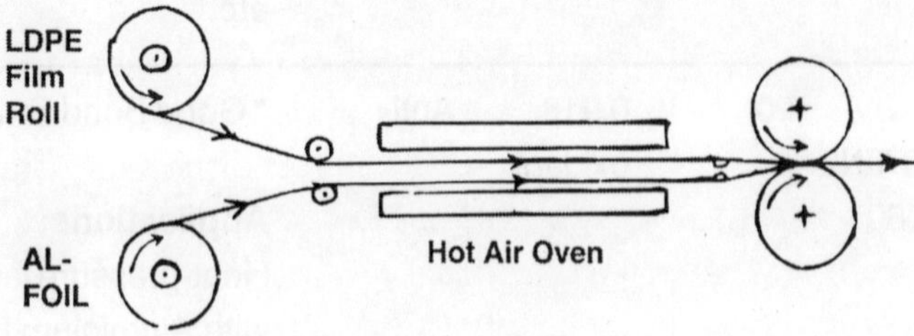

Adhesive Lamination Process

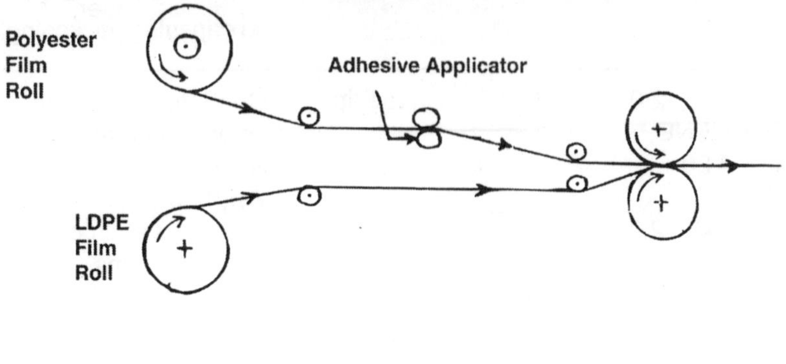

Polymer and Grade	Average Melt Flow Index gm/10 min	Average Density Gm/cc	Additives	Characteristics and Applications
LDPE INDOTHENE 1070LA17 and INDOTHENE 20FA060	7.0 7.0	0.917 0.918	No additives No additives	* Very good bond strength adhesion to substrates. * Low Neck-in and fluctuations of Neck-in. * Suitable for high line speeds. **Applications :-** Extrusion coating on various substrates such as HDPE Woven Fabric, Poster Paper, Kraft paper, Glassine Papers, Jute Fabric, Aluminium Foil etc.
LDPE INDOTHENE 18LA060	7.0	0.918	Anti-oxidant	* Good Bond Strength. **Applications:** Heat-pressure lamination with Aluminium Foii for Pharmaceutical tablets and capsules packaging.
LDPE INDOTHENE 1020FA 20 and FNS 2000	2.0 2.0	0.920 0.920	No Slip No Slip	* Good Bond Strength. * Good Puncture Resistance. **Applications :-** Adhesive Lamination with Polyester films.

LLDPE INDOTHENE-LL	1.0	0.920	No Slip	* Good Bond Strength. *Good Puncture Resistance * Very good heat sealability
LL20FAO/0 and LL20FA020	2.0	0.920	No Slip	**Applications :** Adhesive Lamination with Polyester Film.

16

Co-extruded Film Manufacturing

Appropriate packaging of food products is essential in developing and developed countries, sometimes with varying requirements. Individual plastic materials may not pro-vide all the requisite properties with regard to barrier to water-vapour, gases and volatiles, resistant to product action, sealability, strength, printability and opacity. Hence, composite structures, both laminations and coextruded structures are expected to provide the following properties :

- Structural - physical strength, impact and puncture resistance.
- Performance - machineability, sealability, temperature resistance
- Barrier - water-vapour, gases, aroma, light
- Appearance - clarity, opacity, gloss, feel.

The diversified nature of food product characteristics and exacting shelf-life and marketing requirements have resulted in the development of co-extruded multi-film structures. Co-extrusion is the process of extruding simultaneously various polymeric materials from different extruders through a single die system to form a composite structure.

Generally webs of 2 to 7 structures are formed on co-extruding machines for non-compatible or dissimilar structures, bonding or 'tie layer' are employed. Commodity plastics form the contact and outer layers while middle layers are made of high barrier resins to retain their properties and economise the structures. Co-extruded films have already entered the food packaging field in sectors hitherto occupied by rigid structures and laminates. The sector is a growing field with many potential applications in near future.

Co-extruded Film Manufacturing

For the co-extrusion process, blown film lines and also cast film lines are being used. In the latter process, the polymer meet is extruded through a flat-section die and is deposited over a chilled roll. These have better gauge uniformity and optical properties, but the equipment is costlier and has less flexibility.

In the more common blown or bubble method, the meet from the die is blown into a bubble-form of controlled size by passing air under pressure, which is maintained by pinch-rollers at the end of the die while at the other, the air pressure stretches the film and reduces its thickness *(Fig. 16.1)*. The stretch provided in the machine direction by the pull of the pinch rollers, in the transverse direction by the air pressure inputs a 'bi-axial' orientation of the molecules. This imparts mechanical strength and clarity to the films thus the properties are more 'balanced'.

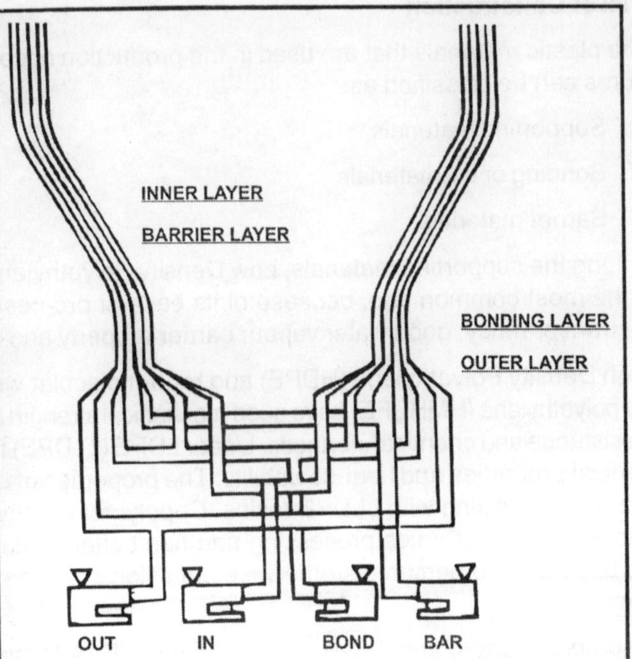

Fig. 16.1 : Co-extrusion Line With Four Extruders.

The co-extruded bubble is cooled and solidified as a tube by externally blown cool air. The bubble is made into a lay-flat tube by the use of collapsing frames. The tube can further be converted into printed rolls, pouches, bags etc. of the designed sizes.

The main advantages of the blown co-extruded film process are:

1. The well established blown-film lines are relatively easy to handle.
2. It is possible to extrude very thin layers.
3. The lines are very flexible = the film width and thicknesses can be adjusted easily through extrusion speed and blow-up ratio.
4. Due to the rotation of the die and cooling ring, the film webs are even and free to circular bumps.
5. It is possible to wind the film either as a tube or as a flat film.

A typical 5 layer co-extruded structure is shown in *Fig. 16.2.*

Material of Construction

The plastic materials that are used in the production of co-extruded structures can be classified as:

a) Supporting materials,

b) Bonding or tie-materials

c) Barrier materials.

Among the supporting materials, Low Density Polyethylene (LDPE) is still the most common one, because of its ease of pro-cessing, seal ability , transparency, good water vapour barrier property and cost.

High Density Polyethylene (HDPE) and High-molecular weight high density polyethylene (HMHDPE) have good mechanical strength and better heat-resistance and chemical inertness. Linear LDPE (LLDPE) has better mechanical properties and heat-sealability. The properties of LDPE can be improved by mixing with LLDPE resins. Copolymer of ethylene and vinyl acetate EVA also aids processing and has better sealability and can be used up to 8 percent as otherwise adhesion surface may pose problems.

Ionomers (Surlyn) and Acrylic acid copolymer (EAA Primacor) due to their excellent sealing properties - sealing integrity through contamination with even fats, oils and powders hot-tack strength, resistance to seal deterioration, better abrasion and puncture resistance.

Among the bonding material or the-layers or CXA (co-extrudable adhe-sive layer), copoly-mers based on polyethylenes, poly acrylic acid, poly vinyl acetate and other adhesive permulations are used[3]. These act as bridge between dissimilar webs such as polyolefins and polyamides or ethylene-vinyl alcohol films. It has been shown that adhesion of PA 6 to EAA is superior to that of EVA and Ionomer films *(Fig. 16.3)*.

Barrier Materials

Polyamide-6 (Nylon-6) polycaprolactam due to its excellent oxygen and aroma barrier properties and mechanical strength has wide applications on the food packaging field. Currently, PA film with good transparency are available, but due to its strong curling tendency, it is mostly used in 5-layer structures.

Copolymer of polyethylene with polyvinyl alcohol EVOH or EVAL films are made of hydrolyzed copolymers of vinyl acetate and ethylene. They offer outstanding gas barrier property and excellent resistance to aroma and flavour permeance, thus making them unique for food packaging applications. EVOH is available in a range of types with percent ethylene mol concentration of 32 to 45. As the material is sensitive to RH, it is used as centre or 'core' layer in co-extrusion structures *(Table 16.1)*.

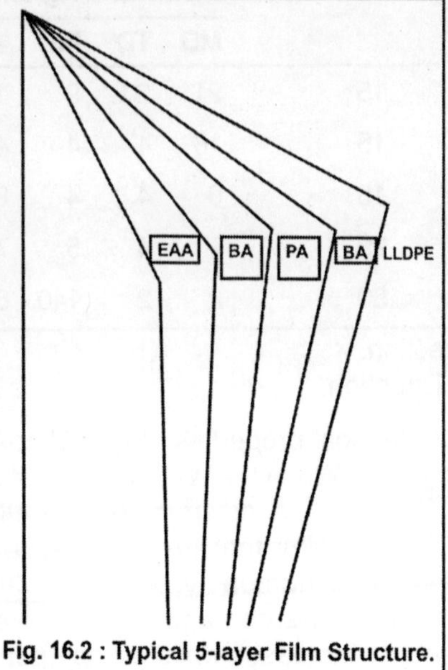

Fig. 16.2 : Typical 5-layer Film Structure.

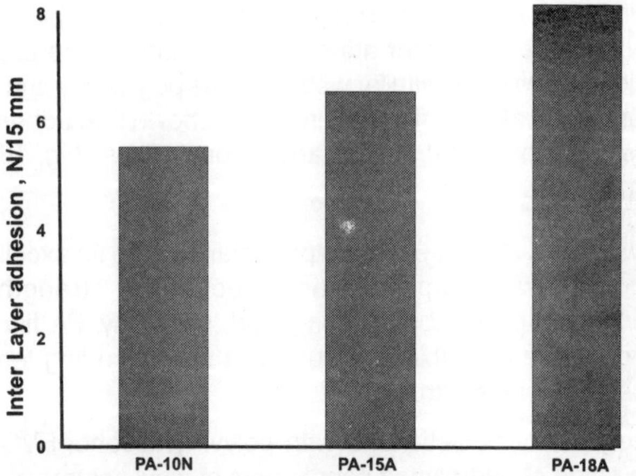

Fig. 16.3 : Inter Layer Adhesion Strength.

Table 16.1: Properties of EVOH Films

EVOH Film grade	Ethylene mole%	Thickness μm	Tensile strength kg/mm2		Tear Strength Kg/cm		WVTR g/m^2 24h. 40°C/90%RH
			MD	TD	MD	TD	
EE-XL	32	15	21	20	9	10	40
EE-H	38	15	16	4	4	40	70
EE-F	32	15	9	4	4	8	100
EE-E	46	20	7	4	5	7	35
LDPE	100	50	2	2	140	60	9

MD-Machine Direction.
TD -Transverse Direction.

The physico-chemical properties of typical co-extruded structures are shown in *Table* 16.2. When the WVTR values of polyolefinic films are low, the OTR of only PA-6 based structures are effective barriers. The different grades of EVOH films that are available, depending on the mole percentage of ethylene homopolymer have different permeability characteristics. As the percentage of ethylene increases, water vapourimper meability increases while oxygen permeability increases.

Some EVOH copolymer film is sensitive to external relative humidity, the dependence of RH is very pronounced at higher val-ues as indicated in *Table* 16.3.

Although PA-6 is an effective oxygen barrier EVOH has better barrier property due to less hydrophilic nature while polyethylene terephthalate (PET polyester) is not dependent on external RH *(Table 16.4).*

It is also to be noted that PA-6 and EVOH are excellent aroma barriers *Table* 16.5. The transmission rates to permeants such as d-limonene, methyl salicylate, benzaldehyde and hep-tane as shown in the *Table* 16.5 Indicate that these are very effective barriers having permeability coefficients in the value 10^1 to 10^3 while commodity plas-tics such as PE and PP in the *Table* 16.5,10^5 to 10^6. This clearly indicates that the co-extruded films based on PA and EVOH are very effective as packaging materials for oxygen and aroma sensitive food products.

Designing Barrier Structures

The selection and design of barrier systems for finite barrier permeable food packages depends on:

1. Selection should be compatible, i.e. with respect to performance and compliance to rules and regulations.
2. Tolerance levels of the food product with respect to water vapour, oxygen and losses of components such as aroma and colour should be established.

Table 16.2 : Physio-chemical Properties of Co-extruded Films.

Film Structure	Thickness microns	Tensile Strength kgf/15mm		WVTR g/m2.24h.		OTR ml/m² 24h.atm. at 27°C
		MD	TD	38°C/ 90% RH	27°C/ 65% RH	
PP/BA/PA-6/BA/EAA	90	3.22	2.86	4.13	1.12	45
LLDPE/BA/PA-6/BA/EAAA	90	3.18	2.91	5.36	1.54	46
HDPE/LDPE/EAA	120	2.36	2.04	2.05	0.56	766
HDPE/BA/PA-6/BA/EAA	120	2.91	2.68	3.03	.0.86	45
HDPE/LDPE/HDPE	100	2.28	2.09	2.24	0.74	852
LLDPE/BA/PA-6/BA/EAA	80	2.68	2.59	4.60	1.36	45
LLDPE/LDPE/HDPE/HDPE/EAA	100	2.86	2.22	1.91	0.60	5.30

Table 16.3 : Oxygen Transmission Rates (OTR) of EVOH Films.

EVOH film grade	Thickness µm	35°C0% RH	OTR ml/m2 24h.atm at 20°C		
			65% RH	85% RH	100% RH
EF-XL	15	0.4	0.3	1.0	6.0
EF-H	15	0.4	0.3	1.5	15.0
EF-F	15	0.5	0.5	2.0	25.0
EF-E	20	3.2	1.5	3.3	10.0
LDPE	50	6000	2700	2700	2700

3. Barrier properties of the packaging materials which are required to maintain the qualities within the tolerance limits.
4. Corresponding barrier thicknesses should be established.
5. Positioning of the barrier system relative to others to reduce curling etc., and minimizing effects of water absorption on barrier properties. The effect of protecting outer polyolefinic layers on cone P A-6 web is indicated in *Fig. 16.3.*

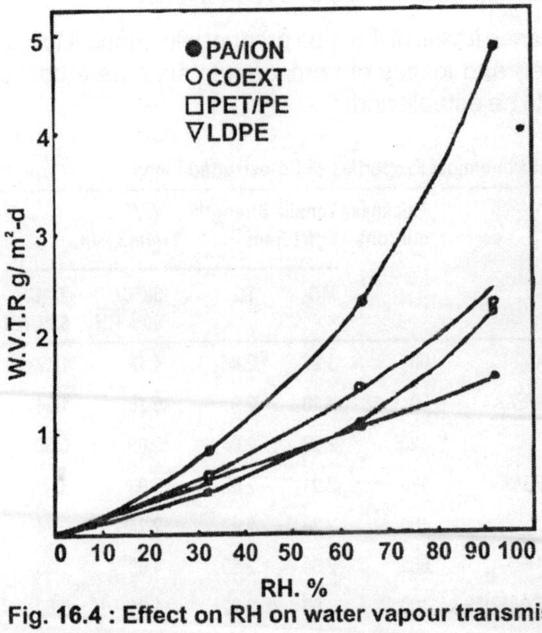

Fig. 16.4 : Effect on RH on water vapour transmission.

The moisture loss or gain in a food product packaged is given by the expression.

M = me - { (me-mo) / In-1
[P/t (A/w) (Po/b) T 1 }

Where

m	=	moisture content of the food product g/100 gdm at time T
me	=	equilibrium moisture content g/100 g at T°c
mo	=	initial moisture content g/100 g.
P	=	Water vapour permeability g.25 μm/m2.24 h of the packaging material.
t	=	thickness of water vapour barrier, μm
A	=	Area of transmission, m^2.
W	=	Weight of food product, g.
Po	=	Water vapour pressure at storage temperature, N/m^2.
B	=	Slope of the moisture sorption isotherm.

Assuming for 100 g of a moisture sensitive product having initial moisture content of 2.0 and critical value of 6% (m) and that area of the package is 450 sq. cm. and the desired shelf-life is 90 days, the WVTR requirement works out to be about 3.2 g/m^2 24 h at 38°C and 90% RH conditions. A co-extruded film of 30μm HDPE/PA-6/50 μm

LDPE would meet this requirement. This shelf-life of 90 days at high temperature/RH condition would correspond to 10-12 months under normal ambient conditions.

Considering an oxygen sensitive product, if 1 litre with an expected storage life of 90 days and maximum acceptance oxygen gain of 200 ppm to reach the maximum critical value, if the total surface area of the package as 0.072 m^2, the oxygen transmission rate of the barrier material as P A-6, as 4.6 ml/ m^2.24 h.atm., the thickness of this material, according to the following formula would be 21.4 μm (5).

$$L = P.A.\Delta Px.\Delta T/\Delta Mx$$

In which 'L' is the film thicken.

'P' is the pressure drop of O_2 between two sides.

A is the area of the package,

$\Delta Mx/\Delta t$ is the transport rate of oxygen.

This indicates a composite co-extruded layer with core polyamide of 25 micron would provide the required shelf-life. However, assuming that

the 90 μm film comprises only polyethylene, the shelf-life would be just 6 **days**. This indicates that for highly oxygen sensitive product such as **edible** oils, inclusion of an efficient oxygen barrier is necessary.

Similarly for food products sensitive to aroma and odour changes, films such as PA6, EVOH or PVDC coatings would provide the required protection.

Applications of Co-Extruded Films

Due to the widely varying properties of co-extruded films of different compositions, they find application in the packing of a wide variety of processed foods, and also allied products such as cosmetics, toiletries

Table 16.4 : Oxygen Transmission Rate (OTR) of Barrier Plastics

Polymer	Sp. Gr.		M.Pt.	Tg.	OTR ml./m².24h. atm	
	amor	crys			20°C/0%RH	20°C/100%RH
MXD6	1.20	1.25	243	64	0.06	0.256
PA-6	-	1.15	215	50	0.5	2.6
PET	1.34	1.40	263	69	1.5	1.5
EVOH (Et 33%)	1.19	-	180	69	0.003	0.375

Table 16.5 : Aroma Transmission Rates of Barrier Films

Permeability @ 25°C dry

10^{-20} x kg. m/m² Pa

Film	d-Limonene	Methyl salicylate	Benzaldehyde	Heptane
Polyamide-6	6.1×10^{1}	1.9×10^{3}	1.6×10^{3}	2.0×10^{1}
Barrier PVDC	1.8×10^{2}	1.6×10^{4}	4.2×10^{3}	8.0×10^{2}
EVOH	4.7×10^{3}	1.8×10^{3}	-	1.5×10^{1}
Plasticized PVDC	8.8×10^{3}	-	2.7×10^{4}	3.2×10^{3}
CPP	1.1×10^{5}	1.6×10^{6}	-	6.2×10^{4}
HDPE	1.7×10^{6}	3.2×10^{6}	-	9.5×10^{5}
LDPE	>HDPE	9.0×10^{5}	1.9×10^{7}	2.1×10^{6}

Table 16.6 : Technical Specification for Spice Powders Packages

1.	Caliper	:	75 to 120 µm
2.	Yield	:	71.68 to 115 g/m²
			13.95 to 8.3 m²/kg
3.	Tensile Strength for 90 µm	:	MD 3.27 kgf/15 mm
			TD 2.82 kgf/15mm
4.	Heat Seal Strength @ 185°C, 15. 7.2 kgf/15 mm	:	MD 2.59 kgf/15 mm
			TD 2.23 kgf/15 mm
5.	Water vapour Transmission Rate g/m².24h at 38°C/90% RH	:	6.0
6.	Oxygen Transmission Rate ml/m². 24h. atm@27°C	:	32

and pastes.

A few of the end use applications are indicated below :

Edible Oils	Coffee
Vanaspati	Tea
Fruit pulp	Spices
Ready-to-serve beverages	Meat Products
Ketcup	Sea Foods
Sauces	Snack Foods

Non-food applications include desirable syringe, saline water, veterinary medicines, cosmetics and toiletries, lubricants etc.

Edible oils and fats : It has been observed that to package double filtered groundnut oil, co-extruded films of (a) LLDPE/E/BA/EAA, Yellow and white pigmented, and (b) LLDPE/LDPE/HDPE/HDPE/EAA with WVTRs of 5.4 and 1.91 g/m2.24 h and OTRs of 40 and 530 respectively provided shelf-life of 45 to 65 days and 30 days at the accelerated and 95 to 180 and 65 days to normal conditions of temperatures and relative humidity.

Polyamide/lonomer puouches containing refined groundnut oil was found to offer shelf-life of 120 days and 60 days at normal and accelerated conditions, while in mono films of LDPE, HDPE and HMHDPE, the corresponding storage lives were 45 and 20 days under the two conditions (2) refined sunflower oil packed in 90¦m. LLDPE/BA/PA-6/BA/EAA and exposed to two different conditions of temperatures/RH has indicated that polyamide based co-extruded film provides adequates protection up to 60 and more than 90 days.

Vanaspati packed in LDPE/HDPE/LDPE co-extruded film, indicated shelf life of 90 and more than 120 days under accelerated and normal or BIS conditions of storage.

Snack Food : The traditional savoury, kodbale packed in co-extruded film of 100 µm yellow pigmented HDPE/BA/PA/BA/EAA having WVTR of 3.02 and 0.42 at 38C/98% RH and 27C/65% RH respectively and OTR of 55.4 ml/m^2. 24 h atmosphere at 27°C provided shelf-life of 60 and 120 days under the accelerated and normal conditions. Gas-flushing with nitrogen extended the shelf-life.

Spices and spice products : Packaging and storage carried out on curry powder packed in 100µm LDPE/BA/PA-6/BA/LDPE at three different temperature /RH conditions indicated it provided good protection against loss of volatile.

Studies on the keeping quality of pickled chicken in pouches of white pigmented LLDPE/BA/PA-6/BA/EAA of 100µm thickness having WVTR of 3.66 g/m^2.24h. at 38C/90% RH and OTR of 4.4 ml/m^2.24h. kPa at 27C indicated protective functions similar to that of metallised polyester / HDPE/LDPE pouches. The findings have indicated that both types of pouches could offer 90 to 180 days shelf-life under high and normal conditions to temperature and relative humidity.

A typical specifications for spices packaing is shown in table 16.6.

Other food products: Jelly crystals requires good protection from moisture ingress and loss of aromatic substances. Storage studies on the product packed in LDPE/BA/PA-6/BA/LLDPE of of 100 µm with WVTR values of 3.6 and 1.1 g/m^2. 24 h at 38C, 90% RH and 27C/65% 65% RH conditions have indicated that the material provided shelf-life of 45 days and more than 180 days under the two storage conditions.

Pedha: This intermediate moisture milk product, with initial moisture content of 14% equilibrating to 0.84 a_w at 27C, and packed in 75 µm LLDPE/BA/EAA having WVTR of 4.5 g/m^2.24 hand OTR of 50 ml/m^2.24h at 27C and packed with Free-Oxygen-Absorber (FOA) was found to extend the shelf-life to 42 from 15 days.

Conclusions

The co-extruded films due to various advantages have already found applications in a wide variety of food packaging applications. With the introduction of newer plastic materials, their usage will comprise many specialized food packaging applications as well as several non-food items.

Abbreviations used in the text :

HDPE	:	High-density polyethylene
HMHDPE	:	High-molecular-weight HDPE
LLDPE	:	Linear low-density polyethylene
EAA	:	Ethylene-Acrylic acid copolymers
PA-6	:	Polyamide-6 (Nylone)
EVOH	:	Ethylene-vinyl alcohol copolymer
OTR	:	Oxygen transmission rate
PET	:	Polyethylen terephthalate
WVTR	:	Water-vapour transmission rate
PVDC	:	Polyvinylidene chloride copolymer
BA	:	Bonding Agent (Tie-layer)
MXD-6	:	Meta xylilene diamine polyamide
CPP	:	Coast Polypropylene

17

Production of Breathable Films and Laminates

Introduction

The very first breathable films for the hygiene industry were developed in Japan as early as 1983. The production of breathable films commenced in the USA in the middle of 1990; since circa 1995 these products have also conquered the European market and the market shares continue to increase from year to year. The normal way to produce a breathable film is to prepare a basic material respectively a matrix (PE or PP) with 40-60% calcium carbonate to a compound or masterbatch. Further processing to a film is performed on flat film or blown film lines with subsequent stretching. Triggered off by stretching, the calcium carbonate crystals partly break off from the polymer matrix. This leads to the formation of micro-channels in the film cross-section, which allow water-vapour to penetrate at a later stage.

Raw Materials

Basically the raw material for breathable films are PE (for hygiene industry) or PP (for building industry) with approx. 45-70% calcium carbonate.

Material Drying/Material Feeding

To make sure that the raw material for the production of breathable films has the lowest possible dampness, the material is predried prior to processing using a dry-air drying unit. Too high a residual dampness would lead to holoo in tho unctrotchod and stretched film. Vacuum suction conveying units are used to load the drying hopper and the extruders. Dust protected gravimetric dosing units are used to feed the individual components.

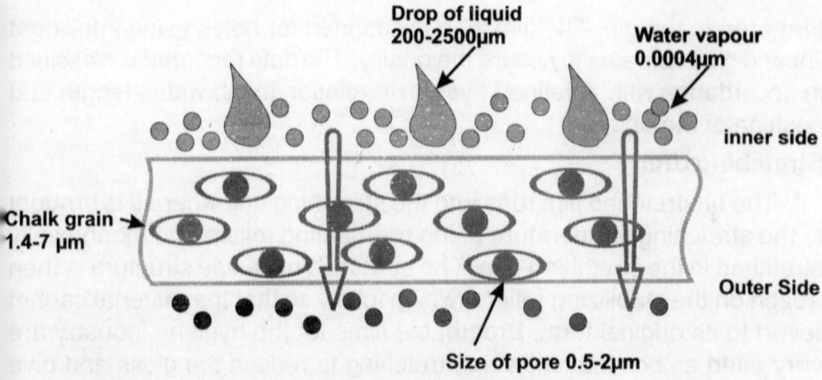

Mode of Operation of breathable films

Extrusion

Very high demands are made of the extrusion of breathable films in as far as quality is concerned. The high performance one-screw extruders used have a long processing unit with a diameter of 28 to 33. The screw diameters range as a rule between 75 mm for co-extruders up to 150 mm for the main extruder. Hydrautically operated piston filters are used for melt filtration as well as screen belt filters.

Feedblock /Die

Breathable films are mostly made of three layers, and sometimes only of one layer. In the case of a three-layer structure, the outer layers are made 100 % of new material, recycling material is used for the middle layer.

Chill and Take-Off Unit

To begin with the melt web is cast on a matted steel roll with a diameter of 800 mm. The chill roll which follows is a high-polish roll with a diameter of 400 mm. The basic frame comprises a solid slide wall and the first measuring frame is directly assembled on the chill unit.

Thickness Measurement Device and Web Inspection

Cast film lines with a stretching unit are equipped by SML with two thickness measurement devices, the first primarily measure the primary film and the second measure the secondary film after the stretching unit. A flat thickness profile is set on the second measuring frame. The system works out a target profile for the first measuring frame, which takes the origin of the film into consideration when stretching. This information, is furthered to the die. The film web is scanned for holes using intelligent linear digital cameras to assure the quality. The data recorded is classified in accordance with a defined system in relation to the width, length and position of the object.

Stretching Unit

The unstretched film runs into the stretching unit where it is brought to the stretching temperature using pre-heating rollers and monoaxially stretched in the stretching gap. The stretched molecule structure is then frozen on the stabilizing rollers, which follow so that the material cannot revert to its original form. Breathable films for the hygiene industry are very often embossed following stretching to reduce the gloss and give the film a textile touch.

Unwinder

The fully automatic unwinder for non-wovens is based on the turret winder principle and is positioned above the lami-nating unit.

Laminating Unit

Hot melt laminating units are used to be able to laminate the breathable film with the nonwoven. The hot melt is always applied to the nonwoven and then laminated with the film. Most of the hot melts used for laminating are glues on a rubber basis.

Edge-Trin Cutting/Recycling

The edge of the film is always cut in front of the stretching unit, the laminating line and the winder. Provided that this is purely film, it can be fed back into the process. This recycling is performed either using a horizontal scraptruder or an inline-recycling unit.

Winder

The SML Aerofilm Winder 2000 was specially developed to wind breathable films and laminates. The maximum mechani-cal winding diameter possible equals 1200 mm. This winder is a horizontal sliding winder.

There are two large applications for breathable films and laminates

Applications Build-up

1. Hygiene products such as babies diapers, adult incontinence products and ladies' hygiene products.
2. Construction films such as under-roofing laminates and housewrapping films. Moreover breathable films are used for protective clothing and packaging.

18

Manufacture of Extruded Thermoplastic Foam

Foam plastics are widely used in several applications and find tremendous potential in a developing country like India. Foams are used in various shapes, e.g. single layer foam sheet used for thermal insulation, impact absorption, marine floatation and packaging. Building and construction industry uses low density foam products as expansion joints.

This article attempts to explain some basic infor-mation about extruded foam, their uses and basic features of machinery required to produce them.

A foamed thermoplastic uses a specific thermo-plastic and an additive that produces gas, which after processing, yields solid structure having voids (cells) surrounded or partially surrounded by the solid polymer. The foam can be classified as "high density" or "low density" foam, depending on the final density. High density foams can have density not substantially less than those of unfoamed polymers. High density foam can have lowest density of 0.4g/cc. On the other hand, low density foam can have final density as low as 0.025g/cc. This compares with normal density about 0.9g/cc of un-foamed low density polyethylene. Extruded foam products generally use PS (Polystyrene) to produce EPS foams and LDPE (Low density polyethylene) to produce EPE foams.

Fig. 18.1 clearly show the cells formed in the foamed product making it light weight compared to unfoamed polymer. The control of cell size in processing is very important and it determines the final property of the foam and also whether it is ofhigh density or low density category.

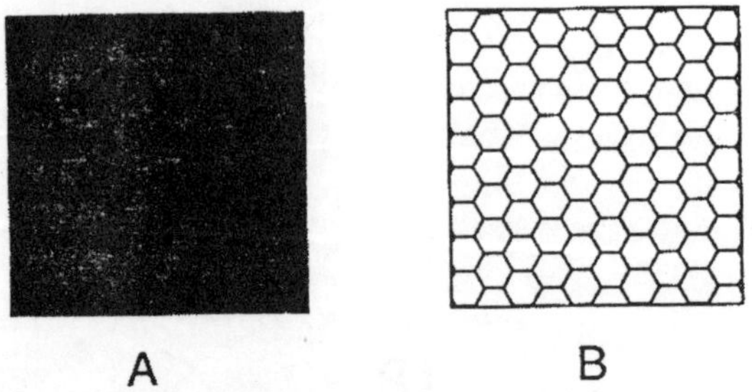

Fig. 18.1 Illustrative examples of section through unfoamed polymer shown in Fig. A) and in foamed polymer shown in Fig. B) The volds (cavities) caused by the foaming agent is clearly shown resulting in low density of product compared to unfoamed polymer.

HIGH DENSITY FOAMS

High density foams are primarily used as permanent structures being sought for rigidity with weight reduction e.g. replacement for wood in doors, windows and mirror frames and furniture components. In automotive, it is used in paneling, glove box door, instrument panels, vehicle crash barriers etc.

LOW DENSITY FOAM

Most low density foams have densities down to 3% than those of unfoamed polymer. Generally, low density foam is defined as foam product having density of 10% to 20% of unfoamed product. They can further be classified as rigid or flexible foam. Rigid foam is formed when base polymer is rigid (e.g. polystyrene) while flexible foam is formed when the base polymer is flexible, e.g. LDPE (polyethylene). This section mainly refers to production technology for LDPE low density or EPE Extruded foams.

Extruded low density foam competes with traditional insulation products such as fiberglass and mineral wool as well as thermoset rigid polyurethane. It also competes with traditional shock mitigating products as foam rubber and straw as well as thermoset flexible polyurethane. Extruded low density plank is used to protect large and heavy shipments.

EXTRUSION: A PRIMARY PROCESSING TECHNIQUE FOR POLYMERS

Extrusion belongs to that class of primary processing technique for polymers in which single or twin screws rotate inside a stationery barrel heated electrically. The principle of conventional single screw extrusion can be understood with reference to Fig. 18.2.

The screw rotates inside a stationery barrel. The mechanical energy for rotation is supplied by y duty gear box and electric motor. The barrel has a vertical feed opening through which the raw-materials are picked by the rotating screw(s), melted and conveyed forward in the barrel. The heat required for melting the polymer is supplied by electric heaters wrapped round the barrel plus friction heat generated due to mechanical energy being supplied by the rotating screw. The melted polymer is mixed homogenously and pumped past suitably shaped orifice fitted to the discharge end of the extruder. This process produces continuous, long lengths which are cut in-line or wound on rolls.

As is clearly shown in Fig. 18.2, the extruder screw is divided into 3 zones, viz. feed, transition or compression and meter or pump zone. The functions of the various zones are clear from their respective names.

Table 18.1 :Typical Markets for High Density Thermoplastic Foams

Market	Aplications
Furniture	Panels, frames, tables, seating, bed structures, drawers, and drawer fronts.
Cabinetry	TF, stereo component cabinets, equipment housings.
Material Handlings	Pallets, milks, and soda cases, containers
Industrial	battery cases, underground conduits, handholds, transforme housings, trash containers, equipments covers and doors.
Consumer	Recreational, musical toys, coolers, totes, mirror and picture frames, calender and business card sheets, miscellaneous.
Construction	Shutters, shingles, windows, doors.
Appliances	Washer tops and doors, dishwashers tops, tubs and bases, air conditioner housing and bases.
Automotive	Decorative paneling, glove box door, instrument panels, seat frames, fan shrounds, fender liners, vehicle crash barriers.
Marine	Fascia, seating, fish boxes, cabin structure.

The feed zone which has greatest depth serves to convey the pellets forward for other zones, the transition zone has tapered core which allows for gradual compression of the pellets to help in compaction and melting of the raw-materials, while the pump zone has shallow depth constantly over its length and serves to maintain the pressure required for pumping the melt through the die opening. The ratio of flighted length of screw to its diameter is referred to as "Length-to-Diameter Ratio" of the extruder and is generally in range of 24:1 to 30:1 for conventional extruders the ptich of screw flight being equal to diameter of the screw. The shaped product as it emerges from the extruder mostly needs additional handling (cooling/sizing) by other eqipment (post extrusion equipment) placed in-line to give the required dimensions on the final product and also collect it suitably.

All forms begin with microscopic voids that grow on nucleating sites in the polymer melt (see Fig. 18.3). All micro bubbles initially grow as isolated cells in an infinite medium of gas-laden polymer. The final product density depends on the blowing gas concentration, the rate at which the gas diffuses out from the matrix, the polymer melt temperature and external constraints on the foam as it expands, as well as upon the

Table 18.2 :Typical Markets for Low Density Foams.

Market	Aplications
Comfort cushioning	Automotive, transportation, furniture seating, mattresses, bedding and carpet underlay.
Flotation	Marine pier buffers, in-place flotation for small vessels, marine life vests, pool accessories, child toys.
Shock mitigation	Package protection for light bulbs, eggs, fruit, electronics, furniture, and machinery, surface protection for furniture and movers as overwrap, crash barriers, etc. transportation of glasswares, protection of mirrors, paintings, etc.
Thermal barrier	Sidewall and roofing insulation for coolers, tanks and reservoirs appliances and hot water insulation, insulative packing containers for beer, carry outo.
Miscellaneous	Disposable dishes and plates, egg trays, etc.

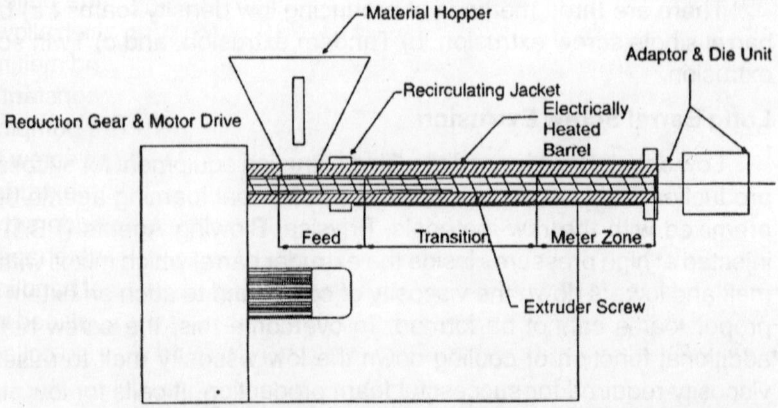

Fig. 18.2 Schematic of Conventional Single screw Extruder

external calibrators used after extrusion. In high density foams, bubble shape is typically spherical to ovoid and bubble growth is restricted by cold metal constraints, blowing agent concentration and rapidly decreasing melt temperature. In low density foams, the growing cells thin the polymer into membranes. In the free foaming process, the foam is allowed to expand freely in atmosphere as it comes out of the die. It has limitations on dimensional control of the foam, whereas in the calibration process, there are calibrators placed after the extruder which constrain the foam and fix its dimensions.

In general, all foams have primary characteristics of the respective unfoamed polymers. The final thermal and mechanical properties of the foam are determined primarily by the foam density.

Chemically Expanded Foams

Chemically expanded foams are produced on conventional extrusion equipment by mixing the polymer with ingredients like nucleating agent, filler and certain exothermic chemicals e.g. Azodicarbonamide (AZ), which decomposes by the heat inside the extruder, at approx. 200°C and produces gases which serve to expand the product as it emerges from the die. However, this process can be used only for producing high density product. Foam density can be 40-50% of the base polymer density.

Low Density Process

This process is used to produce very low density foam in the form of sheet less than 12 mm in thickness, profile, rod, pipe or foam netting.

There are three methods of producing low density foams : a) Long barrel single screw extrusion, b) Tandem extrusion, and c) Twin screw extrusion.

Long Barrel Screw Extrusion

Low density foams need modified extrusion equipment for successful production. This is because instead of chemical foaming agents being premixed with the raw-materials, Physical Blowing Agents (PBA) are injected at high pressures inside the extruder barrel which mixes with the melt and lowers down the viscosity of compound to such an extent that proper foams cannot be formed. To overcome this, the screw has an additional function of cooling down the low viscosity melt to raise the viscosity required for successful foam production. It calls for low shear screw design in the cooling zone and additional cooling by water circulation to remove the excess heat from the compound. The final section consists of a specially profiled discharge screw to provide high pressure for pumping through the die and prevent premature foaming inside the processing equipment. It is very essential to maintain the compound inside the extruder and die at a pressure well above the partial pressure of the PBA to prevent premature foaming. The single screw extrusion equipment is 45 to 50 diameteres long for low density foam production. The PBA, unlike the chemical foaming agents, do not react chemically to release gases, since it is direct gas injected into the Fig. 18.4: Tandem extruder. For efficient pumping, however, all PBAs are injected through metering pumps as liquids. Most common PBAs are butane, liquid CO_2, isopentane, dichlorodiflouromethane (R 12) etc. However, R12 is now banned by most countries due to depletion of the protective ozone layer of atmosphere. Most common gases used for low density foam production is butane. Since this gas is highly inflammable, proper safety measures should be followed inside the plant to avert accidents.

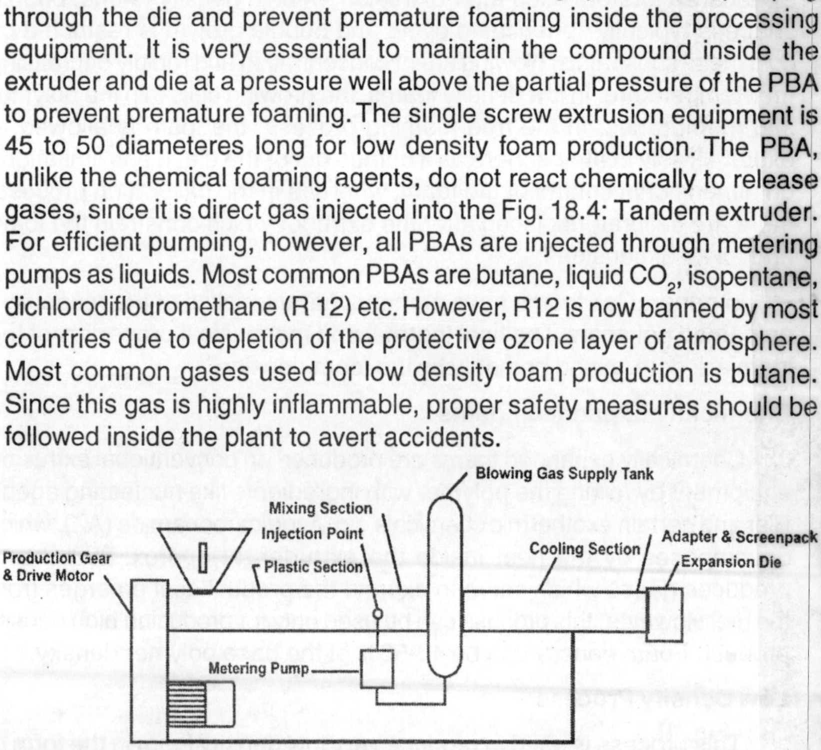

Fig. 18.3 : Schematic for Low Density Foam (EPE) Long Barrel Extruder.

The drawback ofthe above extruder is that good cooling calls for low screw speeds (to minimise frictional heat) while plasticizing calls for medium screw speeds. This results in compromise with consequent reduction in output because of low screw speeds. The advantage is low initial capital cost because one single extruder is used for plasticizing and cooling.

To eliminate this drawback, the tandem extrusion technique is used.

Tandem Extrusion

This uses two separate extruders - the primary extruder is used for plasticiz-ing while the secondary is used for cooling. The two extruders are connected by a suitable pipe. The output of the primary forms the input to the secondary extruder.

In this case, the primary extruder is a separate unit with its own drive unit and can run at higher speeds to supply more production. Typical speeds are 75-100 RPM. The screw design includes the conventional

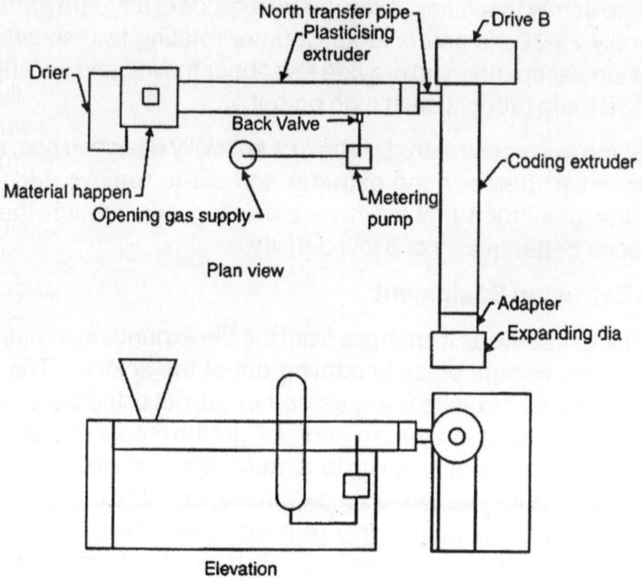

Fig. 18.4 : Tandem Foam Line for producing Low density Separate Extruders.

feed, compression and meter zones in this section. There is an additional mixing zone to mix the blowing agent with the polymer homogenously.

The secondary extruder- which is called as cooling extruder is of higher size (diameter) and runs at low rpm to supply more output and less shear energy for efficient cooling of the melt and PBA mix. Typical speeds range between 20-40 RPM. They have deep cut flights and large diameter to provide large heat dissipation area for cooling the melt. The screw channel depth is constant to provide minimum shear to the melt. The cooled mass is discharged through the die unit and the foam is formed immediately as it exits the die.

Twin Screw Extrusion

The twin screw extruders consist of twin screws inside a stationary single barrel. The screws fully intermesh to provide self-cleaning while running and minimum material hold-up. The two screws are either co-rotating (rotating in same direction) or counter-rotating (rotation in opposite sense).

Twin screw machines provide good mixing and high output compared to single screw machines. Twin screw extruders for foam production are generally 25-30 diameters long. Counter rotating twin screw machines run at slower speeds and provide low shear mixing and cooling required for good foam production at high output.

Some twin screw extruders have a specially designed heat exchanger (static mixer) between the extruder and die to remove additional heat from the gas-laden mass before extruding out through the die. This produces better quality and low density.

Post Extrusion Equipment

The extrudate as it emerges from the die expands in all directions due to the rapid escape ofgases coming out of the solution. The product is either allowed to expand freely as it emerges out of the die, or as is usual, sized against the calibrator or mandrel to get the proper size of product. For producing single layer sheet up to 12 mm thick, annular dies are used with due allowance for the blow-up or expansion ratio and the product is drawn over a mandrel, which not only removes extra heat, but also sizes the product. The bubble is slit to get a single layer sheet which is passed over several idlers and finally wound in rolls. For producing foam pipe, simple circular die with a central core or pin is used. For producing a rod, a plain circular hole is used as die. For producing foam netting, specially designed dies with mechanical drives are used to make the open work structure of netting foam. Their design is held proprietary by manufacturers. In all these dies, the die orifice size is generally much smaller to account for expansion while the product emerges from the die.

It should be noted that, if foam products need additional processing, e.g. coating with a thin layer of high density polymer, then sufficient time period should be allowed for the PBA to diffuse out completely, since after coming out of the die, the PBA continuously diffusing, and air diffuses in, long after the foam has been formed. There should be sufficient long-term warehousing period before surface finishing or coating is applied, so that reheating in subsequent processes will not allow gases trapped inside to escape due to the coating layer. The result may be excessive surface porosity and blistering.

Basic operations required for producing foam product:

- Polymer System Feeding - premix or multiple streams. ft involves feeding the base polymer material in pellet form alongwith additives such as nucleating agents, cell stabilizers, lubricants, etc., either premixed together or metered in accurate amounts via. separate feeders.
- Melting/Compounding - blend the base polymer, disperse nucleating agents, colourant, stabilizers, etc,. in the plasticizing zone of extruder.

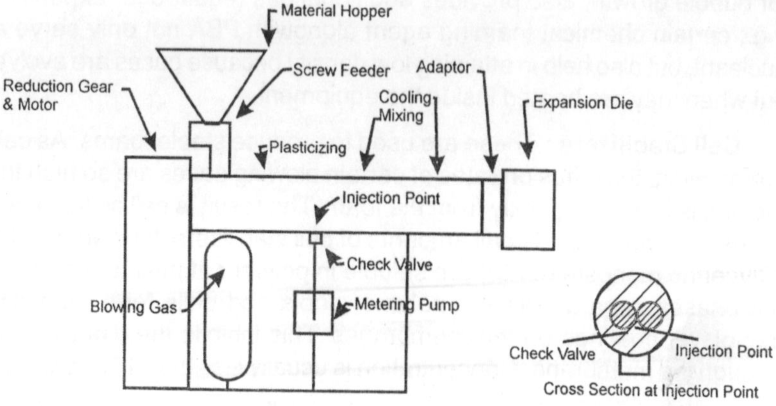

Fig. 18.5 : Schematic of Twin Screw Extruder for Producing Low Density Foams.

- Dynamic Sealing - is special zone designed on the extruder screw to prevent back flow of blowing agent towards the material hopper.
- Gas injection - It is done with aid of high pressure (3000-5000 psig) multi-stage plunger metering pumps over the specially designed mixing zone on the extruder screw.
- Cooling- injection of PBA reduces the melt viscosity. This zone of extruder cools down the compound to temperatures between 80-100°C.
- Pumping - Pumping power for final die flow and maintain the melt at pressures well above the partial pressure of the blowing agent to prevent premature foaming in the equipment.
- Die Forming - To shape the product and allow right bubble growth.

PRIMARY RAW MATERIALS NEEDED IN FOAM PRODUCTION

Foam recipe has two major components: 1) polymer (resin) and 2) foaming agent and minor components called as additives. Most common foaming polymers for Thermoplastics Extrusion are Polystyrene and LDPE (Polyethylene).

Nucleants: Nearly all foams employ nucleating agents in concentration of 1-1.5% by weight. The primary role for a nucleant is to provide surfaces on which bubbles can organize and grow. They provides as sites for bubble growth. Microfine grades provide fine cell structures. Talc is most common passive nucleant used in foam production.

There are also active nucleants which, in addition to providing sites for bubble growth, also provides additional gas required for expansion, e.g., certain chemical foaming agent alongwith PBA not only serve as nucleant, but also help in attaining low density because gases are evolved out when they are heated inside the equipment.

Cell Stabilizers : These are used to produce stable foams. As cells are growing, the diffusion rates of certain blowing gases are so high that the gas is lost very quickly from the foam. The result is cell collapse and excessive shrinkage. Small amounts of cell stabilizers, typified by GMS (Glycerine monosteareate) are soluble in polymer at melt tempera-ture but phases separate as the polymer cools and cells form, providing monolayer coatings on the membranes. This inhibits the diffusion rate through the membrane. Concentration is usually less than 1 % by weight.

In addition to the above primary in-gredients, the compound may include fillers and reenforcing agents, antioxidants, antistatic agents, colourants, fire retardants, external or internal lubricants, etc. but some may interfere with nucleation or cell stabilization and their properties and effects should be carefully studied before using the same.

Processing: For producing chemically expanded foams, all ingredients alongwith the pellets are premixed and loaded in the hopper of the conventional extruder and the material is heated above the melting temperature of the resin. The chemical foaming agent decomposes inside the extruder due to the applied heat and evolves blowing gases required for expansion, as the product emerges out of the die. Inside the extruder, the temperature is maintained from 80 to 250°C rising towards the exit end. Screw rpm is adjusted as per requirement. Satisfactory high density foams about 40-50% density than that of unfoamed polymer are produced.

High density flexible wad sheet is also produced by the above process using "T" die and conventional sheet take-off equipment. Of late, such a sheet is also produced by blowing gas injection process, wherein liquid CO_2 gas is pumped into the melted resin to attain lower densities. Density of around 0.2 g/ cc has been attained by this process.

For low density foam production, it is should be noted that, the blowing gas is externally injected at very high pressures (3000-5000 psig are common) through plunger type multiplex metering pumps and it should be ensured, that, the material is fully molten at the time of injection or gas blowback may occur preventing formation of cells in the foam. High injection pressures are required to ensure maximum solubility and homogenous mixing with the melted resin to achieve lower densities.

Low density process requires more careful setting of the process parameters and in the cooling zone, the temperature is held not more than 80-100°C for PE or PS foams to attain proper melt conditions.

Though all the ingredients can be pre-weighed and premixed in a tumbler mixer and loaded in the hopper, it is desirable to load the components separately by respective screw feeders or gravimetric hoppers for best results. The gas injection should be through non-return or check-valve to prevent any back flow of melt in the injection nozzle and clog the gas lines in event of loss of blowing gas pressure. The expanded product from the die is constrained by calibrators which also serve to cool down the foam. The rigid foam is cut in desired lengths foe storage and flexible foam is wound in large diameter rolls or spools.

Process wastage generated in the process is usually stored in clean area and reground for reuse with the virgin resin.

Gas lines should be insulated to minimise temperature rise of the blowing agents, since they have very low boiling points and it is necessary to pump the gases as liquids through the pumps. Blowing agents can be used singly or in combination (e.g. pentane and carbon dioxide combination) with individual control of dosages in the multi-stage metering pump.

Volatile blowing agents are danger-ous (butane, propane, pentane, etc.), and require careful handling in the plant to save accidents. Certain CFC gases like R 11, R 12 were used with polyethylene, but have now been banned for depicting the ozone layer of atmosphere.

19

Plastic Pipes for Water Supply

It is widely recognised that there is a crucial and urgent need to use water supply resources more efficiently. Plastics can play a crucial role in this endeavour. The material properties of plastics, when combines with committed suppliers and users can ensure easy, safe, contamination-free conveyance of potable water and leakage-free disposal of sewage and wastewater.

However, the present use of plastics in India has been influenced more by economic considerations, than by the inherent properties of the materials. This is illustrated by the fact that over 60% use of uPVC Pipes is by farmers for farm irrigation. To extand and match the global trends of usage of plastic pipes into wider productive areas mandates major changes in approaches and re-affirmation of design and application principles.

On the contrary, the use of HDPE pipes in India is restricted to the exploitation of one particular property of the product, namely corrosion re sistance, thereby becoming more of a discerning engineer's repertoire than the choice of the common man.

High Density Polyethylene (HDPE) Pipes

Polyethylene is highly abrasion and corrosion resistant, and is thereby able to handle a wide variety of slurries, abrasive materials as well as almost all acids, cuastics, salt solutions and other corrosive liquids and gases. Thus the use of this material in India is restricted to the benevolent chemical engineers, as the mateiral producers have not enlightened the civil engineer, on the advantages of PE pipes for water supply.

Water Supply

In many countries, the PE pipe is the standard choice for drinking water mains as well as for service mains. The new generation material in the form of PE 80, PE 100 has also made it possible to use thinner pipe walls and reduce the weight and cost per meter of the pipe for both smooth walled and structured wall pipe systems. Whreas, until the World Bank stepped in to prevent water leakage from corroded metal pipes, the Metro Boards of Chennai and Hyderabad had not even thought of PE ppes, Even then the usage is limited to the loan amount and no attempt has been made by the authorities to make the product usage mandatory.

Non-use of PE pipes for service water lines can be attributed to non availablility of easy to fit compression fittings. One cannot expect the water supply engineers to recommended buttwelding for the service lines. There are over fiteen quality producers in the World for compression fittings and it requires a pioneer to promote indigenous manufacture fo compression fittings. This can significantly affect the market of PE Pipes, in India if the amortization of the compression fittings, moulds is not on the sale of fittings itself but on the PE pipe market that it develops.

HDPE transmission mains are economical even upto 630 mm because of their flexibility; smooth inner surface and low modulus of elasticity (low surge pressure). They are thus ideal for rural water supply mains.

The properties of PE make the pipelines suitable for areas subject to ground movement caused by seismic forces, mining subsidence, and compaction of filled sites of the disturbance caused by the activities of other utilities in the vicinity.

Studies after the Kobe earthquack showed that PE system are able to accomodate severe ground disturbances without being harmed.

Pipe behaviour can be broaded classified as flexible or rigid, depending on how to performs when installed. Flexible pipes can move, of deflect, under load without structural damage, HDPE pipes is an example. The rigid pipe is sometimes classified as pipe that connot deflect significantly without structural distress, such as cracking. Resinforced concrete and asbestos pipes are examples. Thus for underground rural water supply system, there is hardly any alternative for HDPE pipes-limiting factor being effective installation and maintenance norms.

Special Properties of HDPE Pipes

HDPE pipes float on water. This particular property is used for laying the pipes under the sea or backwaters for both effluent disposal and

Water Contamination and Loss in Piped Water Supply

Essential action to ensure that a piped water supply remain safe and sustainable include :

- Preventing contaminations
- Minimising water loss

Contamination of distribution pipelines may arise from :

- Intermittent supply
- Low water pressure on the distribution network
- Leaking Pipes
- Inadequate waste-water collection systems

Water loss (physical loss) often amounting to more than 50% of supplies mainly arises from :

- Leaking pipes, joints and valves
- Overflowing service reservoirs
- Waste water through illegal connections and non-metered house connection

potable water transport. Even electrical cable laying across water bodies can be acheived easily and economically. Only, the State of Kerala has used this particular property of HDPE pipe to deliver potable water to remote hamlets that are otherwise inaccessible.

Yet, a lot needs to be done by the manufacturer so that this particular property is fully exploited : water supply to ships docked in the ports, is one such application.

Industrial Water Piping

Every Industry large, medium or small needs water—drinking water, gardening, water, de-mineralized water, raw water, cooling water, boiler feed water etc. Polyethylene pipes are the best solution for all these applications. A prudent Consulting Engineer, who plays a significant role in selecting/recommending piping material, can draw great economic benefits, by slight modification on how the pipes are supported in "cable rack" type supporting system, in the Industrial scenario.

Large Diameter HDPE Pipes

But fusion welding is the most reliable and convenient method of joining large diameter HDPE pipes. Manufacturers and users in India have taken this as too easy a method and have ignored the need for

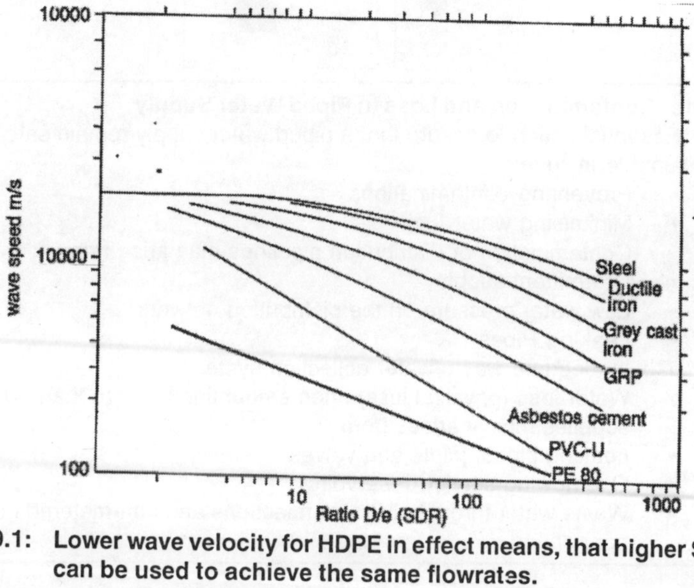

Fig. 19.1: Lower wave velocity for HDPE in effect means, that higher SDR can be used to achieve the same flowrates.

effective machinery and skilled contractors. Large diameter pipes, necessarily supplied in straight lengths are heavy and difficult to maneuver at the best of times and the logistics of butt fusion in the field sometimes needs careful consideration. Aside the butt welding machine required for large diameter pipes is itself a very large piece of equipment and needs to be supported by an equally large generator. A school of Welding to ensure skilled labour availability to the users is need of the hour.

Electro Fusion Welding

Electro fusion welding is used mainly for GAS pipe joining, as it is expensive, because of the cost of fittings. However, as trench welding of HDPE pipes - especially for repair- is unwidely, the electro-fusion welding up to 300 mm NB has been recommended even for water supply pipelines. Also for tapping from main transmission lines, electro-fusion saddle is the only way.

Thus there is need for popularising electro-fusion welding for the benefit of the growth of the HDPE pipe industry.

Corrugated PE Pipes

Corrugated polyethylene pipe has been used successfully for decades in a variety of drainage applications, especially in USA. It's flexibility over concrete and metal has made it the sanitary engineer's first choice. Whereas PVC is the principle material used in Europe, PE is the predominant resin for corrugated tubing production in the USA.

Polyethylene resins provide the physical properties required to meet the structural handling and installtation, environmental stress cracking resistance and long term performance needed for the various end-use applications of corrugated tubing. Corrugated (structured wall) PE has become the principle drainage material used in agriculture, in the construction industry and for highways and roads. In comparsion to solid wall pipes, structured wall pipes provide far higher stiffness and, therefore, improved mechanical behaviour towards external loads. Under-the-building cable conduits could be one such application for corrugated PE pipes.

It is not out of place to suggest that Corrugated PE pipes could be an economical replacement for rigid PVC pipes for irrigation.

PE Fittings

The HDPE piping system is not complete without the fittings. This is one area, the pipe manufacturers in India lacked progress–more so for

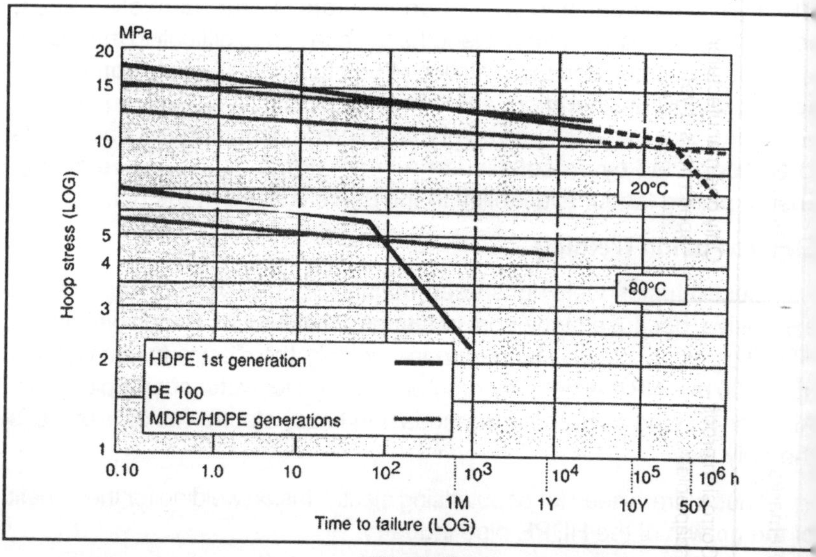

Fig. 19.2

Fig. 19.3

Size (mm)	Water Supply	Industry and GAS
20 mm-110 mm	Compression fittings (PP)	Injection Moulded (IM)/ Electro fusion fittings
125-315 mm	Electro fusion/IM fittings	Electro fusion fittings
>315 mm	Butt welded fittings	Butt Welded Fittings

Size -NB (mm)	Sector	Recommended Product	Remarks	Limitation
15 mm to 50 mm	Building Construction –Inside Plumbing	PE-Al Composite Pipes	Corrosion proof/ adaptable	Only one manufacturer – specs not set yet – fittings standards to be reviewed
	Building Construction –outside Building	PP-Random or PE Pipes/ASTM PVC Plumbing	Till PP random pipes are available PE/PVC Pipes can be used	PP ideal for hot water applications-require Fittings developements/ standardisation
	Industrial Use	PE Pipes	Compression fittings make the ease of installation and maintenance	Availability of fittings need be addressed by the industry
	Municipal water connections	PE Pipes	Compression fittings make the ease of installation and maintenance	Availability of fittings need be addressed by the industry
65 mm to 100 mm	Industrial Use	PE Pipes	Compression fittings make the eae of installation and maintenance	Availability of fittings need be addressed by the industry
	Farm Irrigation	PVC Pipes/ PE pipes	Economical consideration make PVC the ideal choice– In typical terrains PE pipes do make a flexible choice	If pipe is exposed to sun then – PE, buried PVC/ PE, as per convenience and cost economies

	Rural and Semi-urban Water Supply	PE Pipes	Compression fittings make the ease of installation and maintenance	Availability of fittings need be addressed by the industry
125 mm to 250 mm	Industrial Use	PE Pipes	Butt welding is most economical method of jointing	Rugged usage–requires support system for overhead lines
	Farm irrigation	PVC Pipes	PVC-most suitable; economic. However only for buried pipes.	Accessories quality circumspect
	Rural and Semi-urban Water Supply	PVC Pipes	Ideal material, if proper laying precautions are followed	Strict implementation of quality checks necessary – Industry fragmented and requires stricker BIS controls.
300 mm and above	Industrial Use	PE Pipes	Butt welding is most economical method of jointing	Rugged usage–requires support system for overhead lines.
	Rural and Semi-urban Water Supply	PE Pipes	Better impact and water hammer resistance makes PE score over PVC	Butt welding could be difficult to perform in rural areas–Electro-fusion to be persued.

Fig. 19.4

large diameter pipes. Connectivity to valves either by flange or screwing is a question it needs. Also, the method of manufacturing these fittings that ensure leak proof butt welding with matching melt flow rates of the pipe and the fittings is the issue has to be addressed by the industry.

While building homogenous systems, it is necessary to ensure that the pipes and fittings have the same MRS and wall thickness. With the production of pressure tested PE pipe fittings the situation is very different; there is no single technology available to cover the size range of 20 mm to 1000 mm. However the following table can be used as a guideline.

Fig. 19.5

The viability of large diameter fittings can only be determined by testing to try to predict lifetimes under field conditions.

Fittings are also sometimes made from a lower molecular weight of better-lubricated compound in order to facilitate moulding. Such compounds may have somewhat weaker creep-rupture and fatigue characteristics, which may need be compensated by thicker walls or by limiting the maximum servicing conditions of pressure and temperature.

Surge Pressure Capability

Lower modulus of elasticity of HDPE compared to many other competing materials such as Ductile iron, Mild Steel and PVC is great advantage, which needs to be conveyed to the Design Engineer.

Because of this particular property, HDPE pipes can be used with higher velocity, than normally recommended by the practicing civil engineer. Thus, higher flow rates can be designed for the same size of pipe as compared to other material. This is another area one must take into consideration while feasibility studies with HDPE pipes are being conducted (Refer Fig. 1).

PE Resins

HDPE 80, HDPE 80, Blue compounded Resin, Black ompounded Resin, HDPE 100, Bimodal PE are some resin names that are doing the rounds that confuse the innocent pipe manufacturer and the end user. The bottom line however is the fact that the long-term strength of the resin plays a significant role. The long-term characteristics of the material essentially depend on the length of the chains. The greater the number of long chains of a PE product, the higher is its resistance against brittle failures, caused by long slow crack growth.

PE pipes are designed for a fifty year life, based on depreciation of 2% per annum.

Extrapolation methods as described in ISO 9080, esnure that the PE pipes are classified as per the long term stress. Organizations such as German Association of Gas and Water Experts (DVGW) and Bodycote Polymer, Sweeden carry independent tests that help classify the resin.

20

New Opportunities with PP for Window Profiles

Overview

Since 1957, as a result of the intensive development of production technology, Polypropylene (PP) has been produced on a large, industrial scale. This intensive developement–which started with the catalyzer and developed with increasingly sophisticated additive systems–has made it possible for PP, especially during the last two decades, to be applied in several demanding applications including car construction, structural and civil engineering, and the chemical industry.

This article shows the current situation for plastic in the European window market, as well as various trends in the most relevant geographical areas. The core of the article concerns the opportunities of PP as one of the alternatives to traditionally used materials for window profile extrusion. The described Polypropylene window profile system is well documented and some comparisons with existing materials are shown. PP installtions are also described and some general conclusions are stated at the end of the article.

General Properties of PP

Since 1957, PP has been produced on large industrial scale. Intensive development has made it possible for PP to be applied in car construction structural and civil engineering, plastic pipes (13-5) and the chemical industry. The main drivers for the enormous wolume increase of PP has been its excellent mechanical properties, high chemical resistance, and an excellent price/performance ratio.

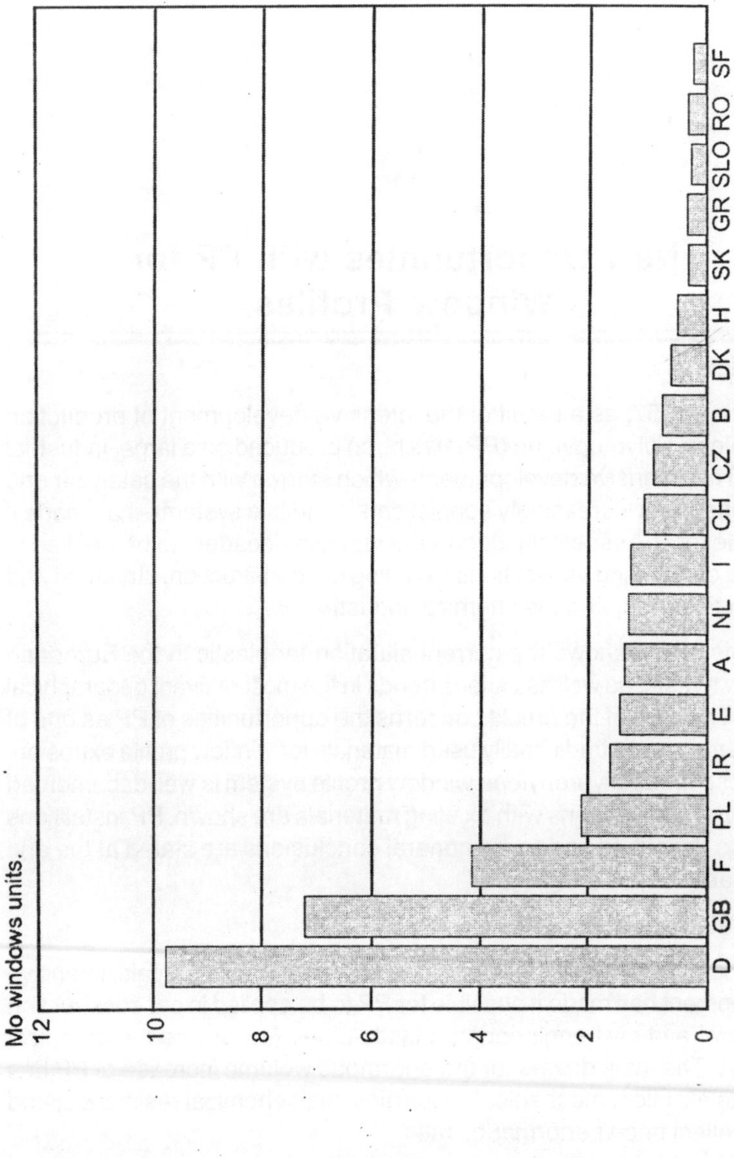

Source : VFF Verband der Fenster-und Fassandenhersteller e.V.7/00

Fig. 20.1 : The European market for PVC windows – year 2000

Profile extrusion is a very new application for PP. This market is dominated by PVC, which has an excellent technical performance and 30 years experience. Neverthless in some markets (mainly Germany, Austria and North Europe), PVC has been under pressure over the last 10 years for ecological reasons. Despite its technical advantages the use of PVC has been prohibited and wood or aluminium has been installed.

This "Green" debate is a very emotional one. There are a lot of arguments against it, but it is a fact of life; and the bottom line is a loss of market share for plastic windows. Compared with other raw materials for windows, PP offers the best environmental image. No legislative restriction are expected , now or in the future. PP can be recycled and reused for the same application or burned without any adverse effects on the environment. Life cycle analyses demonstrate its very high environmenal ranking. PP has good mechanical properties, but it achieve results as good as PVC it is necessary to note some essentially differences between partially crystalline PP and amorphous PVC.

Table 20.1 :

Tailer Made PP	PVC-U
• Single Screw extruder	• Twin-screw extruder
• Co-extrusion	
• Granules	• Powder
• "Flowablility"–value; MFR (230/2.16) 0.45-0.60g/10 min	• "Flowability"–Value : K-value

Profile extrusion

Grades and Properties

Based on the above mentioned market trends, the general properties and potential of PP to be tailor made (i.e. designed for defined application), a number of steps have been initiated in the development of PP grades which can be used for the extrusion of window profiles.

To meet these needs the two grades tailor made for a co-extruded window profile are :

- WA522E, a standard stabilised for mulation as a core material.
- WA590E, a high performance UV-stabilised formulation for the outer layer

Table 20.2

	Value	Unit	Test method
Density at 23°C	1020	Kg/m³	ISO 1183
Melt Index (280°C/2.16 kg)	0.50	g/10min	ISO 1133
Yield strss (50 mm/min)	.4	MPa	ISO 527
Elongation at yield (50 mm/min)	6.5	%	ISO 527
Tensile modulus	2400	MPs	ISO 527
Impact strength (23°C)	34	KJ/m²	ISO 179/leA
(–20°C)	2.5	KJ/m²	ISO 179/leA
Vicat softening temperature VST/B/50	85	°C	ISO 306
Heat distoration temperature	112	°C	ISO 75/B
Ball indentation hardness	72	N/mm2	ISO 2039
Shore Hardness	69		ISO 868

Technical properties of the grade WA522E

Table 20.3 : Comparison of Costs

Material (Wall Thickness	Density g/cm	Volume ratio	Material cost per meter profile
PVC-HI (3 mm)	145	100%	+
PP-Version (3 mm) Core layer Outside layer UV-Stabilised	 1.04 1.04	 70% 30%	 ++
PP-Version (4 mm) Core Outside layer UV-Stabilised	 1.04 1.04	 70% 30%	 +
ABS/ASA -Version (3mm) Core ABS Outside layer ASA	 1.11 1.11	 70% 30%	 0
Homogenous ASA (3mm)	1.11	100%	
Cost relative to PVC-HI			
++...80-100% Costs of PVC-HI		0.....130-200% Costs of PVC-HI	
+ ... 100-130% Costs of PVC-HI		–.....≥ 200% Costs of PVC-HI	

Property	Test standard and parameter	Measured Value	Reference for PVC
Apearance	Outer layer uniformly white, free from voids, crakcs, blisters and other etef.	Outer layer uniformly white free from voids, cracks, blisters and defects	See measured value
Density	DIN 53479	1.04 g/cm3	1.42 g/cm³
Vicat softening temperature VST B 50	ISO 306	83°C	>75°C
Impact strength double-V-notch (r = 0.1mm)	GZ 716/1	39/43 mj/mm²	average>/-40mJ/mm²
Dimensional change after heated storage	DIN EN 479, 100°C,1h	0.43%	>/= 2.0%
Behaviour after heat storage	DIN EN 478, 150°C, 30 min	No cracks blisters, delamination	See measured value
Short-time welding factor	GZ 716/1	0.7	0.8*
Weathering resistance after artificial Weathering (8000 MJ)	DIN EN 513	In accordance with : Colour difference E = 2.1**	E<range 4 in accordance with ISO 105-A03
Tensile modulus from Profile specimen	DIN EN ISO 527	200 N/mm²	.2200 N/mm²

* Requirements on other countries are currently lower (e.g. 0.7).
** Testing is being continued, current status (Xenon 1200): 30000 h.

Ta

Mechanical properties are the same for both grades. For rheological reasons there is no difference between these grades except the UV stabilization.

Processability

Profile extrusion on single screw extruders is not yet 100% "state-of-the-art" with PP compounds. As this extrusion process, unlike PVC, involves a partially crystalline process, it creats considerable demands on moulding and calls for excellent process engineering knowledge of profile extrusion. Current productions run at about half the speed of a standard PVC production. Increasing experience; development in machine technology, and optimised tools will make processing of PP considerably easier in years to come. In the near future we expect to reach a competitive output level of 4m/min with double string tools.

Properties of Windows

There is no standard or "guerichtlinie" which exists for PP windows, therefore all tests have been made following the existing PVC standards. Window profiling made of WAG33E/WA590E fulfill the requirements of RAL-GZ 716/1 as shown in the following table :

Conclusion :

- PP meets the need of window profiles.
- PP is the best alternative to PVC in the market.
- PP window complement rther an oppose PVC Windows.
- PP opens new markets for plastic window products.

21

CORRUGATOR MULTILAYER PIPE TECHNOLOY

History of the Corrugated Plastic Pipe and the Application Fields

Almos 45 years ago the so called corrugated plastic pipe has been introduced into the world market. The birthday of corrugated plastic pipes coincides with the invention of the first corrugator in the mid-1950s, with which the manufacture of corrugated plastic products ventured away from the smooth-walled constructions standard until that time. Before then, continuous plastic pipe or tube of PVC or PE featuring acceptable stiffness had never been produced industrially in such low unit weights.

The very first idea of the corrugated plastic pipes was the flexibility compared to the plain / smooth pipes in those days. Later, another fact, today the most important one, has been introduced into the market. It is actually the biggest advantage of this pipe. You can save up to 60% of the material compared to the old-fashioned smooth pipe having even the very same technical characteristics, having the very same stiffness, having even the very same impact resistance. And this advantage, the saving of material, made this kind of structured wall pipe well known and that successful all over the world.

Transparency "Comparison between smooth ..... "

This comparison has been made for an Asian client. We took his existing smooth pipes, his weight, etc. and tested the ring stiffness that could be achieved with this smooth pipe. This customer wanted us to take the very same outer diameter. Then we calculated a double wall pipe (in this case PVC) with the same stiffness and found out that the material saving reaches a max. of up to 69%. To be honest, it is not a cost saving of 69%, because the material itself for such a double wall pipe is approx. 10-15% more expensive than the material for a smooth pipe. But you can still save up to 40% in material costs.

It you take this value and calculate an order of 200,000m of pipe size 110 you can easily see that it is not only the material where you can save a lot of money.

Transparency "Difference in outputs (corrugated pipe compared to smooth pipe)"

	Corrugated Pipe	Smooth Pipe
Size	110	110 x 3,7
Weight	726 g/m	1767 g/m
Output	400 kg/h	400 kg/h
Output	9,2 m/min	3,8 m/min
Time	362 hours	877 hours

From this simple calculation you can see that you do not only save material but you also save a lot of energy costs, labour costs and storage costs.

Of course it is right that a corrugator, that is the machine the corrugated pipe is produced on, is much more expensive than a smooth pipe production line. But it is only a question of your market's' demand and a short period of time after which the investment into a corrugator has paid for itself.

Corrugated pipes with several layers which are produced in bars or rods can be provided at their end with belled couplings, in line or out line, (depending on the production speed) and with the help of belling machines usual in trade. There are also other possibilities of connecting such as

Blow or injection moulded couplers, in-line injection couplers, rotary welding couplers and others. Depending on the application, nearly all thermoplastic materials are nowadays used for the manufacture of corrugated pipes. The choice of the material is mainly influenced by the following facts.

- Availability and price of the raw material
- Chemical and physical requirement of the final product
- Standards and rules to be met
- Special requirement of the market and the customers

With the long-standing experience manufacturers are able to assist you as to the choice of material, profile proposals will be worked out to optimise the product itself and advises for all questions of production techniques will be provided due to their multiple advantages compared with usual materials, for example low weight, high flexibility, good insulation resistance, big coil length (and therefore less couplers) and high resistance to temperatures and chemical agents these pipes are used for electric installation and cable protection in buildings and machines, cars, planes and even ships. These pipes are also used as cable protection for telephone ducting, optic fibre, power and control lines, wiring harness, conveyor pipes, vacuum cleaner hoses, for washing machines, for medical applications, drip irrigation and much more.

Very large sized pipes, and we are now referring to the manufacturing of pipes up to 2500mm, are nowadays a long lasting alternative to concrete and clay pipes used still today. The excellent resistance against chemical agents guarantees absolute efficiency. In terms of installation time and cost the length of usually up to 6 meters makes a faster installation possible in comparison to the said concrete or clay pipes.

In the US there are pipes on the market up to approx. 1500mm ID for drainage and storm water applications.

In Europe we have big diameter pipes for sewerage applications up to 1000mm OD.

And now this trend can be seen all over the world. Several manufacturing units with these big corrugators have been set up in ASIA.

Another application where these large diameter pipes can be advantageously introduced is as culverts. In developing countries where highways have open trenches / channels running on either side for surface drainage, the large diameter corrugated pipes can be used as culverts at lower cost as well as lower transportation and installation cost.

The main machine to produce these pipes is the so called corrugator, which has mainly three tasks form the pipe, cool the pipe and transport the pipe.

Another very important part of complete line is the so called die head. And there are different die heads for the different pipes that can be produced.

There are die head for single wall pipes

Transparency "single wall die head"

Die heads for double wall pipes where you are using only one extruder.

Transparency "die head PVC double wall pipe"

And special die heads for double wall pipes produced with two different materials or in two different colours.

Transparency "die head PE double wall pipe"

This die had could be connected to two single screw extruder to be used mainly for PE and PP double wall pipes and has several advantages compared to the one for double wall pipes using one extruder only. It is easier to adjust several wall thicknesses within a certain tolerance of course only by changing the output of the two different extruders.

It you want to have more material for the outer wall that means if you need a higher wall thickness you just have to increase the output of the extruder that gets you the outer-material.

Another big advantage especially if we are talking about Polyolefins is that you can use two different materials and or two different colours. 1\vo different materials could also mean for example a PE double wall pipe could become flexible just simply by using a MD or LDPE for the inner wall and a HDPE for the outer wall. Then it is possible to coil such a double wall pipe and you could save a lot of money because you are going to save couplers and fittings.

Another advantage of this system is that you can easily use different materials, that means for example a second grade material or recycled material. That allows again a saving of money which of course nowadays is very important.

Transparency "disc die head"

This new technology was specially developed for the production of large sized polyolefins pipes. This construction allows for a relatively short die, resulting in :

- reduction in weight of the die
- reduction of the length of the flow channels
- reduction of the heat energy consumption
- easier mass temperature control
- increase in output
- easier in handling

This new DISC DIE HEAD Technology for double wall pipes can be used with either one extruder together with a material distributor box or two extruders with the relevant inlet pieces.

The die head and the die set itself includes of course the so called tightening mandrel or the cooling mandrel depending whether you are producing a single or a double wall pipe. The tightening mandrel gets us the possibility of creating an inner forming pressure wherever it is necessary, for example if you are going to produce an in-line coupler. The cooling mandrel, necessary for double wall pipes, cools and smoothens the inner surface of the double wall pipe. A double wall pipe is more or less calibrated inside by this mandrel and outside of course by the mould blocks.

Variety of Corrugator

As the corrugated pipes range from 3mm to 2000mm there are naturally a variety of corrugators offered for different range of sizes, different outputs desired by producers and in accordance with the international pipe standards so that such a corrugator normally covers a wide range of such a standard.

For example corrugator UC 250 (UC stands for Universal Corrugator) covers the diameter range' from 40 up to 250mm a.D. and therefore the whole drainage pipe range (from 50 to 250 mm) and for example the whole cable protection range from 40 up to 200 mm according to international standards, here the German drainage pipe standard DIN 1187 and the new European standard for cable protection pipes the EN 50086. Thus it is possible to produce on only one corrugator the whole program of pipes. Whether this is the most economical solution or not - I don't like to comment on it. It is a calculation you have to do on your own.

In the latest developments starting from the UC 75 up to the UC 1500 the new technology features the horizontal open design, the direct cooling of aluminium mould blocks, the vacuum forming unit and the quick exchange of mould block system became from the very beginning the most successful system ever produced.

Newest and hard to top technology.

Transparency "horizontal open design"

From our corrugator UC 75 up to the biggest corrugator we now have the so called open horizontal design. That means the mould blocks are not any longer guided in closed channels.

The mould blocks are mounted on mould block carriers made of special steel. These carriers are guided very accurately by special guiding plates. The mould blocks are driven by an lower and upper synchronised A.C. driven gear drive and it is therefore not possible that the mould block can tip during the forming process. Therefore the mould blocks are gUided very precisely and a flash or marking at the pipe itself is not as big as it could be with other systems.

Both of the mould block halves are driven by means of a common drive which enables a perfect synchronisation of both of the mould block halves. This results in a perfect product where we have only very small markings on the pipe, almost not possible to see.

The open design of our corrugators allows an easy access to all parts at the machine, so that maintenance and handling is not any longer that complicated. Changing of parts under the corrugator is not any longer a time wasting matter, you can do it now within a very short period of time.

The open horizontal design also features an easy disassembling of the mould blocks even in the middle channel. That means in case of troubles you can open the mould blocks at the rear and simply take it out of the middle channel.

The horizontal design allows even bigger pipe dimensions at relatively low extrusion height. The system that made the new technology so successful is the new cooling method.

Transparency "cooling system"

This system now allows outputs we only dreamed about before.

The cooling medium is now led directly into the forming blocks through a special distribution system. That means every mould block is connected to the system. Every mould block gets a constant through flow of cold water and therefore guarantees a high heat transfer. The combination of this cooling method and the usage of aluminium as the material for the mould blocks get us incredible output rates.

Another important fact to improve the quality and the output of the finished product, the corrugated pipe is the vacuum forming.

Transparent "Vacuum mould blocks"

The vacuum is taken from the upper part and the different zones can be regulated individually. Especially when you want to produce Polyolefins and bigger pipe dimensions we would say it is a must to have the vacuum forming. It gives you a better outer shape of the profile and it ensures a much longer direct contact of the material and thus results even in higher output possibilities.

A development, a special feature, that resulted from our daily experience from our own pipe production is also the so called quick exchange of mould block system. As I told you before the mould blocks are no longer connected to each other, they are mounted on the so called steel mould block carriers.

These carriers are equipped with a special tension bolt that fixes the mould block to the carrier.

In case you are going to change the pipe dimension you don't have to disassemble connecting links or screws any longer, you just open or loosen the quick release nut by means of a socket wrench, uncouple the direct cooling water hoses, you tip the mould block forward and remove it from the carrier, you place the new mould block onto the guiding carrier, you tighten the nut and connect the water hoses. And that is all you have to do. Such a change could be done within seconds for one half of the mould block. Changing a complete set of mould blocks is now no longer a matter of hours, but of minutes only, depending on the number of mould blocks your corrugator has.

Again we want to point out the advantages of this new technology that puts you ahead of your competition, that gives you the chance to head for new skies.

Transparency "UNICOR's advanced technology"

General Information

On corrugators from 3 mm up to 500 mm that means starting from the baby corrugator the DC 15 up to the DC 500, the so called closed mould block chain system is used.

For corrugators bigger than 500 mm the so called Shuttle System is used. The mould blocks do not any longer consist of a closed mould block system. This system now consists of only a few mould blocks driven by a special moving unit as you can see on the transparency sheet.

The small number of mould blocks allows an quick exchange and therefore shortens the pipe dimension changing time. Further more it gets you a great saving in investment costs.

Machinery manufactures having their own pipe production units are gaining day by day all information

Multilayer Pipe Technology

1. History of the pipe

Not too long ago, all house installations have been made with metallic pipes, such as black steel, galvanized steel or copper. For decades, severe problems, like corrosion, and material built-up (encrustation) had been taken for granted. ~ ***Picture corrosion, encrustation***

In the middle of the seventies, the search for solutions had led to a result, and for the first time ever, plastic pipes made from PE, PP and PB have revolutionized the sanitary and heating installation markets.

With the introduction of plastic pipes, corrosion problems were no longer existent. These plastic pipes have many advantages like no encrustation, light weight, resistant to many chemicals, the first time long coils could be produced, etc.

However, a new problem, the rapid aging of plastics subjected to permanent loads of high temperature and pressure, was the new challenge for researchers and industry.

Again one was looking for solutions and, as a result, the CROSS LINKING of PE, either by means of electronic rays or with chemical catalysts like silane or peroxide, was introduced.

Cross linking increases the toughness and long-time resistance of PE to heat and breaking. Through the cross linking process, a change in the structure of the plastic molecules, from linear to cross alignment is achieved.

Now, since corrosion was no longer a problem and the resistance to heat and breaking was acceptable, another problem, namely the oxygen diffusion, an attribute of all plastic materials, still had to be solved. Because of the diffusion of oxygen through plastic pipe walls into the water of for instance a closed circuit heating system, permanent corrosion of metallic components of that systems, such as boilers, pumps, valves etc. is caused.

A solution to this problem was promised by the development of the so-called Diffusion tight PEX pipe. By means of a very thin extruded skin of extremely expensive and intensely oxygen tight plastic, the relevant requirements of the DIN standards with regard to the oxygen diffusion tightness of a heating pipe were barely fulfilled.

Although the Diffusion tight pipe represented a substantial improvement compared to normal plastic pipes, decisive disadvantages did still exist.

A) The very thin EVOH skin can be damaged very easily (for instance when dragging a coil of pipe over a rough concrete floor at a building site).

B) At higher water temperatures, the oxygen permeability of the diffusion harrier increases proportionally to raising temperature.

In one sentence: This pipe represented an improvement but no solution.

In the late seventies, for the first time, experiments had been carried out with metal-plastic-composite-material and during the 1980's proper manufacturing techniques had been developed.

At last, the "Ideal pipe", the pipe of the 3rd generation, was available. A composite pipe which combined the advantages of metal and plastic, without the specific disadvantages of both materials.

Advantages like metal

- the multi-layer pipe has an extremely high long-time rupture strength and is very well suited for higher temperatures and pressure.
- Multi-layer pipe is 100% oxygen diffusion tight
- multi-layer pipe has a negligibly small length expansion tendency at high temperatures
- multi-layer pipe can be bent by hand or with relevant tools, without spring back effect.

At the same time, multi-layer pipe offers the indisputable advantages of plastic:

- absolute corrosion resistance
- no material built-up or wear

- light weight
- very small friction resistance
- indifferent to most aggressive mediums such as acids or alkaline solutions

Multi-layer pipe belongs to the new generation of supply pipes which in the foreseeable future will supersede traditional pipe systems made from metal or pure plastic on the world markets.

The multi-layer pipe has the follOwing specific advantages.

- has a very smooth bore and so no encrustation is possible
- is absolutely corrosion free
- has small heat expansion like metal pipes and unlike normal plastic pipes
- the pipe is flexible and comes in rolls of long lengths in sizes up to 32 mm thereby reducing the need for expensive fittings. At the same time it has form stability, due to the aluminum layer and retains the shape in which it is bent, reducing the need for elbows pr angles.
- it is 100% oxygen tight and does not permit oxygen permeation
- has excellent long term rupture strength and accelerated laboratory tests show a life span in excess of 50 years life.
- It is designed to operate at 95°C at 10 bars pressure
- It has a press-fitting system of Brass fittings, as well as specially designed composite fittings of Brass and Engineering Plastics which are leak-proof
- It is very light in weight and hence easy to carry
- It is resistant to many chemicals
- It is approved for the contact with foodstuff and potable water

The multi-layer pipes has so many advantages over all other conventional metal and plastic pipes that it can be used in practically all applications. Just to mention a few of them:

- water supply in buildings
- radiator connections
- hot water heating systems

- compressed air supply lines
- air conditioning and refrigeration systems
- in ship building
- for the automobile industry
- for airplanes
- in the food industry
- in railway coach building
- in Hospitals
- in gas distribution etc. etc.

With this background on the development of the multi-layer pipe, the many advantages and applications would like to come now to the development of different markets for the different pipes.

Transparency of market shares in different markets

Based on this market data now would like to give an overview where these pipes are produced besides Germany.

Up to now the biggest market is the P. R. China. We have delivered already 20 lines which are producing very successfully. By the end of the year another 5 lines will be delivered. At the end of the last year we entered into a contract to supply 50 lines up to the year 2005. By the year 2002 there will be approx. 70 or more lines working in China from one source alone.

Outlook for Chinese market:

We are the opinion that these figures speak for themselves, especially when in a country Hke China where nobody cares about patents and copyright, we are the number one supplier and all the Chinese copiers have only a minor share.

Our machines are also running in Korea, another country where you can find many similar looking machines. The machine and the parts can be copied but fortunately not the know how.

The special situation in these 2 countries is a very big challenge for us, to be always ahead and not only 1, 2 or 3 steps better. The constant Research and Development being carried out is to the advantage of our customers. The new developments are always put to test under normal working conditions in our own production units before they are commercialised.

In addition to the 2 named countries we have production lines based on our technology all over the world. India being a very large market for Galvanised steel pipes has tremendous potential for several units, as the Multi Layer Composite Pipes can be produced and sold at prices lower than Galvanised steel pipes even though they are far superior in all respects.

Before I finish please allow me to point out a few highlights of themachine technology. When we talk about multi-layer production lines.

- We are talking about modern, most advanced completely computer controlled lines.
- We are talking about change over times from one size to another of less than 1 hour
- We are talking about short lines with a length of max. 35m resulting in savings in investment, and recurring cost of heat, light, etc.
- We are talking about lines producing very good pipe quality within 2 weeks after arrival, . and installation of the line.
- We are talking about lines which have proved their suitability in different countries and varying conditions operating on round the clock production.

22

Option for Cable Conduit Systems

In today's business world, high performance communication networks have already become indispensable and they will become even more important in the future. The internet for example, with its easy communication and data transmission possibilities is almost as important for modern business transactions as the telephone. In addition, an increasing number of private users are using services such as internet shopping, internet banking and availing themselves of the enormous amount of information provided by the internet. Currently, there are more than 16 million internet users. This number is expected to rise to 60 million over the next five years.

The growth rate of Germany's telecommunications market is approximately four times higher than that of the rest of the country's economy. Therefore, this market segment has the most promising growth potential world-wide. For a reliable simultaneous transmission of large amounts of data all over the world, high-performance transmission media are a prerequisite.

Over the past few years, optical cables made from glass-fibre materials which allow high transmission rates have consolidated a strong market position. Glass-fibres offer transmission rates which arc a thousand times higher than those of conventional copper wires. The transmission capacity of one ton of copper material equals that of one kilogram of glass. It is worth noting however, that new technologies have helped to increase the transmission capacity of copper enormously.

Glass fibres were discovered as a transmission media in 1970. They have been used for commercial applications since the 1980s. For transmission purposes, glass-fibre cables are combined to form a strand. For these strands, cable manufacturers produce cable conduits resembling the sheathing produced for copper wires. These cables are laid under ground or under the sea, more rarely they are installed over land.

- high transmission rates;
- high interference resistance;
- long working life;
- flexjbility, since their capacity can be increased by new technologies even at a later date.

Is Satellite Technology an Alternative?

Considering the fact that in Germany, UMTS licenses have only recently been sold for an inconceivably high amount of money, one might be led to surmise that the future of data transmission lies with satellite technology instead. This technology will certainly be used in the future, however will not replace but rather add to the range of transmission media such as optical cables. The reason becomes clear in a comparison of the two systems which is shown below:

Table 22.1 : Comparison between glass fibre and satellite technology.

	Fibre optic cable	Satellite
Transmission rate	very high (in a recent laboratory experiment, the transmission rate of a fibre optic cable was found to amount to terra bit per second (1010). For comparison: 160 giga bit (10^9) equals 2.5 million telephone calls conducted at the same time.	Lower UMTS - Technology : 2 mega (10^6) bit/sec.
Working life	Providers demand a working life of at least 30 years	10 to 12 yrs.
Delay	Low, depends on the distance: Under-the-sea cables between Europe and USA cover approximately 10,000 km	Long delays, because the information is transmitted over 36,000 km to a satellite and back
The system is suitable for:	high-population areas due to the advantages mentioned above	remote areas with a low number of users

The Structure of Fibre Optic Cable

A modern fibre optic cable with a diameter of 11mm as introduced in this example, consists of a centre elements with a diamter of 2.5 mm. This centre element is made from steel wire or glass fibre reinforced plastics. Six so-called leads, small plastic tubes in most cases made from polyester with a diameter of 2.45mm are grouped around this centre element. Each tube contains twelve glass fibres of various colours which together with their protective layer, have a thickness of 250µm. In this example, the fibre optic cable consists of 72 individual fibres. The centre element and the leads are encapsulated by an outer layer. They are referred to as the stranded cable core. The next layer consists of extending elements in the shape of plastic yarn made from aramid. These may be encapsulated again by a metal fibre. The fibre optic cable is encapsulated by a plastic layer with a thickness of 1.5 mm. This layer is often made from polyethylene. One lead can never contain more than twelve glass-fibres since more than twelve different colours cannot be distinguished during excavation works, especially in insufficient light. If a cable with a higher number of glass-fibres is required, the diameter of the centre element can be increased which allows more leads to be grouped around it. It is also possible to stand twelve glass-fibres making up several layers of glass-fibre strands inside the cable. The most common modern glass-fibre cables contain between 60 and 144 individual fibres.

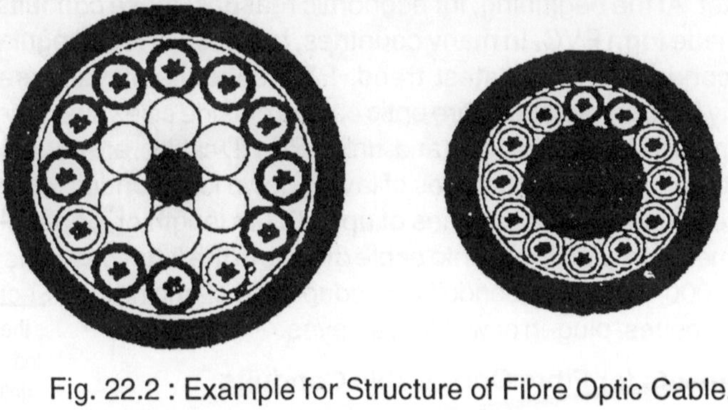

Fig. 22.2 : Example for Structure of Fibre Optic Cable.

Underground Installation of Fibre Optic Cables in Cable Conduits.

Apart from long distances such as the distance between Europe and the USA which is bridged by sea cables, most fibre optic cables are laid underground. The most important requirement to the observed for these high-quality underground cables is their protection against rodent damage. During production, a steel plate armour can be applied to the cable or a specially hard or slippery plastic material can be selected for the outer sheathing. This layer may be made of polyamide. Another protection method consists of inserting the cable into a cable conduit. The first two methods do not really offer sufficient protection for these high-grade transmission media, most modern optical cables are protected by cable conduits made from PE-HD. These have advantages such as :

- reliable rodent protection,
- sufficient protection of the cables in unusually stony ground or during tectonic movement,
- cable conduits fulfil two purposes at the same time: two cables can be inserted into the same conduit and old cables can be replaced by new ones,
- repair works can be carried out easier,
- protection against damage during excavation work which may occur at a later date.

The production of cable conduits in series began as early as the 1950s. These conduits were developed for the protection of copper cables and low and high voltage lines. Due to their advantages over conventional cable protection systems such as corrosion resistance and their flexible and easy installation, the plastic conduits quickly gained a substantial share in the market. At the beginning, for economic reasons, these conduits were mostly made form PVC. In many countries, because of legal regulations, PE-HD conduits are the latest trend. PVC conduits playa lesser role especially for long-distance fibre optic cables outside cities since they can only be produced in short lengths and, unlike PE-HD cables, are not windable. Especially for modern techniques of laying down long conduit routes, it is advisable to use conduit bunches of up to 500m length or, depending on their diameter, to wind them onto cable drums. In the latter case, they may be up to 3,000m long. The conduits are coupled by clamping joints, screwed coupling sleeves, plug-in or welding sleeves.

Requirements for Fibre Optic Cable Conduits

In principle, optical cables can be inserted into existing conduits. If there is not engough room, the old cables which are mostly made of copper, can be taken out and replaced by fibre optic cables. If the conduits are wide enough, the new cables can simply be added to the old ones. It is also possible to use empty conduits with wide diameters which may contain all supply lines including the fibre optic cables.

This report will deal with those cable conduits which have been specially produced to protect fibre optic cables. Normally, these conduits have diameters of 40 mm to 50 mm. Despite the fact that there are no legal regulations and the requirements are different for each of the various conduit producers and cable installation companies, there are some basic criteria for cable conduits which can be generally applied. These are listed below.

- long lengths for easy installation,
- simple joining methods,
- prevention of oval shapes,
- dimensional stability even under underground load stress,
- compressive strength for the cable insertion process (usually PN 10),
- low frictional resistance of the inner conduit wall to facilitate cable insertion.

Installation Techniques

In the area of cable conduits the so-called alternative installation techniques are considered as effective as the conventional technique consisting of excavating earth with a digger to produce a cable duct. Specialist installation techniques include methods such as horizontal flushing, tilling, the use of so-called ground rockets and insertion by ploughing. In this report, the installation of cables by ploughing will be dealt with in more detail since, according to our knowledge, this is the most widespread method. A cable or piping plough opens the ground for the length of the entire route. In combination with a special device for cable drums, the plough can open the ground and lay the cable conduits in one step. The ploughs can install conduits at a speed of 10 m/min, depending on the condition of the soil with up to tweenty cable bunches being installed at the same time. These ploughs are available as self-propelled or traction models. On rough ground, the plough has to be pulled by a tractor. For economic reasons, it is quite common to lay down several conduits at the same time even if not all of them are used at the time of their installation.

Techniques for Inserting Cables into Cable Conduits

Fibre optic cables can be inserted into conduits with several different methods. If the distance short, the cable can be pushed into the condit. Another method involves pulling the cable into the conduit with the help of a rope which was inserted into the conduit during production. This technique is also used for short distances. For long distances, there are basically two methods of cable insertion, consisting of water-assisted and air-assisted cable insertion. While water-assisted insertion, as the name says, involves the use of water and sufficient pressure to insert the cable into the conduit, the second method uses only compressed air. In Europe, the air-assisted method of "blowing" the cables into the conduits became the most widespread. With a pressure of 10 bar the optical cables can be inserted into the conduits over a distance of up to 3 km. Characteristics such as compressive strength, prevention of oval deformation and low friction between the inner wall and the cable are of the utmost importance especially for this technique.

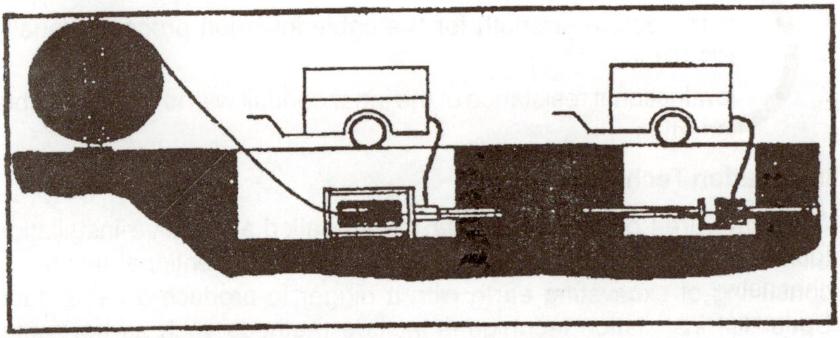

Fig. 22.3: Air assisted inserting of cables, Peter, Lancier GmbH & Co. Kg.

Especially in high-population areas, cable ducts, mostly located at points of inter-section, are left open to allow easy access. These are often lined with concrete. Currently, there is a trend for cable ducts to be lined with plastic due to the superior efficiency of the material. Again, for economic reasons, long-distance cables have as few ducts as possible. For these applications, the conduits are coupled with metal sleeves which are equipped with so-called positioning aids. These are also used along the conduit route to ensure easy detection of the metal-free conduits in case of defects. Each cable duct usually contains a spare piece of wound-up cable which can be used to replace the broken piece of cable during repair works. The broken piece is then removed and the new piece inserted into the conduit. With his method, there is only one junction point instead of the usual two.

This method is especially useful for the sophisticated technique used for joining individual glass-fibres. Glass fibres are joined by splicing which means that prior to joining, the cable ends are melted with an electric arc.

Linking a cable with 144 individual fibres takes approximately twelve hours. It is important that the connection of the fibres is not detrimental to their transmission capacity and does not reduce it by more than the authorised 0.1 db.

Conduit Types

Irrespective of the technique used for inserting the cables into the conduits, it is useful to ensure a low level of friction between the inner conduit wall and the cable itself. Therefore, in addition to the smooth PE-DH conduits conventionally used, conduits with mondified inner walls can also be used.

Fig. 22.4 : Example of Conduit Types.

The German telecommunications company "Deutsche Telekom" requires with forty grooves evenly distributed along the wall circumference. Other network providers and cable installation companies also use grooves of different size and thickness. Their production is easy. An existing PE-HDpipe extrusion line for example, only needs to be fitted with an extra-mandrel with a corresponding profile. These conduits have the advantage of a reduced contact area between their inner wall and the inserted cable.

Another popular method of reducing friction between the inner conduit wall and the inserted cable is the co-extrusion of an additional layer of silicone-modified polyethylene onto the inner conduit wall. This requires retrofitting the extrusion line with a co-extruder and a two-layer co-extrusion die. Naturally, the investment costs and the additional material costs incurred using silicone increases the price of the end product.

However, the application of silicone to the conduit wall facilitates the insertion of the cable. The silicone layer on the inner conduit wall reduces the friction coefficient immediately. Insertion of the cable is markedly facilitated - applying the same amount of force and energy will thus lead to the insertion of longer cable sections. Moreover, with this method less coupling points are required which reduces the overall costs.

0-0

As an alternative to co-extrusion, silicone can be sprayed onto the inner conduit wall.

In additions to single conduit, multiple conduits are also available on the market.

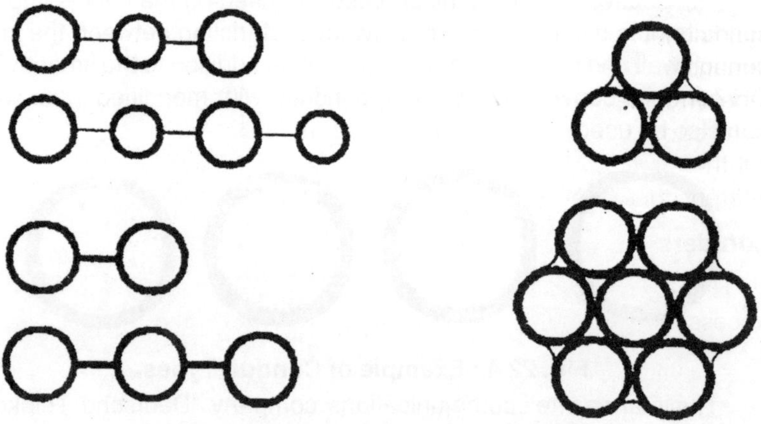

Fig. 22.5: Example of multiple conduits.

They consist of a combination of conduits with the same or differing dimensions, which can be tailor-made to suit individual customer requirements. The connection of the single conduits can be made by solid links or flexible hinges. The extrusion of such combinations requires specially designed dies and corresponding calibration units. Alternatively, in a second cycle applying a flexible plastic layer, single conduits can be connected to multiple ones. Another possibility is the encapsulation of a conduit bunch with a thin outer layer. All these methods open up a wide variety of conduit combinations.

It is difficult to predict which conduit model will be proved the most cost-efficient in its practical application. If required, it might prove useful to install a more sophisticated and therefore more expensive conduit since this may save excavation and installation costs in the end. It is not possible to make a general statement. Much to the contrary, when deciding for or against a certain conduit type it comes down to individual experience.

Extrusion Lines for Cable Conduits

PE-HD cable conduits are produced on conventional pipe extrusion lines. Single-screw extruders ensure continuous material conveying, homogenous melting of the plastic material and constant pressure build-up. Conventional pipe dies in various designs are responsible for an even melt distribution around the circumference of the conduit. Calibrating sleeves of various standard designs can be used to promote a constant predetermined outer conduit diameter.

Standard PE-HD pipe producers can easily extend their production range to include conduits without any additional investment since their equipment usually already accommodates conduit dimensions. Since the demand for cable conduits is on the increase, some pipe producers may benefit from optimising their existing lines to suit this specific application. At the same time, if necessary, new extrusion lines could be modified to suit the specific production requirements of this market segment with different consequences for individual line components.

Extruders

High-performance single-screw extruders should meet the following process requirements:

- high torque for high melt throughput rates,
- high and pulsation-free melt throughput,
- thermal and material homogeneity,
- prevention of material degradation or cross-linkage, i.e. shear and melt temperature control,
- wide processing range ensures high flexibility,
- low wear,

The experience of many years has shown that extruders with a grooved barrel in combination with barrier screws are the most efficient for combining a high melt capacity with an excellent material homogeneity. The grooved barrel leads to a high specific melt throughput rate. The barrier screw ensures a specified material shear in the barrier gap which leads to a good homogeneity of the melt at low material temperatures. Old machines which have not been fitted with the actual grooved feeding sections and barrier screws can be retrofitted with the new processing units to improve their capacity. The improved performance of the feeding section promotes higher specific throughput rates. The required screw torque can be achieved by changing the reduction gear ratio. It the drive motor performance remains unchanged, this change will improve the melt quality at a lower screw speed. The reduced specific energy input into the material may lead to a minor increase of the melt throughput rate. A more powerful drive motor however, will lead to a marked increase in the melt throughput rate.

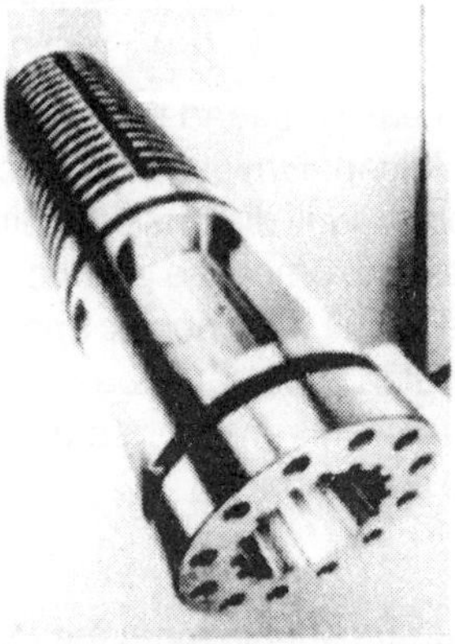

Fig. 22.6 & 22.7: Grooved Feeding Section, Barrier Screw.

Currently, the relevant throughput rates for cable conduit production of 300 kg/h up to 1000 kg/h can be achieved on machines with screw diameters between 60mm and 120 mm. The processing lengths range between 30 D and 33 D.

Pipe Dies

Pipe dies are used to ensure an even distribution of the melt around the pipe circumference. The pipe die should suit the specific properties of the processed material. It should also be adapted to suit the respective melt throughput rate and pipe dimensions. Dies in general should have a low pressure consumption rate which helps to keep the melt temperature low. This also reduces material degradation and increases the melt throughput rate. High melt temperature can have a detrimental effect of the throughput rate of the entire line. On the whole, dies have to be designed to promote an even melt distribution at a low pressure consumption.

The most popular dies used for PE-HD processing are lattice basket dies and spiral mandrel dies.

The main advantage of lattice basket dies for the production of PE-HD cable conduits is their low pressure build-up. Thus, high melt throughput rates at low melt temperatures become possible even for those small to medium-sized pipe dimensions commonly used in cable conduit production. The melt distribution is always good, regardless of the processed material and the operating point.

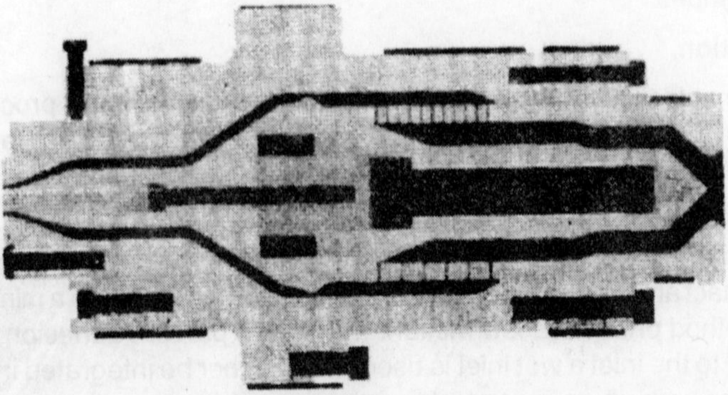

Fig. 22.8 : Lattice Basket Die.

Spiral mandrel dies have many properties which can be useful for the production of cable conduits. One example is the co-extrusion of a thin inner layer. Several spiral can be interlocked to allow multi-layer solutions for products of small dimensions. Spiral mandrel dies can also be used where cross-head dies are required. They can be fitted with a side-feed system and annular groove pre-distributors which allows the insertion of a traction rope or the injection of friction-reducing materials into the finished conduit.

Fig. 22.9 : Spiral Mandrel Die.

On their outside, the conduits are marked with colour-coded stripes. Both types of die can be fitted accordingly with co-extrusion rings for colour stripes.

Calibration

The selection of the calibrating sleeve depends on the processed polymer and the take-off speed. Several different types such as disk calibrating units or sleeves with water inlet can be used for PE-HD processing.

During disk calibration, the pipe is completely enclosed by water. The contact area between the sleeve and the pipe is reduced to a minimum. This method ensures a low friction. In order to prevent adhesion of the material to the inlet a wet inlet is used. It can either be integrated into the sleeve or be built as a separate spray ring. The separate ring can be more readily adapted to different materials and take-off speeds.

Disk calibrating units are used especially for small high-speed pipe dimensions. They are used for pipes with diameters of up to 50mm. They are suitable for extrusion speeds of 50 m/min or more depending on the pipe dimensions and the processed material. The current throughput rates for cable conduits can most certainly be supported with this type of calibrating unit.

Calibrating sleeves are used for pipes with low take-off speeds. For the pipe dimensions relevant to this report, they are also operated with a water-inlet. Directly downstream from the material intake section, the sleeve is fitted with an adjustable water ring. This wets the entire pipe surface with water. The water film between pipe and sleeve works like a lubrication layer which prevents the material from sticking to the sleeve's surface.

Cooling Section

At the end of the production, the finished pipe has to be cold enough to prevent deformation from outer stress which is exerted by processes such as the contract pressure form the caterpillar take-off or the tensile force exerted by the winder. Practical experience has shown that unwindable pipes require an end-of-line inner wall temperature of 50°C to 70°C. At this temperature however, cable conduits which are wound onto drums would be deformed by the tensile force of the winder. After the winding process, they would no longer be round but too oval in. shape. In any case, the temperature of the inner wall should be below 40°C. This requirement markedly increases the cooling section necessary for windable pipes processed at the same pressure level. Hence, the cooling section of existing lines for the production of PE-HD cable conduits is of special importance.

The cooling sections of small extrusion lines producing pipes with an outer diameter of 20mm to a maximum of 63 mm are generally designed for windable cables since they are often the main product in the range. For the most part, the extruders used have screw diameters of 60 mm and a maximum throughput rate of 300 kg/h.

Pipes with a diameter range of 40 mm to 50 mm can be produced on larger machines with higher throughput rates. An extruder with a screw diameter of 90 mm with the appropriate die can easily produce 600 kg/h. On the market, these machines are often combined with downstream equipment which allows the production of pipes with an outer diameter range of 125 mm to 250 mm. The production range of these pipe lines focuses on unwindable pipes with large diameters. The cooling sections arc also designed for PNIO products. Hence, the production of windable pipes on the big lines which are currently on the market is limited by the length of their cooling section. Often, the production halls are also not long enough to accommodate these long lines, thus an extension of the cooling section is often not possible without drastic changes.

There are two possibilities for benefiting from the higher throughput rate of existing extruders for windable pipes in existing production halls. The first method involves retrofitting the downstream equipment as a twin strand line. This would reduce the length of the cooling section by half. If an extruder has the capacity, the throughput rate can be doubled. The disadvantage of this method is the high amount of investment costs and the reduced line flexibility. Another possibility to use the existing hall dimensions involves a diversion of the pipe. With help of diversion rollers the pipe could be redirected back to the extruder at the end of the cooling section. Take-off units and winders need no longer be placed at the end of the cooling section but could be positioned at the side of the line. This solution is only useful for small pipe diameters and proves inconvenient for freight management, since the finished pipes have to be transported across the production hall.

Newly planned production halls for PE-HD cable conduits should therefore be constructed to accommodate a sufficiently long cooling section which allows for a high take-off speed.

Take-off Devices

Take-off units for PE-HD cable conduits should allow high take-off speeds. Double-action belt take-off units fulfil this requirement. They should be fitted with mechanically operated fixed stops, since they handle the pipe on only two pressure points. Fixed stops prevent excessive deformation of the pipes by limiting the feed travel of the belts.

Multi-caterpillar take-off units are technically more sophisticated. Hence, they are more expensive. Using four pressure points on the pipe for example will cause only minor deformation. Moreover, these units allow a higher transmission of take-off force.

Machine Control

The coordinated interaction between control unit and all line components is paramount for a smooth production process. Different market requirements call for customised automation solution with a strong focus on the benefit for the customer. Inflexible automation concepts are a thing of the past, automated production requires specialised solutions instead.

The most important reason for the automation of a pipe extrusion line is the need for simpler process control, minimum use of material and central access to information and documentation of all process and product data. The degree of automation should match the requirements of the individual situation.

The systems available for pipe extrusion lines often integrate the control of gravimetric and wall-thickness sensors and thus offer a high degree of production data acquisition. In combination with the corresponding product control circuits, the systems can help save material costs by optimising the product. The higher the product requirements, the more useful automation concepts for extrusion lines turn out to be. The discussion concerning 100% wall thickness measurement for the production of PE-HD pressure pipes for gas or water supply is one example of the relevance of this statement.

Compared to the situation for pressure pipes, the requirements for PE-HD cable conduits are currently not that high. Nonetheless, within reasonable investment costs, modern line design should sup'port the simplification of processes, the documentation of quality and the reduction of material costs. A flexible automation system for instance, which allows for the integration of co-extrusion processes and which can be upgraded for ultrasonic measuring technology will meet all requirements for an easy line operation. With its weight per meter control device an additional weighing unit will reduce material consumption and ensure product quality control at the same time.

Naturally, a line producer with the overall responsibility will be competent to co-ordinate the individual components for optimal and efficient operation. The co-ordination of line components is an important aspect for all line operators. However, the importance of this aspect increases with the demands on the pipe extrusion line.

Example of a Suitable Pipe Extrusion Line

Optimising existing extrusion lines is one possibility for pipe producers to meet the increased demand in PE-HD cable conduits for the telecommunications market. Alternatively, new market shares can be acquired if the production capacity is increased by investment into new machine technology. Which requirements do new extrusion lines for these products have to meet, how could they be implemented?

For these new lines, as for all investment products, efficiency is paramount. In practice, this entails high throughput rates and line speed in combination with high product quality and a low use of material. One example of how this can be achieved entails modern control technology and high line availability. These rather general requirements become more specific if applied to PE-HD cable conduit production. For this market segment, the following characteristics are especially important:

- high extruder output rate,
- good melt distribution in the die at a low pressure build up,
- calibration suitable for high speeds,
- a sufficiently long cooling section for windable pipes,
- and a control unit with modern control circuits ensuring minimum material costs.

To allow a flexible reaction to market requirements, the line should also offer

- the facilities for the co-extrusion of inner layers,
- or, alternatively, devices for the injection of friction-reducing substances,
- the facilities for inserting a traction rope,
- downstream equipment supporting a wide rallge of pipe diameters,

- a control system which can be adapted to suit the ever-increasing market requirements.

A line which meets all these requirements could have the following features:

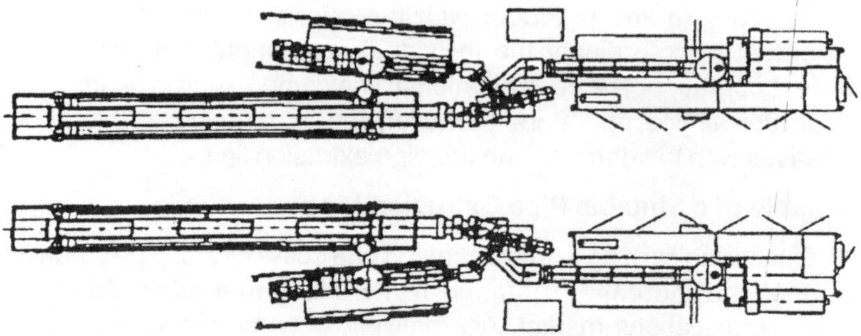

Fig. 22.10 : Extrusion Line Example, Layout.

Fig. 22.11: Extrusion line example, Extruder.

An extruder with a screw diameter of 75 mm and a process length of 30 D is the basic equipment. Its melt capacity for PE-HD amounts to apprcximately 450 kg/h. The machine is fitted with a two-layer spiral mandrel die for pipe diameters ranging from 20 mm to 125 mm. This die allows the production of smooth pipes and pipes with an inner profile. If required, a silicone-modified layer may be applied to the inner pipe wall. Moreover, the die is designed with a cross head which allows the insertion of a traction rope. This flexible die concept meets the entire range of market requirements.

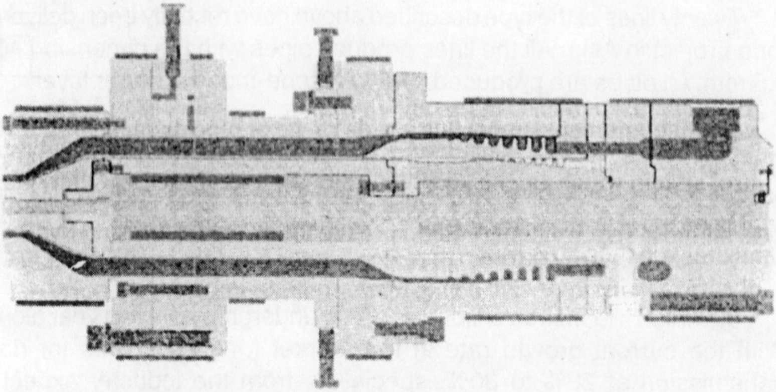

Fig. 22.12: Extrusion Line Example, 2-layer Die.

A co-extruder with a screw diameter of 45 mm and a process length of 25 D applies the inner layer. The machine has melt capacity of 100 kglh which is also suitable for thick layers and high line capacities. Both layers of melt are side fed into the die. To save room, both extruders are connected to the die with an angular adapter. Thus, both units can be placed in an offset position in the direction of the extrusion. The rear of the die is unobstructed and can be used for storing a rope pulley. Another co-extruder with a screw diameter of 25 mm in combination with the relevant co-extrusion ring marks the pipe with different colour-coded stripes.

All units of the downstream equipment support a pipe diameter range of 20 mm to 125 mm. Therefore, the production range of the entire line is not limited to cable conduit production but can be used for other applications. The six-metre vacuum tank in combination with a disk calibration unit ensures the dimensional stability of the pipe. The entire cooling section is 50 m long which guarantees sufficient cooling of the pipe for a line capacity of at least 450 kg/h. A double-action belt take-off is used for high take-off speeds.

A machine control unit controls all line components. Both extruders are fitted with weighing units. These units control the inner to outer layer thickness ratio. Integration of the take-off controls the pipe's overall weight per metre. The control system is flexible and can be retrofitted with an ultrasonic all thickness gauge for controlling the minimum wall thickness of the pipe.

Twenty lines of the type described above have recently been delivered for a project in Asia. All the lines produce pipes with the dimension 40 x 3.5 mm. All pipes are produced with a silicone-modified inner layer.

The interval between the investment decision and the successful start-up of the lines was shorter than five months. Within such short notice, production capacities of more than 500,000 m of pipe per day could be achieved.

Future Prospects

80 million kilo metres of fibre were laid underground in this year alone. With the current growth rate in the market for glass fibres for data transmission at 20% to 30%, specialists from the industry expect a volume of 100 million kilometres of fibre for the next year. There seems to be no end to the progression of cable networks. Installation of glass-fibres for long distances and as yet unexplored city networks as well as the substitution of copper wires with glass-fibre cables for the short-distance connection to the private customer offer an enormous potential. Up to now, private customers have used the existing cables, but their transmission requirements are on the increase. Moreover, we can expect that new providers and new media will require increasingly powerful cable networks. For the cable conduits market this means that high-performance extrusion lines have to be available for this growing demand.

ALL FOLLOWING PROJECT REPORTS ARE READILY AVAILABLE

FOOD, AGRO FOOD, PROCESSED FOOD, AGRO PLANTATION, CULTIVATION, FARMING, DAIRY/MILK, TOBACCO/PAN MASALA, BREWERY & DISTILLERY, EDIBLE OILS, EOU FOOD PRODUCTS AND ALLIED PRODUCTS

- Alcoholic Beverages & Venegar From Coconut Water
- Alcohol Drinks From Ethyl Alcohol By Mixing Of Various Flavours
- Amla Fruit Products With Preservation Tomato Sauce, Pickles Jam And Jellies
- Anti Scale Compound For Adding Into Sugar Juice Boiling
- Apple Juice Concentrated & Dehydrated Fruit & Vegetables
- Artificial Fish Meal For Poultry Feed
- Automatic Biscuit Making Plant
- Automatic Bread Making Unit
- Baby Cereal Food And Milk Powder
- Baby Corn
- Bacteria For Cane Juice
- Baker's Yeast
- Bakery Industry
- Banana Puree
- Barley Malt
- Beer & Wine
- Beer Plant (Brewery)
- Bidi
- Bidi & Cigarette
- Biscuit Plant
- Bread (Automatic Plant)
- Black Pepper (Spices)
- Bread And Biscuits
- Breeding Farm
- Broiler Chicken
- Button Mushroom Cultivation & Processing
- Canning Of Rasagullas In Metal Cans
- Caffein From Tea Waste
- Canning Of Fruits & Vegetables
- Casein From Milk
- Casein And By-Products
- Cashew Fruit Juice From Cashew Fruit Apple
- Cashewnut Kernel Extraction From Cashewnut Fruit
- Cashewnut Shell Liquid & Kernel Processing
- Cashew Feni
- Catecheu (By Chemical Process)
- Cattle Feed From Tapioca
- Chewing & Bubble Gum
- Chicken/Sheep Meat Processing
- Chocolate (Milk)
- Cigarette And Beedies
- Cocoa Butter From Cocoa Mass
- Coconut Water (Coco Jal) - Packed
- Coconut Products & By Products Process Complex
- Cold/Soft Drinks
- Collection Of Milk And Milk Making Powder
- Collection Of Milk And Packing In Polythene Pouch (1/2 Kg.1 Kg. & 2 Kg.)
- Condensed Milk (Sweetned)
- Cold Storage
- Confectionery Industry (Toffee & Candy, Semi-Automatic Plant)
- Confectionery Unit With Toffee, Candy, Chewing Gum And Bubble Gum
- Corn Flakes
- Country Liquor From Molasses
- Custard Powder
- Cigarette
- Dairy Farm And Dairy (Milk) Products (Pasteurised Milk, Butter, Ghee, Paneer)
- Dairy Farm To Produce Milk & Packing In Pouches (50%) & Can(50%)
- Dairy For Milk Processing
- Dairy Farming (Buffalo)
- Dairy Farming (Jersey Cow)
- Dal (Pulse) Mill Unit
- Dehydration Of Carrot & Garlic
- Dehydration & Canning Of Fruits & Vegetables
- Dehydration Of Figs
- Dehydration Of Fruits And Vegetables By Vacuum Drying Method
- Dehydration Of Fruits And Vegetables By Iqf Technology
- Dehydrated Onions And Onion Powder
- Drinking Water (Packaged)
- Dry Ice By Breaking Of Air
- Drying Of Red Chillies, Haldi, Dhania, And Green Peas
- Egg Powder (40,000 Eggs Processing Per Day)
- Export Of Processed Foods And Marine Products
- Fish Canning & Pouching
- Fish Farming (Prawn & Other Marine Products)
- Fish Meal
- Flour Mill And Mustard Oil
- Flavoured Milk
- Food Colour & Orasted Groundnut Gram Peas, Etc In Pouches
- Frog Legs Processing
- Frozen Meats Processing
- Food Flavours (Whisky) Vodka, Grape, Butter Scotch)
- Food Products Complex (Dehydrated Onions, Garlic Powder & Flakes, Cattle Feed, Tomato Powder, Tomato Products, Canned Fruits & Vegetables, Tomato Pure, Ground Nut Oil, Refined Oil, Dehydrated Grapes Etc.
- Banana Powder & Waffers)
- Freeze Drying Coffee Manufacturing Unit (Processing) And Packaging In Glass Bottles
- Fruit Juice, Jam, Jellies & Allied Products
- Fruit Juice, Pickles Processing And Canning
- Fruit Juice Making & Packing In Plastic Container/Pouches
- Fruit Processing (Jam & Jellies)
- Fruit Pulp & Juice Concentrates
- Fruit & Vegetable Drying (Freeze Drying Method)
- Ginger Oil
- Ginger Paste
- Ginger And Garlic Paste
- Goat Farm
- Goat & Sheep Farming
- Gram Dall/Pulse Mill
- Grape Dehydration
- Hard Boiled Candy (Toffee & Candy)
- Herbal Cigarettes
- Honey Processing & Packaging
- Honey Coated Cashewnuts, Peanuts And Other Nuts
- Ice Cream Of Different Flavours
- Ice Cream Stabilizer
- Ice Making Plant
- Icing Sugar
- Indian Made Foreign Liquor (I.M.F.L)
- Instant Food (Idli Mix, Dosa Mix, Gulab Jamun Mix)
- Instant Food (Instant Food & Fast Food Parlour)
- Instant Noodles
- Instant Tea
- Instant Tea From Black Tea
- Integerated Starch Baking Powder/Yeast Industry
- Integrated Unit Of Dairy Farming, Milk Collection And Processing, Fish Farming, Poultry Farming And Hatchery
- Iodized Salt
- Iodized Salt (Ordinary Moisture-Less/Free Flowing In Plastic Bags And Containers)
- Jam, Jellies, Fruit Juice & Allied Products
- Katha And Cutch
- Khandsari Sugar

Market Survey Cum Detailed Techno Economic Feasibility Report on all Projects are available Contact.
"ENGINEERS INDIA RESEARCH INSTITUTE". 4449, Nai Sarak (D), Main Road, Delhi-110006 (India)
Ph. : 09811437895, 9811151047, 91-11-23918117, 23916431, 23947058, 64727385, 45120361
E-mail : eiriprojects@gmail.com, eiribooks@yahoo.com • website: www.eiri.in, www.eiriindia.org • www.eiribooksandprojectreports.com

ALL FOLLOWING PROJECT REPORTS ARE READILY AVAILABLE

- Khandsari Sugar & Imfl
- Lactic Acid From White Sugar By Fermentation Process
- Lactose & By Products Processing From Milk
- Liquid Glucose And Its Bye Products
- Macroni And Vermicilli
- Malt Extraction From Barley
- Mango Processing (Mango Pulp, Juice & Slices)
- Mayur Brand Type Chewing Tobacco
- Mineral Water
- Milk Preservation & Marketing To Whole Sellers (Inpouch Packing By Uht Technology)
- Milk Processing And Packaging Of Milk Products
- Milk Products (Casein, Lactose, Ghee & Whey Powder)
- Milk Toffee
- Mini Flour Mill
- Mini Sugar Plant
- Misri (Pearl Sugar Candies)
- Modern Rice Mill
- Murabba
- Mustard Oil Extraction & Refining
- Mutton Tallow
- Namkeen Industry (Bhujia, Chana Chur Etc.)
- Namkeen (Kurkure Type Snack Food
- Namkeen With Kurkurre Type Snack Food
- Namkeen & Sweets
- Non-Basmati Rice From Paddy
- Oleoresin, Essential Oil, Dyes & Powder Of Spices
- Oleoresin Extraction From Diptero-Carput Turminatus And Pinus Khasyana
- Oleoresin Extraction From Chilli
- Pan Masala With Packing In Pouches And Tin Cans
- Pan Masala, Tobacco, Zarda & Kimam
- Packaged Drinking Water
- Packaged Coconut Water (Coco Jal)
- Paneer From Milk
- Pappad Plant
- Papain From Papaya (Papaya Latex)
- Pectin From Mango Peel Pectin From Apple Pomace
- Phyto Tea (Herbal Tea)
- Pickles And Sauces
- Pickles Murabba Etc. (Veg. & Non. Veg.Pickles)
- Piggery Meat Process
- Pine-Apple Juice Preparation & Packaging
- Potato Chips/Waffers
- Potato Powder
- Pouch Filling & Packaging Of Edible Oil & Ghee
- Poultry Feed
- Processed Foods & Spices (Eou)
- Processed Readymade Food
- Processing Of Fruits & Vegetables
- Puree, Paste, Juice And Ketchup From Khajoor (Dates)
- Rabbit Farming

EIRI
We Create Industrialists

- Rasgullas Making & Canning In Metal Cans
- Ready To Eat Processed Cooked Food
- Ready To Eat Retort Packed Food
- Ready To Eat Snack Food (Crax, Roll & Ball Type)
- Rice & Corn Flakes
- Rice Noodles
- Roasted/Salted/Masala,Cashew Nuts, Almonds & Peanuts
- Roller Flour Mill (Atta, Suja And Maida)
- Salt Licks For Cattle
- Sattu
- Sausages Food Casing
- Soft Drinks (Cold Drinks)
- Soft Drinks Essences
- Soft Drinks (Non Carbonated) Mango,Licchi, Pineapple Flavours Frooti Type In Tetrapack)
- Softy Ice Cream Cones (Fully Automatic)
- Soft/Cold Drinks (Cola, Orange, Lemon Etc. Flavours)
- Soyabean Products
- Soyabean Bariyan
- Soya Milk & Paneer
- Spices/Masala With Formulae
- Spices And Namkeen (Integrated Unit)
- Snack Food (Kurkure Type)
- Starch & Allied Propduct From Broken Rice
- Strawberry Cultivation & Processing
- Sugarcane Juice Preservation
- Sugar Cubes From Cane Sugar
- Sugar Plant
- Supari (Sweet) – Betel Nut (Synthetic)
- Sweet Aroma Betel Nut
- Synthetic Tallow
- Tamarind Juice Powder
- Tamarind Juice Concentrates
- Tea & Coffee Processing & Packaging
- Toffees, Golies, Candy (Hard Boiled)
- Tomato Products
- Tomato Ketchup, Tomato Puree And Tomato Juice (Tomato Products)
- Trading Business Of Spices & Pan Masala
- Tuity Fruity
- Vermicilli (Including Roasted Vermicilli)
- Virgin Coconut Oil
- Vodka From Potatoes
- Wallnut Processing
- Wine, Brandy, Whisky &Champagne
- Wine From Dates
- Yeast From Molasses
- Zarda, Kimam No. 60,90,120,160,240,300 & 400 (Tobacco)
- Zarda Kimam And Tobacco
- Zarda-Zafrani (Babachhaptype)

GUMS AND ADHESIVES

- Acrylic Adhesive
- Adhesive (Different Types)
- Adhesive (Fevicol Type)
- Adhesive For Stickers
- Adhesive Based On Vinyl Acetate
- Adhesive Based On Polyurethane
- Adhesive For Band Aid (Johnson & Johnson Type)
- Adhesive Industries (Laminated, Sticker,Ddl & Other Types)
- Adhesive For Gasket (Liquid/Paste)
- Araldyte Type Adhesive
- Alkyd Resin
- Bopp Self Adhesive Tapes
- Cyanoacrylate Adhesive
- Ester Gums
- Fevicol Type Adhesive
- Guar Gum
- Gum Bottle (Pvc)
- Gum For Pasting Labels
- Leather To Leather Adhesive
- Liquid Adhesive For Corrugated Boxes
- Office Paste
- Poly Amide Resin
- Pressure Sensitive Adhesive
- Pvc Indulation Tapes
- Printing Gums (Guar Gum Based)
- Rubber Adhesive
- Self Adhesive Labels
- Starch And Dextrin Based Afhesive
- Surgical Adhesive Plaster
- Synthetic Rubber Adhesive
- Synthetic Adhesive For Decorative Laminate Bonding
- Tapioca Starch Adhesive
- Vinyl Ester Adhesive
- Vulcanising Adhesive Formulation Vulcanizing Rubber Solution/Cement For Automobile Tyre
- Urea Formaldehyde Resin
- Water Based Latex Adhesive

Contact EIRI

for required Project report apart from this list.

Market Survey Cum Detailed Techno Economic Feasibility Report on all Projects are available Contact.
"ENGINEERS INDIA RESEARCH INSTITUTE". 4449, Nai Sarak (D), Main Road, Delhi-110006 (India)
Ph. : 09811437895, 9811151047, 91-11-23918117, 23916431, 23947058, 64727385, 45120361
E-mail : eiriprojects@gmail.com, eiribooks@yahoo.com • website: www.eiri.in, www.eiriindia.org • www.eiribooksandprojectreports.com

ALL FOLLOWING PROJECT REPORTS ARE READILY AVAILABLE

PAINT, ENAMEL, SOLVENTS, THINNERS, INKS & VARNISH

PAINT, ENAMEL, SOLVENTS, THINNERS, INKS & VARNISH

- Acrylic Emulsion Paints
- Acrylic Cement Paint (Dry Powder)
- Aluminium Paint
- Automobile Paints
- Ball Point Pen Refill Ink
- Bituminious Road Emulsion
- Bitumen
- Bituminious Felts For Water & Damp Proofing
- Bituminious Road Emulsion Rapid Medium & Slow Setting
- Buffing & Polishing
- Cement Paint For White & Grey Cement
- Dispersant
- Dry Distemper
- Dry Distemper & Cement Paint
- Duplicating Ink Black For Gestner Duplicator
- Emulsion Paints (Water Based)
- Hammertone Paint
- Insulating Varnish & Wire Enamel
- Iron Oxide Pigments
- Insulating Varnish (Poly Vinyl Butyral Based, Ffc Grade)
- Lime Colour (Cement Colour)
- Synthetic Red Oxide For Floorings
- Solvent & Thinners
- Marking Inks (Water Proof)
- Metal Naphthanate (As Drier For Paints)
- N.C.Putty
- Offset Printing Ink
- Oil Bound Distemper Paint
- Paint Brushes
- Paint Manufacture For Rolling Coating Of Aluminium And Steel Coil
- Paint Removers
- Paint Industry
- Paint & Varnish
- Picture Varnish
- Powder Coating Paint
- Printing Inks (Offset,Flexo & Roto Gravure)
- Primer Paint & Enamel Paint
- Putty & Water Proofing Paint
- Printing Inks (Flexo-Graphic Ink)
- Putty (Metal Casement)
- Red Oxide Primer (Anti Corrosive)
- Refrectory Paint (Graphite Based)
- Screen Printing Inks
- Silk Screen Printing Ink Formulation For Plastic, Paper, Cloth
- Stamp & Pad Ink
- Stoving Paint
- Spirit Soluble Maleic Resin
- Texture Paint
- Thinners And Its Allied Products
- Toner Ink
- Varnish Thinner (Solvent)
- Vacuum Metallizing Lacquers
- Wood Primer

PHARMACEUTICAL, DRUGS, AYURVEDIC/HERBAL COSMETICS & MEDICINES, HOMOEOPATHIC MEDICINES, HOMOEOPATHIC MEDICINES, DISPOSABLE SYRINGE, DENTAL COLLEGE & FINE CHEMICALS ETC.

MEDICINES, HOMOEOPATHIC MEDICINES, DISPOSABLE SYRINGE, DENTAL COLLEGE & FINE CHEMICALS ETC.

- Aromatic Pills
- Alumina From Bauxite
- Aspirin
- Ayurvedic Pain Balm Ointments
- Ayurvedic Churan And Tablets
- Ayurvedic Tablets (Hajmola Type)
- Ayurvedic/Herbalpharmacy
- Ayurvedic Sherbats
- Ayurvedic Products
- Bulk Drugs (E.O.U)
- Blood Bags
- Calcium Gluconate
- Capsule, Tablet & Injection With Modern Instruments
- Cashew Feni
- Chloroquinone Phosphate (Bulk Drugs)
- Clinical Thermometer
- Dental Clinic
- Dental College
- Dental Grade Eugenol
- Dextrose Monohydrate, Liquid Glucose
- Dehydrated Onion & Onion Powder
- Dextrose Powder (Anhydrous From Starch)
- Dextrose Saline Solution
- Distillery (I.M.F.L)
- Disposable Needles For Syringes
- Disprin
- Distilled Water
- Empty Hard Gelatine Capsules
- Fairness Cream
- Filling & Packing Of Capsules
- Glucose - D - Powder
- Glycerine
- Hair Colour Mate (Formulations And Process Only)
- Herbal Cosmetics
- Herbal Shampoo
- Herbal Shampoo And Cream
- Herbal Hair Oils (Ayurvedic)
- Homoe & Bio-Medicines With Mother Tincture
- Homoepathic Medicines
- Hypodermic Needles
- I.V. Fluids
- Ibuprofen
- Infusion & Transfusion Sets (I.V. Set)
- Injectable For Pharmaceuticals
- Injection Ampoules Packaging Box
- Integerated Surgical Cotton
- Ice Making Plant
- Ice & Cold Storage
- Lactose & By Products Processing From Milk
- Lichen (Jatamansi Charila)
- Liquid Glucose And Its By-Products
- L-Lysine Monohydro Chloride
- Liquid Glucose From Potatoes
- Medical College
- Methanol (Hpcl Grade)
- Nicotine From Tobacco Waste
- Ointment-Ayurvedic (Yellow & White)
- Pharmaceutical And Food Grade Gelatine
- Pharmaceutical Industry (Tablets, Capsules, Liquid, Gel, Ointment Powder Injectable)
- Pharmaceutical Unit (Eou) With Formulations, Injectables, Etc.
- Pyridine & Derivatives
- Salt (Iodized Salt)
- Saline & Injection Water
- Saline Water & Dextrose Solution (I.V.Fluid In Plastic Bottles)
- Sorbitol
- Starch (Maize)
- Surgical Adhesive Plaster
- Surgical Bandages
- Surgical Gloves
- Surgical Cotton
- Surgical Cotton And Bandage
- Synthetic Camphor Powder
- Tablets & Capsules
- Tissue Culture
- Tincture From Rectified Spirit
- Trimethopime
- Veterinary College With Hospital
- Veterenary Medicines (Only Formulations)
- Vitamin 'C', Sorbitol' Anhydrous Dextrose, Starch

Market Survey Cum Detailed Techno Economic Feasibility Report on all Projects are available Contact.
"ENGINEERS INDIA RESEARCH INSTITUTE". 4449, Nai Sarak (D), Main Road, Delhi-110006 (India)
Ph. : 09811437895, 9811151047, 91-11-23918117, 23916431, 23947058, 64727385, 45120361
E-mail : eiriprojects@gmail.com, eiribooks@yahoo.com • website: www.eiri.in, www.eiriindia.org • www.eiribooksandprojectreports.com

PHARMACEUTICALS & DRUGS TECHNOLOGY WITH FORMULATIONS

ISBN. 81-86732-52-7 # ₹ 950/-

Tablet & Capsules, Lubricants & Disintegrants, Pan Coating, Oral Preparations Mixtures, External Preparations, Ear Drops, Mouth Washes, Nasal Drops, Ointments, Creams & Eye Preparations, Antibiotics, Formulations, Packaging, Tablets including Amoxycillin, Analgin, Ibuprofen, Injectables, Liquid Orals, Capsules & Dry Syrups, Eye & Ear Preparations etc.

MODERN PACKAGING TECHNOLOGY FOR PROCESSED FOOD, BAKERY, SNACK FOOD, SPICES & ALLIED FOOD PRODUCTS

ISBN. 81-86732-28-4 # ₹ 600/-

Latest methods of Packaging Technology of fruits/veg. growers ,Spices mfrs., Snack food mfrs., Bakery Mfrs., and Edible oil mfrs. etc. Suppliers of Plant and Machinery have also been incorporated.

BOOKS ON SYNTHETIC DETERGENTS, SOAPS & DETERGENTS

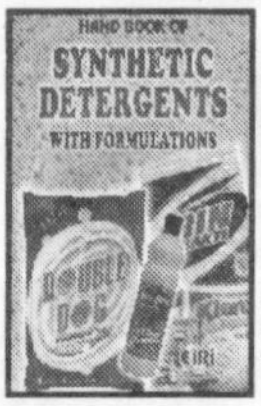

HAND BOOK OF SYNTHETIC DETERGENTS WITH FORMULATIONS

ISBN. 81-86732-43-8 # ₹ 900/-

Group of Synthetic Detergents, Synthesis of Detergents, Manufacture of Synthetic Detergents with Formulae, Testing of Detergents and Soaps, Project Profiles, Suppliers of Machinery and Raw Materials, Acid Slurry, Sirf Excel Type Detergent, Ariel Type Detergent, Dry Mix Process, Dry Clean Unit and much more others etc.

MANUFACTURE OF HOUSEHOLD SOAPS, TOILET SOAPS & OTHER SOAPS WITH FORMULATIONS

ISBN. 81-86732-53-5 # ₹ 750/-

Soap base manufacture, Solid, household and toilet soaps manufacture, Production of soap base, Perfuming, Manufacturing process & formulations, Miscellaneous formulae, Scourig bar, Detergent cake & powder, Toilet & herbal soap, Laundry soap, Liquid soap, Complete plant Suppliers, Suppliers of chemicals, Present manufacturers etc.

BOOKS ON ESSENTIAL OILS, PERFUMES & FLAVOURS

MODERN TECHNOLOGY OF ESSENTIAL OILS

ISBN 81-86732-71-3 # ₹ 850/-

Essential Oils Technology, Essential Oils and Flavours, Production of Essential Oils & Oleoresins, Herb & Oil Yield in Different Ocimum Species, Kewda Essential Oil and Attar, Mint Oil, Lemongrass, Palmarosa Oil, Musk, Java Citronella, Bio-Chemical Studies, Patchouli Oil, Rose-Scented Geranium, Basil Oil etc.

ESSENTIAL OILS PROCESSES & FORMULATIONS HAND BOOK

ISBN. 81-86732-39-X # ₹ 650/-

Essential Oils by Steam Distillation, GC-MS studies, Essential Oil from Cinnamomum, Kewda flower distillation, Composition of essential oil frombottle brush, Composition of essential oil from flowers of Keora, Manufacturers/ Exporters of Essential oils & Aromatic Chemicals with Machinery.

HAND BOOK OF ESSENTIAL OILS MANUFACTURING & AROMATIC PLANTS

ISBN. 81-86732-27-6 # ₹ 650/-

Rose oildistillation, extraction of essential oils, Uses of indigenous aromatic plants, essential oil bearing plants status,fractionation of essential oil, essential oil of hyptis suaveolens poit, super critical fluid extraction, ginger oil, Jasmine, rose etc..

HAND BOOK OF PERFUMES WITH FORMULATIONS

ISBN. 81-86732-42-X # ₹ 750/-

Creating a Perfume, Flower Perfumes, Colognes, Raw Materials, Classification, Packaging of Perfumes, Testing of Perfumes, Aromatic Perfumery Compounds, Scent & Perfume, Spray Perfume, Suppliers of Raw Materials .

HAND BOOK OF PERFUMES & FLAVOURS

ISBN. 81-86732-30-6 # ₹ 600/-

Perfume, Formulary of Perfume & Flavour, Natural Odours Simulated with Aromatic Chemicals, Simulated Flower Scents, Simulated Marine Scents (Algae), Plant & Equipment Suppliers, Suppliers of Raw Materials, Suppliers of Perfumes. Project profiles etc.

HAND BOOK OF FLAVOURS TECHNOLOGY

ISBN 81-86732-98-5
₹ 750/- or US $ 100/-

The book cover flavour analysis, Chemistry of flavours, Off-flavours in foods, Manufacturing processes of flavours, Plant materials used in flavouring, Principal Essential Oils used in Flavourings, Application of flavourings in food processing, Quality control, Non-Alcoholic Flavours, Flavours fruit (whiskey, vodka, Grape, Butter Scotch & Rum), Terpeneles Menthol Crystals.

ENGINEERS INDIA RESEARCH INSTITUTE Mobile : 9811437895, 9811151047
4449, Nai Sarak, Main Road, Delhi - 110 006 (INDIA) Ph. 91-11- 23918117, 23916431, 23947058

BOOKS ON THINNER, PLASTIC FILMS, PLASTIC WASTE RECYCLING, ROTATIONAL MOULDING, MAIZE, INJECTION MOULDING, PLASTIC MATERIALS & POTATO

MANUFACTURING TECHNOLOGY & FORMULATIONS HAND BOOK ON THINNERS, PUTTY, WALL & INDUSTRIAL FINISHES AND SYNTHETIC RESINS

ISBN978-81-89765-32-3

₹ 900/- **Pages- 339**

The book covers Thinners, Inorganic Pigments, Titanium Dioxide Pigments, Organic Pigments, Extender Pigments, Putty, Glaxing, Compounds Caulking, Compounds and Sealants, Paint Driers, Paint Additives, Architectural Paints, Industrial Finishes etc.

ROTATIONAL MOULDING TECHNOLOGY HAND BOOK

ISBN- 978-81-89765-25-5

₹ 750/- Pages- 212

The book covers Innovative Rotomoulding, Technology of Rotational Moulding, Rotational Moulding Process, Roto moulding Technology Details, Materials that can be Roto moulded, Roto moulding Machines, Design Consideration for Roto mould Containers, Rotational Moulding Process Control, Rotational Moulding of Nylons, Moulds Fabrication for Roto moulding, Roto moulds for Cast Aluminium, Pin-holes and Bubbles in Roto moulded Products, Rotational Moulding of Liquid Polymers, Powdering Thermoplastic and Quality Consideration, Plastic Water Storage Tanks (HDPE), Sintex Type etc.

PLASTIC WASTE RECYCLING TECHNOLOGY

ISBN 978-81-89765-30-9

₹ 750 **Page No. 238**

The book covers Introduction, Details of Polymers , Types of Plastics, Identification of Plastics, Recycling of Plastic Waste, Recycling of Thermosets, Chemical Recycling, Recycling Commodities Plastics, Recovery of Chemicals from Plastic Waste, Factors Affecting Recycling Process, Automatic Scrap Recycling, Reclaiming Polyamide Spin Fibres, EPS-Recycling from Post-Consumer Expanded Polystyrene, New Patented Processes, Environmental Health and Future Prospects, Recycling Polyester Resins, Polyurethane Waste Recycling, Recycling and Government Policies, Identification of Plastics, Plastics and the Environment, Recycling An Industrial Approach etc.

INJECTION MOULDING OF PLASTICS

ISBN 978-81-89765-20-0

₹ 750/- Pages-319

The book covers Injection Moulding, Setting-up-Mould and Machine, Effect of Processing on Mechanical Properties, Mouldflow, Computer Controlled Automatic Injection Moulding Machine, Maintenance of Injection Moulding Machine, CAE and CAD Technology in Moulds Making, Injection Moulding process, Specialised Injection Moulding Process, Troubleshooting in Injection Moulding, Injection Moulding of Thermosets, Injection Moulding Machine, Design for Injection Moulds, Designing Moulds for Thermoset Processing, Injection Moulded Plastic Components, Plastic Moulded Toys, Plastic Injection Moulding Products, Plastic Injection Moulding Items etc.

HAND BOOK OF PLASTIC MATERIALS AND PROCESSING TECHNOLOGY

ISBN 978-81-89765-26-2

₹ 750/- Pages 231

The book covers Introduction of Plastic Materials, Polyethylene, Linear Low Density Polyethylene (LLDPE), Polypropylene, Copolymers of Ethylene, Polystyrene, Acrylic Plastics, Poly (Methyl Methacrylate), Acrylic Fibres, Poly (Vinyl Acetate), Poly (Vinyl Chloride), Polytetrafluoroethylene (PTFE), Coumarone-Indene Resins, Polyacetals and Polyethers (Acetal Resins), Polyamides, Polyimides, Polyesters, Polyurethanes, Polycarbonates, Epoxy Resins, Cellulose Plastics, Phenolic Resins, Amino Resins, Silicones, Additives for Plastics, Polybutylene Terephthalate, Polyethersulphone, Nylon, Polyvinylidene Fluride etc.

POTATO AND POTATO PROCESSING TECHNOLOGY

ISBN- 978-81-89765-29-3

₹ 750/- Pages-264

The book covers Introduction, Origin, Description of Plant and Flower Parts, Nutritive Value, Growth and Development, Agro-Techniques, Management of Water, Weed Management, Seed Production, Handling of Post Harvest Potato, Prospects for Potato Exports, Quality Parameters that influence Export Quality of Potatoes, Areas Suitable for Producing Seed Potatoes, Areas Suitable for Producing Processing Potatoes, Grading of Potatoes, Packing of Potatoes, Potato Storage, Quality Requirements, Potato processing , Dehydration of Vegetables, Potato Based Textured Snacks, Potato Chips/Wafers etc.

TECHNOLOGY OF PLASTIC FILMS

ISBN 978-81-89765-28-6

₹ 650/- Pages 165

The book covers Introduction, Theoritical Aspect of Die Design, Plastic Packaging Films, Oriented Packaging Films, Orientation Techniques, Technology of Commercial Shrink Films, Stretch Films and Laminates , Properties of Heat Shrinkable Films, Coextrusion, Different Types of Die, Detailed Drawings of 100 MM Mandrel Type Dies, Chilli Roll Casting of Film, Internal Cooling of Blow Films, Side Fed Co-Extrusion Film Dies, Materials of Construction for Dies, Temperature Control in Dies, Die Maintenance & Care, Production of Blow Films, Polythylene Film Manufacture and Control, Water cooled Polypropylene Film, Orientation of Film, L.L.D.P.E. Film Extrusion, Coextrusion Dies for Manufacturing Flat Films etc.

TECHNOLOGY OF MAIZE AND ALLIED CORN PRODUCTS

ISBN 978-81-89765-17-0

₹ 650/- Pages-258

The book covers Corn, Types of Corn, Botany of Corn, Cultivation Practices, Carbohydrates and Related Compounds, Quality Factors, Traditional Food Products from Corn, Corn Milling, Products and their Uses, Processing Ready-to- Eat Breakfast Cereals, Popcorn, Formulated Puffed Snacks, Manufacturing Corn Chips, Maize Products, Maize Starch, Sweet Corn, Baby Corn, Extruded Snacks, Corn Flakes, Liquid Glucose, Maize/Corn Oil, Malto Dextrin from Maize, Plant Economics of Non Roasted Corn Flakes (POHA), Starch from Maize, Snack Food, Yeast Dry Powder from Maize, Suppliers of Maize/Corn Processing Machineries, Present Manufacturers/Exporters/Suppliers of Maize and Maize Products.

ENGINEERS INDIA RESEARCH INSTITUTE Mobile : 9811437895, 9811151047
4449, Nai Sarak, Main Road, Delhi - 110 006 (INDIA) Ph. 91-11- 23918117, 23916431, 23947058